Nine Suitcases

Nine Suitcases

A Memoir

BÉLA ZSOLT

*Translated from the Hungarian
by Ladislaus Löb*

Schocken Books
New York

All rights reserved under International and Pan-American Copyright
Conventions. Published in the United States by Pantheon Books,
a division of Random House, Inc., New York, and simultaneously in Canada
by Random House of Canada Limited, Toronto. Originally published in
weekly installments in Hungary in the journal *Haladás* from May 30, 1946,
to February 27, 1947. Originally published in book form in Hungary as
Kilenc Koffer by Magvento Koenyvkiado, Budapest, in 1980. This translation
originally published in Great Britain by Jonathan Cape, London.

Pantheon Books and colophon are registered trademarks of Random House, Inc.

Library of Congress Cataloging-in-Publication Data
Zsolt, Béla, 1895–1949.
[Kilenc koffer. English]
Nine suitcases / Béla Zsolt ; translated from the Hungarian by Ladislaus Löb.
p.   cm.
ISBN 0-8052-4204-X
1. Zsolt, Bâla, 1895–1949.   2. Jews—Hungary—Biography.   3. Holocaust,
Jewish (1939–1945)—Hungary—Personal narratives.   I. Title.
DS135.H93Z7513   2004   940.53'18'092—dc22   [B]   2004045313

www.pantheonbooks.com

Printed in the United States of America

First American Edition

2   4   6   8   9   7   5   3   1

Translator's Introduction

Béla Zsolt was born in Komárom, northern Hungary, on 8 January 1895. From the outbreak of the First World War in 1914 he served in the Austro-Hungarian army on the Russian front, until he was gravely wounded in 1918. While still in military hospital in Nagyvárad (today Oradea, Romania), he began to make his name as a writer and journalist. In 1920 he moved to Budapest, and over the next two decades became one of Hungary's most prolific and best-known authors.

Between 1925 and 1943 Zsolt produced ten novels and four plays, as well as a large amount of political and literary journalism. He contributed copiously to the radical liberal press, and in 1929 was appointed editor-in-chief of the journal *A toll* (The Pen). A sophisticated bohemian, he spent much of his life in the Abbazia Café and other fashionable coffee houses haunted by the writers, artists and intellectuals of Budapest, arguing, conducting political and cultural campaigns, smoking and drinking to excess, and damaging his already weakened health.

In his writings Zsolt assumed an aggressively liberal stance. While he had little sympathy for the far left, he took every opportunity to denounce the conservative establishment that had ruled Hungary since the failure of the bourgeois-democratic revolution of 1918 and the short-lived communist regime of 1919. He opposed with particular ferocity the rising movement of folksy populists, both in the arts and in politics, who decried urban Western civilisation and championed a chauvinistic system based on the alleged strength and purity of an unspoilt Magyar race rooted in the Hungarian countryside. In their turn, the adherents of this ideology, which was closely related to the German Nazis' cult of 'blood and soil', vilified Zsolt as a decadent, bourgeois, cosmopolitan enemy of the Hungarian nation. Since their outlook was profoundly anti-Semitic, they naturally also attacked him as a Jew. Ironically, Zsolt's own social criticism was often directed against the same targets. His best-known novels—*Gerson és neje* (Gerson and His Wife), *A dunaparti nő* (The Woman from the Danube Embankment) and *A kínos ügy* (The embarrassing affair)—were harsh satires on the contemporary middle classes of Budapest, and above all the Jews among them.

In the early years of the Second World War the Jews of Hungary were not yet being exterminated on an industrial scale, like those of German-occupied Eastern Europe. Nevertheless, there was harsh anti-Jewish discrimination, and in 1941–2 some 100,000 Jewish men from all walks of life were drafted into the forced-labour service and put to work in the Ukraine as part of the Hungarian army, which was fighting side by side with the Germans. Conditions were atrocious. Apart from starvation, disease and exposure to all weathers, the men were brutally ill treated by their rabidly anti-Semitic guards. In August 1939 Zsolt, with his wife Ágnes, had taken refuge in Paris, but shortly after the outbreak of the war, at her insistence, they had returned to Hungary, and in the summer of 1942 he too was sent to the Ukraine. As a prominent Jewish member of the political opposition, he was treated with particular viciousness by the Hungarian soldiers and officers, but his influential friends in the capital succeeded in bringing him home in late 1943. Soon after his return to Budapest he was thrown into the notorious political prison in Margit Boulevard on charges of incitement and horror-mongering. In January 1944 he was released after four months' detention, and travelled to Nagyvárad with his wife to recover at her parents' home.

Meanwhile Hitler had lost his faith in his Hungarian allies, and on 19 March 1944 German troops invaded Hungary. Within weeks, the entire Jewish population of the country, with the exception of those in the capital, was rounded up, 'ghettoised' and deported to Auschwitz, mainly by exceptionally sadistic Hungarian gendarmes.* Between late April and mid-July some

---

* In Hungary different aspects of law enforcement were entrusted to two different forces, the 'police' and the paramilitary 'gendarmerie'.

430,000 reached the death camp, where 100,000 men and women were selected for forced labour, and the rest immediately gassed. On 15 October, after an attempt by the regent, Miklós Horthy, to extricate Hungary from the war, the fascist Arrow Cross party seized power and unleashed a reign of terror, in which half of the 200,000 Jews remaining in Budapest were murdered, before they could be liberated by the Red Army in early 1945. When the war started, the Jewish population of Hungary numbered about 725,000: when it ended, about 260,000 were still alive. From Nagyvárad, between 27 May and 3 June 1944, some 19,000 were taken to Auschwitz, nearly 90 per cent of whom died. Zsolt and his wife managed to escape from the ghetto, go underground in Budapest, and eventually find a safe haven in Switzerland as members of the 'Kasztner group'.

When the deportations began in the spring of 1944, the journalist Rezső Kasztner and some other members of the Hungarian Jewish community embarked on an adventurous rescue enterprise, involving a number of Nazi officers including Adolf Eichmann and possibly acting with the approval of Heinrich Himmler. They were to supply the Germans with 10,000 trucks and various consumer goods from abroad, in exchange for the lives of a million Jews still surviving in Hungary and elsewhere in Eastern Europe. Neither of the parties could have regarded this as a realistic proposition, but the German side may have hoped that it could lead to negotiations for a separate peace with the Western Allies, while the Jewish side hoped to gain time and keep alive as many Jews as possible until the final collapse of the Third Reich.

The deal came to nothing, but in the course of the negotiations Kasztner succeeded in saving a group of 1,680 men, women and children, for a ransom of $1,000 per head, raised mainly by American and Swiss Jews. The group was selected by a small committee, including Kasztner, from Jewish communities all over Hungary. It consisted of wealthy people who were able to contribute to the ransom, prominent figures from political, religious and cultural life, and some ordinary individuals, who somehow managed to gatecrash. Their train left Budapest on 30 June and arrived at the concentration camp of Bergen-Belsen on 8 July 1944, where they were to await the outcome of Kasztner's negotiations. Three hundred and twenty reached Switzerland on 21 August, and the remaining 1,360 on the night of 6/7 December 1944. Among the latter were Zsolt and his wife, who had been invited to join the group by Kasztner. Zsolt's mother, brothers and sisters, his wife's parents and her thirteen-year-old daughter by her first husband were killed in Auschwitz. Kasztner himself—after being accused of collaborating with the Nazis for his own profit, and losing a libel case he brought as a result—was murdered, apparently by right-wing extremists, in Tel Aviv in 1957. In 1958 he was posthumously rehabilitated by the High Court of Israel.

In June 1945 Zsolt returned to Hungary and immediately resumed his political and journalistic activities. He played a leading part in the creation of the Hungarian Radical Party, and he founded the weekly journal *Haladás* (Progress), with himself as editor-in-chief and main contributor. While the party initially failed to gain any parliamentary seats, the journal soon became a powerful voice, indicting the continuing influence of former fascists and the persistence of corruption and anti-Semitism under the country's new communist rulers. In 1947 Zsolt was elected to parliament, but soon came under increasing pressure to toe the communist party line. In the autumn of 1948 he was admitted to a sanatorium in Budapest, where he died on 6 February 1949, at the age of 54. His wife had committed suicide in 1948 after publishing the diary of her dead daughter, which had been preserved by the family's loyal Hungarian cook (*The Diary of Eva Heyman*, translated by Moshe M. Kohn, Jerusalem: Yad Vashem, 1974, New York: Shapolsky, 1988).

Nine Suitcases was originally published in *Haladás* in weekly instalments. The first instalment appeared on 30 May 1946, and the last on 27 February 1947. The last two instalments are fragments of Part II, which was planned, but never written: they describe some episodes of Zsolt's train journey from Bergen-Belsen to Switzerland. Part I is complete in itself. It ends with Zsolt's arrival in Budapest after his escape from the Nagyvárad ghetto, as does this translation.

An edition of *Nine Suitcases* in book form was announced in

Haladás for the autumn of 1947, but never materialised. Perhaps Zsolt was too ill to organise the publication, or no longer willing or able to do so, as a result of many hostile personal or political reactions to the serial. For some decades after his death he remained out of favour with the ruling circles, not only because he was an anti-communist and a Jew, but also because any public discussion of anti-Semitism and the Jews' fate in the Second World War was frowned on throughout the Soviet bloc. As a result, the first Hungarian edition in book form did not appear until 1980. It is likely that Zsolt would have tidied up the few minor inconsistencies in the text if he had had the opportunity to prepare it for publication himself. The first edition in any other language was an incomplete German translation of Part I by Angelika Máté (Frankfurt am Main: Neue Kritik, 1999), which breaks off at the end of Chapter Thirty-six.

Nine Suitcases is one of the very first—and most important— memoirs of the Holocaust ever written. It is by pure historical accident that no English translation has been undertaken before now. When Zsolt first published the serial, there was practically no 'Holocaust literature'. More than half a century later there is an enormous volume of writing on the subject, but Zsolt's work remains unique. Concentrating mainly on his experiences as an inmate of the ghetto of Nagyvárad and a forced labourer in the Ukraine, he provides not only a rare and extremely perceptive insight into Hungarian fascism, but a shocking exposure of the depths of cruelty, indifference, selfishness, cowardice and betrayal of which human beings in general—the victims no less than the perpetrators—are capable in extreme circumstances, created by human beings themselves. The bleak series of horrors, interspersed with moments of grotesque farce, acidic irony and grim wit, occasionally relieved by memories of kind deeds, paints a nightmarish picture of a world without hope that has lost all its values and meaning.

Apart from being one of the earliest, Zsolt is also one of the most accomplished writers of the Holocaust, who can bear comparison with Primo Levi, Elie Wiesel or Imre Kertész. *Nine Suitcases* has sometimes been described, incorrectly, as a novel. It is a horror story but, sadly, a true one. Certainly, there are dialogues that Zsolt could hardly have memorised in those exact words, some minor inaccuracies about dates and names, and some narrative details that he may have deliberately arranged in such a way as to underline their symbolic significance. However, he was not only a creative writer, but also a highly skilled journalist who, in this instance, was reporting with the events still fresh in his mind, and whose memory may have been sharpened beyond the normal degree by the appalling nature of his experiences. For all the brilliant imaginative qualities of the writing, the salient facts are authentic and can be corroborated from other sources. Zsolt was spared Auschwitz, but he nevertheless witnessed, or personally suffered, some of the worst atrocities of the Holocaust. His account is an extraordinary monument to human evil.

It may be worth mentioning that the translator once had the opportunity to observe Zsolt at close quarters for a period of five months. Zsolt is unlikely to have taken much notice of an eleven-year-old child, but the child had been told that Zsolt was an important person. Sallow-faced, emaciated, desperate for cigarettes, he gathered groups of followers around him, with an air of distinction that the child did not fully understand, but could clearly sense. The time was the second half of 1944. The place was the concentration camp of Bergen-Belsen.

Ladislaus Löb

One

So, here I am, lying on my mattress in the middle of the synagogue at the foot of the Ark of the Covenant. The light that consultant Németi inked hospital-blue the day before yesterday flickers. Outside, foreign aircraft are flying over the town, but this doesn't bother us. The star, our stigma, excludes us not only from life's amenities but also from its fears. We aren't afraid of air raids, or any other kinds of death. The dead are lying here next to me: on the mattresses to my right and left there are diabetics in a coma, angina patients, uraemics, people with galloping TB who haven't been looked after during the last few weeks, and suicides who are being brought in on stretchers day and night, generally in pairs, mostly couples, including doctors who had poison at hand and knew the exact doses.

Next to the terrible WC there is a laundry turned into a morgue, but by yesterday half a dozen legs, naked and waxen, were hanging out of the half-open door. The gendarmes allow no funerals. 'They'll all be taken care of together,' the gendarmerie colonel says with icy humour, and the bodies continue to pile up. At the top of the pile, as high as the ceiling, are the naked bodies of two children.

That is why nine dead men and women have been left in the synagogue, decomposing in the stifling heat. My neighbour on the next mattress, Uncle Niszel, the old leather merchant, went with great difficulty—at home in normal circumstances, according to his doctor, he would have had the 'beautiful death' his heart disease had been promising him for years—falling peacefully off his chair, surrounded by his family. Here, in the synagogue of the wonder-rabbi of Wisznice, which is now the ghetto hospital, weighed down by his ordeals, he kept puffing for a day and a half, with his mouth open, rhythmically, like the small steam engine at the timber yard. The whole ward was bored with the poor devil, the amateur nurses shook their heads in disapproval, and three impatient patients, who were after his mattress near the Ark of the Covenant and closer to the window, inspected him every quarter of an hour, interrogating the dazed doctor in his white coat as to how much time the old boy had left. Finally he died at about ten o'clock, but wasn't carried out, because there was no room in the morgue. Even so, the three patients, in their pants and vests, who had hoped to grab his mattress, fell out over the succession, although they eventually contented themselves with sharing out the old man's possessions—his felt slippers, brown blanket and personal bedpan—and slunk away in the blue darkness, each with his booty.

The nurses fluttered ineffectually, before huddling together again in the corner. They were middle-class girls from good families, who hadn't been trained for the work but had fought to get it, because those who sported a nurse's bonnet were able to move freely in the ghetto. The other girls, in groups of sixteen, were stuck in dirty, unfamiliar rooms, where they weren't even allowed to go near the window and every gendarme was entitled to use his weapons against them. Here, in the wonder-rabbi's two-storey synagogue with its large courtyard, the ghetto was freer and more cheerful. On the mattresses unwashed patients lying in their own filth puffed, panted, moaned, prayed and swore, and during the first two days caused a lot of trouble: they needed to be washed, to be given bedpans and enemas, to have their temperature taken and to be fitted with compresses. During the first two days the doctors too fought with all their strength: they administered injections, flushed out the stomachs of suicides, carried out operations and, on the top floor, even carefully delivered babies. Then the rumour spread that the ghetto would be deported. Thirty cattle wagons were shunted on to the industrial siding that cut across the enclosed part of the town. Now the doctors faltered, became absent-minded, dropped out from time to time, went back to their relatives several times a day, clearly in order to discuss whether it wouldn't be better to exterminate all of them. The nurses, for their part, disappeared or sat down on the long bench near the morgue. They were clean, well dressed, with nice hairstyles, and men gathered around them as they had on the promenade. The conversation was entertaining, as it had been in the world outside, but more outspoken, because after two days here the girls overacted the part of the liberated and experienced professional who is familiar with every dirty secret of the human body.

So, when the contenders for Uncle Niszel's mattress pillaged his body in the dark, the girls fluttered and huddled. Then one of them—a tall, blonde, pretty girl of about twenty with a slight squint—separated from the group and set out unsteadily towards the Ark of the Covenant. She stopped and squatted down at the edge of my mattress.

'Mr Hirschler,' she whispered, 'that friendly gendarme was here just now. He said that from tomorrow they'll be beating people up to make them admit where they've hidden their jewellery. They'll do it in alphabetical order, and my father's name starts with B.'

'Have you hidden anything?'

'Yes. My father has high blood pressure. He wouldn't be able to bear a single blow.'

'Then it might be wiser to tell, so they don't hurt him.'

'But they'll beat him all the same.'

'Well, then . . .'

'The gendarme says', she whispered, bending close to my ear, 'that if I go to bed with him he'll save Daddy. I know your real name, Mr Hirschler. I've read things you've written . . . You could advise me.'

I wouldn't have felt particularly guilty in this situation, in this hell, this synagogue of the wonder-rabbi, if I had advised the girl to give in to the gendarme. So many things had been lost since 19 March.* There are really no bogus, high-flown sentiments left in me. I'm saying this as one who has lost not only all his belongings, but something very important, something vital: above all else, I have lost my homeland. This homeland has always meant more to me than to most people around me: it exercised me feverishly when I was writing, speaking or dreaming, and

* On 19 March 1944 the Germans invaded their ally Hungary.

there were years, particularly the years of my youth, when, for example, I hardly took notice of love because of it. That was the time when after the failure of two revolutions,* for nearly a decade I waited for my political ideas to prevail, for my exiled role models and friends to return and save my homeland from the crooks and bunglers. Yes, I waited for nearly ten years, in which I had no lover. And when I had tired of waiting and almost renounced the game for the duration of my life, I married, clutching at privacy as a shipwrecked man clutches at a plank that might help him reach some shore—although I must admit I had no illusions about the shore. But, for all my conscious efforts to abandon 'my crazy ideas and whims', I was time and again dragged out of my private idyll, which had soon staled, by my social passion: the most simple-minded reason for hope was enough to make me forget where I lived and where a person living with me was waiting with my dinner. A few months after my divorce from my first wife we tried to trace the events leading up to our slow, bitter drift apart. 'What started the trouble', she said, 'was that I was all of eighteen years old and married for six weeks when you woke up one morning and said "Bethlen!" instead of noticing—with the March sun shining on our bed—that it was the first day of spring.'

Indeed, I hated Bethlen† with a personal passion, because with his determination, ruthlessness and stubbornness he was gradually destroying all hope of the return of the revolution. I had experienced the collapse of my ideas and my homeland too early, when I was hardly eighteen, and it wasn't only my political, social and philosophical illusions that collapsed, but almost everything else. This collapse has remained the sharpest break in my life to this day. It extinguished what had been burning in me with even hotter and brighter flames than the social passion— the lyrical and the aesthetic. And it nearly turned me into a nervous and physical wreck: it caused painful disturbances in my sex life, and many years of insomnia, lack of appetite, many types

* In 1918 and 1919 respectively there was a liberal and a communist revolution in Hungary.
† Right-wing prime minister of Hungary from 1921 to 1939.

of self-flagellation and waste of energy, which drove me close to a state of frenzy. I spat blood, ran a fever—Sándor Bródy* said that I wouldn't last till the spring—and sat in cafés till dawn, hating and hoping. I know that this gnawing political grief contained many different things, for instance bitterness over the collapse of my personal ambitions, but whatever the case, by the time I was twenty my youth had gone. Over the next few years, time and nature numbed and even healed many wounds, but I never again knew what it was like to be really well. Whatever I ate or drank left a bad taste, and whenever I wasn't fully absorbed by the hatred or enthusiasm of the political and related intellectual battle I felt that I was committing an infidelity. Even while making love I felt guilty about squandering something that should have been reserved for my one and only important passion. At the same time I almost began to worship men older than myself whom I believed to have purer and more faithful passions than I did. For a long time I refused to accept, even when I experienced it face to face, that many of them, despite their patriotic sorrow, were seeking a separate peace and, being corrupted by clever compromises, were slowly slipping across to the other side.

Yes, it was Bethlen who gradually decimated the 'inner emigration', in which we had lived in heroic sterility till the death of Lajos Purjesz.† People would cross over and, with some traces of pride left, invent an ideology for their treason. *Fühlung mit dem Feinde*—direct contact with the enemy—had to be maintained. They did maintain it, making money and carving out successful careers in the process, by publishing a newspaper that served Bethlen under the pretext of being in oppostition to him—while a few of us were left behind on our own, and even among us the majority only used our political *salon des refusés* as an alibi for laziness, tiredness and lack of talent to forge ahead elsewhere.

* Prolific novelist, critic and journalist, precursor of modern Hungarian literature (1863–1924).
† Lawyer, journalist and editor of several anti-establishment liberal journals (1881–1925).

Never had an idol made of ice been able to arouse more fiery feelings of attraction in coldly calculating usurers, big industrialists, lawyers with large offices, and cynical careerists, than Bethlen. And there could hardly be a society whose so-called elite—both Christians and Jews—could have wallowed in its own paltriness and weakness more lustfully than it did in the shade of Bethlen's pompous arrogance and ruthlessness. I hated him also because I couldn't resign myself to being intellectually and morally helpless against him. I pounced wildly on his speeches, in which lack of logic was masked by acoustic vigour, and aristocratic conceit masqueraded as intellectual superiority and manliness. I dissected and laid bare his contradictions, his reckless immorality and ignorance. It was useless. I didn't convince or change a single mind. Eventually even people who shared my viewpoint began to rebuke me for making a fuss and hurting those whom I couldn't help anyway. I was helpless but didn't budge. Eventually Bethlen became a symbol of all my public and private failures: the rock on which I foundered. This fruitless, childish struggle—which Bethlen for his part also experienced as a struggle, although I discovered this only after his fall— became an obsession. Is it surprising that on that morning I woke up with his name in my mouth, and our bed, with the sunshine on it, couldn't relieve this obsession? Yes, it was my delusion that I had to change the order of the world, the order of my homeland, before I could be happy in my house and in my bed.

Bristling with mines, traps and savage thugs,
Ours is no world for kisses and hugs.

This is what I wrote at the time, because I felt that with every kiss I was obeying a bitter, dangerous coercion.

Two

So I have lost my homeland—and a lot more—since 19 March. A postcard arrived at the address of an Aryan friend, written by my mother when she was already in the cattle wagon at Komárom station. I don't even want to think this right through: so my mother is no longer at home in the house in Úri Street that she hardly ever left in fifteen years and where I used to drop in, admittedly not very often and not very eagerly, as if I had never gone away. We would always start our conversation in mid-sentence, as if I had just popped out of the room or been called to the phone and we had resumed at the comma. She had been a very beautiful woman, as mothers generally are in their sons' memories, chaste, naive but wise, critical but credulous where I was concerned, with no illusions, except about me. To me she was timelessness and permanence itself, the centre of my emotional map, which had proved more constant than anything or anyone else. I could never imagine that one day I would go home and she wouldn't be in her place, at the centre, that she would no longer be alive. I never tried to torture myself or indulge in a vision of visiting my mother's grave. I had faced my own death several times as a young man in the First World War, and had fervently wished for it on wintry roads during the Second—but my mother, to me, was like Mont Blanc: she would always be there, even when I was gone. Now she would turn seventy-five in the cattle wagon, with her hair as white as Mont Blanc in dull weather.

I felt as if the mountains had toppled.

And how many more things have been lost! Yet of my so-called human dignity I lost none. When civilised people are devoured by cannibals, it can only hurt physically. Can the bite of a savage's fang cause moral pain? All the while they tortured me as a Jew, giving rein to their envy and loutish greed—first by the laws they had designed to deprive us of our money and our civilised pleasures, the informers and detectives they sent after us, and the loud-mouthed, mechanically rowdy press campaigns they conducted against us; then in Russia with cables and lashes—I was only troubled by the physical and material inconveniences and ill-treatments, but could never be hurt morally or emotionally. Rather, I always suspected that through their venomous, seemingly studied hatred they were trying above all to prove to themselves what they were unable to believe: that they really felt superior to me. I didn't hate them—you can only hate someone you could also love. I was merely sickened by these common criminals, press whores, venal poets and clowns, and butchers' dogs turned wolves. I was repelled by them, I despised them—and, face to face, perhaps revealed too much of my arrogance, like the haughty white man in a topee of the English adventure story for boys, who keeps flaunting his loathing for the blacks, high on their stolen rum, and who excites them to further cruelties through his superiority. And because they noticed my hauteur they often treated me with particular cruelty. But, as I say, their laws, their dirty words and their lashes only hurt my skin and my flesh, and even now that they have dragged me to this ghetto I feel like the doctor in the mental hospital in Poe's short story, who has been put into a straitjacket and locked in a cell by the rioting lunatics. Now they are living in the doctors' quarters, waving the instruments and drugs— transformed into murder weapons and poison in their hands— and cutting up the medical books into sheets of toilet paper. Yet they are not too mad to steal the doctor's money, watch, clothes and whatever else he has . . .

Three

They have taken everything away from me—these gendarmes with their red faces, their thick cheekbones, their eyes like black buttons, their chins, made to look even more beastly by the tight straps of their helmets. They looted our apartment, gobbled up everything in our kitchen, and slung on to their truck the nine suitcases that held all my possessions, my clothes and my wife's clothes and all the necessities and small luxuries we had collected in our lives: the objects, the fetishes. With these nine suitcases we had arrived in Paris one day before the war, never intending to return to Budapest. In the second month of the war, we brought the nine suitcases back from Paris, or rather—as I will explain later—the nine suitcases brought *us* back. Then they were put on top of a wardrobe and I never saw them for two years, because I was in Russia, where I had only a knapsack, and in the prison in Margit Boulevard,* where I had only a shoe box for my food. And when I got out of the prison a few weeks ago my wife decided to put everything we had back into the nine suitcases and bring them here to Nagyvárad, to my father-in-law's house, because here they would certainly be in no danger from bombs. We brought the nine suitcases back on 16 March, the Germans arrived on the 19th; then the gendarmes came and took them away. Now I don't even have a shoe box under my mattress—I have nothing. An acquaintance gave me a box of biscuits yesterday, and that's all the luggage I have. Everything I had has become national property. The 'nation' first broke into my father-in-law's small house, which it looted, turned out my pockets like a pickpocket, and finally kicked me with its gendarme boots when, with nothing but the clothes I stood up

---

* Notorious political prison in Budapest.

in, without a penny or a crust, I wasn't quick enough to slip away through the ghetto gate under cover of the large crowd milling there.

Before this I had had two personal contacts with robbers and thieves.

When I was a young child a cobbler called Buzgó, a professional burglar, looted our home. When a policeman brought him along to confront him with my mother, he wrung his hands and apologised in tears, returning everything he had taken. On another occasion a barber's apprentice called Eszlényi stole my wallet on the tram. Some other people noticed and handed him over to the police. He was doubly unlucky because in my wallet there was nothing but a ticket for a dress rehearsal at the Comedy Theatre. He pulled such a disappointed and desperate face over having risked everything for such a lousy theatre ticket that I begged the policeman to let him go.

But the 'nation' wanted everything: the gendarme even pocketed a season ticket to the zoo belonging to my wife's young daughter. It, too, became national property . . . That is what I have lost, among many other things, since 19 March.

And now here is this blonde girl with the long legs and the squint, almost touching my nose with her knees, and asking me to advise her whether or not to lose her virginity to the gendarme who is going to save her father from being beaten. What should I say to her, whose fate, by the way, leaves me frighteningly cold? In 1942 out there at Skarzysko in Poland I saw the *Feldbordell**
with the Jewish girls from Vienna and Bratislava pulling up weeds between the rails in their 'spare time', cheerfully supervised by a gauche German railwayman, and—the first thing that horrified me—laughing lewdly and dementedly. From time to time the railwayman playfully smacked their bottoms with his cane, without hurting them. The girls were still wearing clothes from good department stores and boutiques, albeit frayed and filthy, and half of them had bulging bellies. We were just starting out for forced labour in Russia—with our horror and pity still fresh— and they had been there for a year, corrupted by being assigned

* field brothel

10

to service German soldiers in the red huts as they passed through on leave. Naturally for a voucher issued by the *Verpflegungszentralstelle*.* When, with horrified gentleness, I addressed one of them, who was called Ilse like a Hanover patrician, she answered in an offhand manner, with crazy laughter, almost in the tone of the streetwalkers on the boulevards. '*Ihr seid Juden?*'[†] she asked contemptuously, barely deigning to speak to us since we were irrelevant to her occupation, and added abruptly: 'You'll kick the bucket, just like us!' Another girl, in the last stages of pregnancy, who was carrying some mouldy bread in a music case, asked us: 'Have you got any German books? I've just finished what I had today. I've got a few days left to read a new one if it isn't too long.—'Why have you only got a few days?'—'Because then I'm going to die. Wait a moment . . .' and she counted on her fingers. 'Seventeen or eighteen days. Then I'll be in labour. Then they're going to take me behind the bushes and bang . . . *Dort ist der Hurenfriedhof*.[‡]

That was where they killed and buried the girls, behind the bushes, because they didn't want them to give birth to mongrels, and also simply because they were Jews. The girls didn't mind becoming pregnant: they didn't have the strength to commit suicide and this was the certain death they longed for. Meanwhile they still enjoyed life, even their helpless bodies were forced to enjoy it—and they hated themselves for it. And sometimes they would even sing, if the soldiers made them drunk. They got the novels from the soldiers. The novels were about blonde German women and U-boat sailors. They read them avidly, with the unlucky ones being taken away mid-novel and never knowing what happened next to the blonde and the captain. They would snatch a glance at the very end, however, before being loaded on to the NSKK[§] truck that disappeared with them behind the bushes.

I saw the same again later in Russia, besides similar and worse things. How am I now supposed to advise this girl on whether or not she should go to bed with the gendarme?

* Central Supplies Office
[†] Are you Jews?
[‡] That's where the whores' cemetery is.
[§] Nationalsozialistisches Kraftfahrzeugkorps = National Socialist Motor Corps

Should I make a question of conscience out of it—should I stop her or should I accept responsibility for starting her off towards the *Hurenfriedhof*? I must admit that if this girl were lying in the morgue, with her long legs hanging out of the half-open door, I would walk past with indifference and apathy. There are friends of mine lying among the bodies, men and women I've known and been friendly with for decades, and I think with cold inertia even of them. Death in this place is a good 'assignment'. The dead aren't driven out at daybreak to work for the SS, they aren't beaten till they hand over their jewellery, and they won't have to set out in the cattle wagons. Sooner or later they will be released from their boarded prison and allowed to stay here in Nagyvárad, in the Rulikovszky cemetery under the old elms or the Velence cemetery with its acacias under the shadow of the Calvary, in the micaceous sand that consumed their ancestors. The gendarmes and the SS don't want to consume the dead, only the living. I wouldn't care in the slightest if this girl were dead. One more dead. And if she asked me whether she should commit suicide I certainly wouldn't advise her against it. But should she go to bed with the gendarme for her father's sake? No, I'm not going to advise her, I'm not going to provide her with any authorisation. She can do what she wants, I won't interfere. Not because of Skarzysko . . . and not because of other things. Perhaps it's the indestructible petty bourgeois in me that is protesting and I take the whole business too seriously even here. Certainly it's pointless for me to regard her virginity as a more complex problem at this moment than her life, for which I wouldn't give a damn. After all, I know, because my friends in London sent me the detailed report from Poland through the messenger from Ankara in 1942—I know that all of us are going to be gassed.

'I can't rule in this matter,' I say coldly. 'This is something you've got to decide for yourself.'

She was disappointed and for a while went on trying to coax an opinion from me. I could feel that she was hoping for encouragement rather than disapproval. I even briefly suspected that she didn't simply want to sacrifice herself for her father, but was unconsciously seeking a pretext for allowing something that she had been preparing herself for to happen, at the last moment before the world ended. In other words, she didn't want to die without having done 'it'. But perhaps there was something else. When I was renting a room in Budapest, I knew a girl whose father, a stupid, hellishly honest chemist with a crew cut, was taken to the police station on the unfounded suspicion of smuggling sweeteners. The girl worshipped her father, although he had ruined her youth with his tyrannical honesty and had generally done a lot of harm to the family—for instance, by almost letting them starve for the sake of his antiquated business principles. The children had had to take music lessons, although no member of the family was musical. When the old man was arrested and his bullied wife lugged his bedclothes after him in the pouring autumn rain, the girl didn't jump from the top floor in her despair but gave herself to their lodger, a fake-jewellery dealer with crooked ears, polyps in his nose and a dirty collar, a poor devil whom she hated and who hadn't wanted anything from her but had only come in to comfort her in his clumsy way. 'You'll see, Licike, he'll be back by tomorrow morning,' the lodger kept mumbling and afterwards was most surprised and ashamed at what had happened . . .

No, I didn't give the girl any advice and may have been too unsympathetic, because she suddenly got up, smoothed down her skirt, threw her head back and shot off.

Four

In the distance we can hear a dull rumble. The blue lamp has gone out again. Somebody on the mattress opposite is continually muttering: 'Debrecen . . . They're bombing Debrecen. The railway line to the north, so they can't take us away.'

Five minutes later the lamp is burning again. The subdued light throws mysterious, alien shadows on the whitewashed walls of the wonder-rabbi's synagogue. High above are the densely barred galleries where the women, hidden from sight, used to watch the men dancing, as prescribed by the chassidic ritual, and praising God in the jubilant words of the psalms.

Could there ever have been a more improbable adventure than lying at midnight on a mattress in a chassidic synagogue in front of the Ark of the Covenant, now a cupboard for surgical instruments?

I knew hardly anything about these chassidim. Most of what I did know probably came from an accurate and poetic sociography, by the Christian Czech author Ivan Olbrecht, of the northeastern Ukrainian-Hutsul-Jewish mountain people, which gave a moving account of their childlike and idyllic existence in their native villages, their mythology with its many gods, devils and idols, and their outrageous poverty. I also knew that they had a rich folklore that nationalist Jews regarded as their folk poetry, but they always filled me with the same mixture of indifference and distaste, or the same political aversion, as did any hangovers from the pristine state of the nations that narrow-minded fanatics tried to reactivate in the social and intellectual life of today. Naturally I had heard of this wonder-rabbi from Wisznice through my acquaintances in Nagyvárad, who used to treat him, sceptically and half-jokingly, as a kind of soothsayer who gave advice on money and love affairs. But the chassidim from the eastern mountains, at the time of the Jewish festivals, made pilgrimages to him in their tens of thousands, overrunning the city merely in order to get a glimpse of the young lion with his red mane, silk caftan, white stockings, clerical shoes and huge fur hat, as he stepped up to the Ark of the Covenant, prayed, did tearful penance and, shaking his locks, danced on their behalf.

None of this had even curiosity value for me. I regarded it as some kind of 'frill' on Judaism or some bigotry that priests turned fanatical magi used in this as in other religions to cast a spell over primitive people. In summer, when I was relaxing in Nagyvárad, I often drove past the unplastered two-storey red brick house at the edge of the city, the likes of which I had seen in Poland and White Russia, but I never knew that this strange edifice with the unfinished exterior was the home of the wonder-rabbi. In my youth, unaware, I used to speed past this house in a car with my friends who are now here in the ghetto—journalists, doctors, lawyers, would-be women of the world—on my way to the thermal baths of Püspökfürdő and Félixfürdő, where, in the parks and on the restaurant terraces, I would be dreaming and telling lies to the women about Vichy, Aix-les-Bains and Interlaken, although I had never been there . . . Later on I did go to all of them and none was as ravishing as in my lies.

Now I must gather up the facts and details: how did I end up here among the chassidim? It was actually my own fault. I could have gone to many different places if I had tried harder. To Cagnes, Madrid, Lisbon, Marrakesh, even America—I was free to choose where I wanted to go. I had the visa and the money. Now, of course, I'm blaming my feeble indecision, my notorious weakness, my posturing generosity. But let us not deceive ourselves: it's certain that if a man is given the opportunity to choose his destination, he'll leave nothing to chance. It's quite certain that when I took that so-called wrong step home I was only pretending to be indecisive but I really wanted to come home at all costs. At that time, in October 1939, in my unease I knew exactly what risks and what chances I was taking. The war had broken out in Poland. In the evening we Hungarians were sitting in the lounge of the Hôtel de France, in a strange country, with our nerves on edge, arguing about politics and wondering what to do next, when I predicted: 'Don't be surprised if by the end of the war we're in Singapore or Archangel. Unless we die of yellow fever in Saigon.' At that time nobody knew, and even I wasn't quite certain, that I would return home. However, my adventurous predictions were in fact mainly about myself, and therefore I have no right to be surprised that in the third year of the war this former resident of Váci Street* and scaremongering regular of the Carlton Café in Budapest was thrown into a military prison, after trudging three thousand kilometres in the two biggest retreats in military history as the world's most miserable lice-infested forced labourer, and now finds himself here beneath the Ark of the Covenant. Why is this more fantastic than landing up in Singapore, where I would now be a prisoner of the Japanese? The others, with whom I had been sitting in the Hôtel de France, did actually fetch up in Saigon, Marrakesh, Chad and African or Middle Eastern camps, and rumours filtered through to us at home that many of them had died of exotic diseases . . . Well, out there in the Ukraine I almost died of typhus and could have trodden on a mine, like eleven out of my twenty fellow mine-clearers, or been hanged, because in my own way I was constantly asking for it. Nothing that is happening now is fantastic or surprising. Not even that I'm here in the domain of the wonder-rabbi. Not even that by the end of the week they'll have loaded me into a wagon, as they've already done half a dozen times. And if they gas and burn me they'll do it in the same matter-of-fact manner as, once upon a time, they used gas for cooking.

I blame the nine suitcases for bringing me back from Paris, where I was living in a small hotel in the Rue Linné with my wife and my friends, trying to prepare the renewal of Hungary from abroad, and to save our homeland from outside. My wife clung to the nine suitcases tooth and nail, and because there was no room for all nine together on the overcrowded train to the Riviera we didn't go to Cagnes. For the same reason we didn't go to Madrid or Lisbon. In those days it wasn't possible to travel on French trains with luggage. Passengers were sitting on the roofs

---

* Budapest's most elegant shopping street.

and hanging from the steps, robbing each other. The railways wouldn't accept any express goods and there was no question of getting anywhere with nine suitcases. I kept asking my wife to leave with two to start with, and to collect the rest later if possible. But she insisted on all nine. Only one train was prepared to accept the nine suitcases, a train with a sleeping car and a dining car, a train as in peacetime: the Simplon Express. It was a good train, a blue train, leaving from the Gare de Lyon. The *wagon-lit* attendant, as haughtily as in peacetime, lifted the nine suitcases over the heads of the Parisians who, in a panic after the first air raids, were trying to escape without any luggage. The train crossed Switzerland and Italy according to the peacetime schedule. Only, its destination was Budapest . . .

It was finally decided in the Rue de Grenelle that I would end up in the chassidic synagogue in Nagyvárad. I was in a taxi with my wife, bound for 37 Champs-de-Mars to take tea with Dr Diamant Berger, the old doctor who had moved to Paris after the great flood and still spoke French with a Szeged accent.[*] My wife had been deeply upset for days by the events of the war that were now touching us personally, and I had contributed to her anxiety. For instance, when communist deputies and journalists were arrested one after the other and Daladier[†] reconstituted his government with right-wingers and Munich appeasers, I would say to her in bed before going to sleep: 'We must get out of here as soon as possible. Flandin or Laval is coming and there'll be fascism.' Unfortunately, two days later in the Rue St Honoré we met Laval of all people, coming in the opposite direction, with his self-important black goat's face, his white piqué tie providing the beast's white beard. My wife spat in front of him and a commotion followed, before he walked on, smirking, and a kindly disposed policeman gave my wife a thorough lesson on the duties of foreigners. It was after one such incident that she suddenly snapped at me in the taxi: 'Look here, I'm

---

[*] The southern Hungarian city of Szeged had been all but destroyed by a flood in 1879.

[†] Édouard Daladier (1884–1970), Radical Socialist, prime minister of France at various periods.

neither a journalist nor a politician, and I don't care about your ideas. I'm a middle-class woman from Nagyvárad and that's where my parents and my child are. I've no business to be here now there's a war on. I want to be with them!'

From her point of view she was right, but I wasn't being honest when, like a gentleman who knows what he owes a lady, I knocked on the driver's window and said with fierce determination: *'Légation suisse!'* I'm sure I wouldn't have done this, had it not given me the opportunity to disguise my own longing for home with the appearance of angry gallantry. The Swiss embassy was in the Rue de Grenelle. The taxi stopped promptly, and within ten minutes I had a Swiss transit visa in my passport. That was the shore from which I cast off to land in the chassidic synagogue, where I'm now lying near the Ark of the Covenant, hungrily nibbling a leftover biscuit and unable to sleep because I'm being bitten by fleas.

At the other end of the synagogue the old people are lying. There are grandfathers and grandmothers whose families begged for a place for them in the hospital, in order to make their lives in the ghetto easier, and also to get rid of them. One is a crazy old woman with cerebral sclerosis, who is constantly chattering. Now she whimpers in German, breaking the monotonous silence behind the chorus of moans and rattles:

'How much longer are we going to stay here? I'm going home. How much longer are we going to be here?' She gets up and starts to squeeze her possessions into her shopping basket. Now she is looking for something she has lost, and shrieks at her neighbour to return her stolen slippers. The neighbour also gets out of bed and begins to pack while squabbling with her. Within minutes everybody, the whole row where the old people were lying, is packing. Even those who know that they can't go home, and why they can't go home, get excited. The whole ward suddenly seems to realise how utterly insane and impossible it is that people who live here, in this town, in the streets nearby—who have houses and apartments round the corner, with beds pushed together to make doubles, who must open their shops or go to court tomorrow, who have never slept in the same room with others—should be detained here in the synagogue of the wonder-rabbi of Wisznice. Now the old people are milling at the door, storming the exit, and the frightened nurses are trying to push them back, kindly or roughly. All those left on the mattresses sit up, ready to bolt. I also sit up, as if to wait and see whether the vanguard will manage to break out before making my own decision.

The friendly gendarme now pushes the door open, unaware that order has broken down in the ward. He has come to see the girl with the squint, or other girls, while doing his rounds. Whenever he's in the vicinity he drops in for a little flirt. He's crazy about girls, but even when he comes to chat them up, his way of pushing the door open betrays the cruelty of his kind. His boots thump and his weaponry creaks and clinks. The old people, who have gone completely berserk, press past him. The bemused nurses start screaming and weeping in their helplessness. Finally the doctors drive the old people back with their knees and fists, while the gendarme unslings his rifle. In an ominously kind voice that he may have learnt from some army chaplain instructing him about the Christian duties of a soldier he calls out:

'Men and women, listen to me. We go back to our places now, or I empty six bullets into you.'

After a bitter struggle they are back in their places. I also fall back on my mattress, exhausted and defeated.

This was our first and only rebellion. So far they had never really had to use force against us: they passed laws and regulations, and we obeyed. With the respect for the law that had been instilled in us we mechanically fulfilled their most idiotic demands. The only way some of us eluded the laws and regulations was by killing ourselves, instead of them. Otherwise anyone whose bed, house, money, father, child, false teeth or devotional objects they demanded handed over that possession as if in accordance with a new, legal method of paying tax, non-payment of which would incur a heavy fine. If a poster was put up, demanding that we should go somewhere with or without a bundle, we would go wherever ordered, queuing up as if we were waiting to book a railway ticket. If they came to search us in the middle of the night and ordered the whole family to strip, we would stand naked, parents in front of children, pitifully and awkwardly in a row like penguins. Nor, perhaps, did we do everything we were told out of fear, but rather because the state, the Hungarian State, with its intimidating and repressive authority, its traditional moral prestige, was one of those powers that simply had to be obeyed: in other words, we had to render unto Caesar those things that were Caesar's.

That was how they used the victims' own respect for the law as a leash to lead them wherever they pleased, and to have them enforce the laws and regulations against themselves. It was also how they made them do whatever a gendarme, or a lout from one of the urban gangs who turned up occasionally in search of thrills, thought would be an entertaining way to discover just what these inferior beings could be made to do. The stinking pigs would even eat their own excrement, because that was what they were like. They would stand on their heads singing the Arrow Cross marching song—'Now you're singing it, aren't you, you son of a bitch?' With their backs against the wall they would recite, beating their breasts: 'I'm a cheating, stinking Bolshevik Jew!' Meanwhile the men of the law stood behind them with their rubber truncheons, cudgels and elegant pointed gendarme boots, gloating that these bumptious Jews were now crawling before them on their stomachs like retriever dogs. The doddering doctor and the little half-blind teacher got the worst of it. These two were spies: their maids had reported that they were constantly listening to British radio broadcasts. A special helping of fun was provided by fat old people, whom these aficionados of comic films, when they lacked work, would drag out for something to laugh at. They called them Fatso and beat their naked behinds to shreds in front of their thin, grey, dishevelled wives whose eyes had run dry. In these burlesques hunchbacks and cripples provided equally popular heroes. They were forced to play the role of sportsmen, jumping over benches with their hernias, wrestling with each other on rubbish heaps . . .

All this, I repeat, could easily be accomplished because, although nothing experienced since 19 March remotely resembled what had previously passed for a state, nation or society, these people failed to realise to the very end that they were no longer living in a state whose laws had to be obeyed, a homeland that mustn't be hated for ill-treating its citizens—even when the filth was rising mouth-high and they were inhaling the stench of the decomposing bodies of their own parents, their own brothers and sisters, and their own children. They were unable to realise that this state had become a rabid dog, this homeland the free range of bandits.

First to wake up to this had been the old women who had attacked the gendarme when they wanted to go home. They had revealed the last vestige of courage when they had tried to restore the normal conditions in which everybody lives in his own home, tidying up his room in the morning and going about his own business, with the postman bringing letters, the policeman standing at the corner to stop cars running into each other, and gendarmes to be seen only at election time or when they would escort thieving gypsies to prison. 'It's absurd that they're keeping us here,' the crazy old lady with cerebral sclerosis had screeched. It was they, the old ones, who had dared to yell that this was absurd and that they had had enough of such absurdity.

I was tossing and turning on my mattress with humiliation. I was ashamed of not having joined the rebellion. After all, I had been organising the resistance in Budapest with my friends, eminent opposition politicians and journalists, since my return in 1939. We had been conspiring in a back room of the Fészek* Club, and then, when we had become suspects, in private apartments, planning, arguing, blustering and showing off about what would need to be done at the decisive moment and which of us would volunteer to take what action with a cool head and death-defying courage. We had been exchanging letters with people abroad via Ankara, and while in Russia I was going to defect a hundred times. Nothing had come to anything. Now at last there had been an opportunity to do more than shoot my mouth off. Now I could have done something. I could have headed the rebellion, leading the assault of the old men and women, mobilising the gravely ill and dying, and smashing our way past the gendarme with boards from the dismantled Ark of

* Nest

the Covenant, bedpans, crutches and slippers. I could have been a leader who would have awakened the ghetto, torn the gendarmerie colonel's seven proclamations with their death threats from the front doors of the houses, and broken out into the city, not in order to occupy the public utilities or to capture the barracks, but merely, as was our fullest right, in order to go home, lie down in our own beds and crawl under our own eiderdowns, which yesterday were still our lawful civilian shields.

Well, yes, the friendly gendarme, who had already forgotten the rebellion and was bantering with the girls in his Baranya dialect, would have 'done' for us. All right, so he would have done for us. I have no desire to commit suicide. Or to live either. But I lay low on my mattress while the old people were fighting.

Five

I heard the carts on the cobbles, lurching towards the weekly market. The peasants were bringing the 'black' milk, butter, eggs, poultry and early vegetables. They were angry because the Jews had been locked up and prices had fallen. The early vegetables were just beginning, and now there would also be lilies of the valley and guelder roses. Dawn was breaking, the episcopal church struck a quarter to four with a hard and hollow ring. But the bishop didn't hear it, the bishop was asleep, and it was just as well that he was asleep, because if he had been awake, he would have been inciting his followers, even at night, in the Nagyvárad newspapers to devour us before the Germans took us away, suffocated us and burnt us. The cocks crowed in a semicircle around the town, and from the town centre we heard the drawn-out howls of pinschers, wire-haired fox terriers and puli dogs—friends of the children and walking companions of the smart Nagyvárad ladies carried off to the ghetto—scurrying to and fro in the empty flats and deserted courtyards for the third night, in terror and confusion.

Suddenly Dr Németi sat down on the edge of my mattress. At first I didn't recognise him: I had always seen him wearing thick, powerful glasses. Now he wearily closed his red eyelids, or struggled to open them. He had blue eyes like a small schoolboy. He was the last of the doctors to persevere in his role as house physician, carrying out his functions for form's sake. From time to time he still passed through the ward with one or two nurses in his wake, doing his stately rounds. He still grasped a wrist or listened to a heart. He was still the consultant, symbolically performing the ceremony. Perhaps because outside he had been a passionate doctor, always studying, keeping up with international developments, reading the *Münchener Medizinische* and the *Lancet*. And perhaps because on the other side of the fence he had been ambitious, and because even here and now being a consultant carried a certain prestige and power.

'Now it's certain that we're going,' he whispered. 'The colonel has told the caterer. The first transport is leaving on Saturday.'

'It was certain from the first moment that we were going,' I answered coldly.

'Listen, we'll be seventy in a wagon. What's going to happen to these old and sick people?'

I was listening to him, leaning on one elbow. I shrugged stubbornly and irritably.

'After all, you're one of the greatest moral authorities in the ghetto,' he continued, even now in his pompous, thoroughly polished manner. 'Help us doctors make a decision. Some of us insist that doctors must fight for the lives of the patient as if nothing had happened. On the other hand there are those who favour euthanasia.'

I became terribly angry.

'Euthanasia, euthanasia? For God's sake, doctor! Let's drop these refinements. Perhaps you should call a conference at six p.m. in the banqueting room of the town hall under the auspices of the Darwin Circle to discuss principles! Let's not use such beautiful words here. Those times are over once and for all. Can't we stop being "European" even here? My dear sir, what we've got here is the plague and a knacker's yard!'

I know, he didn't deserve this rude outburst, but in this human knacker's yard he infuriated me with his snobbery. It was as if somebody had fallen into a cesspool in his evening dress.

He wasn't offended, but tried to calm me. He was a doctor and knew that in such a situation it isn't possible to predict what will drive a person's nervous system wild.

'What we doctors are asking you', he continued in a simpler, less rhetorical tone, 'is whether we should try to save the seriously ill and the suicides, or let them die.'

'Why are you asking me?' I said defensively.

'You can see the issue more clearly from a philosophical and literary point of view. We doctors are bound by the hippocratic oath and . . .'

I went on trying to decline the responsibility for making a decision. But he was right, time was pressing. It was Wednesday morning, and they would be taking people away on Saturday. By then we would have had to decide whether to kill them ourselves or leave the others to kill them. The previous evening the girl with the squint asked me to decide whether or not she should give her virginity to the gendarme. I didn't advise her. I didn't want to, I didn't dare to accept the responsibility. But I'm sure that even this evasion was a form of protest. I was defending the virginity of a daughter of my tribe from the enemy— well, that's a bit of an exaggeration, I didn't exactly defend her, but I found it easier to reconcile myself to the idea of the gendarme beating her arteriosclerotic father half dead than to imagine him embracing this girl, a daughter of my tribe. No, I wasn't thinking of this particular tribe, of the fact that the girl was Jewish. If she had been the daughter of the Lutheran pastor of Lőcse, with whom I used to wander dreamily down Múzeum Boulevard when I was a philosophy student, even then . . . If she had been the gendarmerie colonel's daughter, whom I used to accompany every morning to mass when she was my fiancée for a summer on Margit Island, even then . . . If after a ship- wreck the natives had tried to rape my English, Russian, Chinese or indeed German female fellow-travellers, even then. Those who travelled with me, were together with me, shared the same fate, were my tribe. This was no gentlemanly chivalry: in this extreme peril the old tribal ritual commanded me not to abandon our women to the lascivious rage of the wild boar attacking us. And the same primeval tribal law called out in me not to abandon our wounded, sick and disabled to the enemy, because we knew the enemy's customs: the first thing he did would be to torture, defile and mutilate them. Oh, I had seen the guard of the forced-labour unit in the Ukraine—a farmhand from Egreskáta—beat my comrade Mannstein to death with a rifle held in both hands, and then urinate on him roaring with laughter. And I had also seen the SS and the Todt organisation* raze a village near Minsk to the ground because the railway line nearby had been blown

* A technical unit of the German army.

up by partisans. First they doused the houses in petrol and set fire to them. When the old men, the women, the children and the dogs—the valuable animals had been stolen beforehand—tried to escape from the rampant flames and stifling smoke, they gunned them down one and all. Then the drunken desecration of the corpses began: the castration with bayonet or pocket knife, the tearing off of women's breasts, the smashing of children's heads against the walls—even dogs' intestines were ripped inside out, and the dead bodies hung on the trees. Very primitive African tribes and nomadic gypsies believe that if the murderer humiliates his victim the victim will not be able to reach the presence of God and accuse his murderer. The rabid gendarmes out there in the town, the demonstrating, singing, Arrow Cross brats, the women guffawing through the fence on their way to mass—what would they do, given the chance, to the eyes, ears, genitals of our wounded, to make quite sure that they couldn't accuse them in front of their god! No. Let us have euthanasia. Let us kill them!

Before announcing my decision I examined myself thoroughly. After all, these people, whom I was now sentencing to death, were strangers—but, to test myself, what would I answer to the doctor if, for example, my mother were lying here, dying, and medical assistance could save her?

It wasn't until the momentary icy spasm wringing my heart had eased that I said: 'Let all of them die in peace.' Yes, I was prepared to commit matricide—fervently wishing that my mother were here and I could kill her before she fell into their hands—before they made a mockery of her body, which I only ever dared to think of consciously as a disguise for her soul.

That was how I killed forty-nine people with a single sentence.

Six

In the morning word gets round that some evil-looking civilians have been billeted in the empty brewery. They are detectives from Budapest, come to seek out the political criminals in the ghetto and to beat people up and make them confess where they have hidden the valuables they should have handed in. So this is what the friendly gendarme meant when he propositioned the girl with the squint.

Even the details of the inquisition are already known in the hospital. Torture chambers have been set up with electric machines that beat, burn, numb and paralyse. These are used mainly on the bodies of women. The men have hot eggs shoved in their armpits, and their soles are beaten with rubber truncheons, their kidneys with sandbags, and their genitals with small metal sticks.

The people in the hospital who aren't seriously ill, or who got in by pushing, first try to persuade themselves that the sick will be spared the beatings. Then the rumour strengthens that only the political criminals are wanted. Those who know who I am blink at me slyly, with relief in their eyes: in their minds they have already handed me over. I don't really believe that the detectives are looking for politicos. On the morning of the German invasion both the Hungarian and the German secret police were already at my front door looking for me, and I'm told that even now there is a detective at the gate of my house in Váci Street, waiting for me to come home. Nevertheless, I don't believe that these civilian detectives with their electric machines have been sent here for characters like me. This gang, the government and its knackers, are after 'loot'. They want money and jewellery, these primitive natives, they want glittering objects. At the beginning of April, when we heard that they

27

were going to search every Jewish house, we first burnt the left-wing books they were constantly excoriating and denouncing as the corruption and poison that was ruining the nation. We thought that on entering the houses they would at once set about the bookcases, looking for Marx and company, or at least for books written by Jewish authors that had been sentenced to pulping. In fact they didn't take the slightest notice of the book-cases as they scraped together everything that was shiny: the Chinese silver dishes, the alpaca-silver fruit bowls, the watches in our pockets and on our wrists, the medallions hanging on thin chains round the necks of little girls. I was certain that even if they stumbled on a political criminal it would be by chance, because their noses were exclusively trained for 'valuables'.

Nevertheless, I naturally prepared myself for the eventuality of being caught. I'm here under a false name, with the forged documents of Samu Hirschler, a businessman from Vásárosnamény. I've grown a Hungarian moustache, like a village shopkeeper who also owns a little land: his clothes are middle class, but his face, his manners and his speech are like those of a peasant, or at least a horse dealer. The main reason why I chose a false and more Jewish-sounding name was that I wanted to conceal my own notorious one. I thought that a name of this type would be lost among twenty-five thousand others. Of course, my political and personal friends in Budapest had planned all kinds of things, such as smuggling me back to Budapest with Aryan papers or sending me across the Romanian border, which was only six kilometres from here. But my wife had been brought to the ghetto with an open wound after a major operation, and although she tried for several nights to persuade me to escape on my own and leave her to her fate with her parents and her daughter from a first marriage, I refused, not only out of a sense of honour but also out of vanity. And, to be quite honest, because this solidarity was a perfect pretext for doing nothing.

I was very, very tired by then. I had scant strength or incli-nation to exert myself in order to live. It was only a few weeks since, after a year and a half of indescribable hardships, I had made my way home from Russia, where I had always envied the people sentenced to death in the hinterland, who only needed to take a few easy steps from the threshold of the condemned cell to the gallows, rather than plodding thousands and thousands of kilometres with a rucksack on their back. Nor did anyone kick them and bash their heads with rifle butts. Judges and prosecutors are cold but correct, and hangmen are also unemotional and businesslike. I was beaten out there for nine days on end by drunken peasant infantrymen on the orders of a gang of officers who wanted to kill me without leaving any 'external signs'. Being killed according to this ingenious method is extremely tiring. By the time a captain arrived as a result of my friends' heated demands to prevent my being 'finished off'— much like the messenger with the white flag who came to save Dostoevsky—I was so tired that I didn't even scramble to my feet from the straw where I was painfully wasting away. When I heard that I was to go home to Budapest I was dismayed by the idea of having to wait for days at a station riddled with artillery shells, then being jolted ten kilometres in a cattle wagon before the train was blown up by a partisan mine, marching another twenty kilometres if I remained alive, boarding another wagon loaded with looted goods, oil drums and White Russian traitors, and when I got home—if I got home—feeling that a whole lifetime wasn't enough to recover from all this.

Then they brought me home, and straight to the Margit Boulevard prison, where I could at last stretch my limbs, lie around all day, stay in one place and stare at the same white walls and the same knob on the same church spire through the cell window. This was good. I almost got my breath back, I almost regained some of my drive, and the political prisoners in the cell began to reawaken my old interests and my political anger, which, like me, had become tired of tiredness. But I only sputtered like a damp fuse and couldn't be properly lit. Tiredness had now become my permanent condition. And somewhere, deep down, I always felt that something even more tiring was on its way. Then a few days before the German invasion I was released from the prison. The cat that played with me as if I were a mouse, having first let go of me when, counter to all theoretical expectations, I came home from the Ukraine, now let go of me again. But I didn't run away from it briskly, like a mouse that wants

29

to live. The mouse was tired . . . Rather than taking to my heels, I just dragged myself along, and instead of slipping out of the cat's reach, listlessly gnawed away at the past. Sometimes I thought that the only reason why the immediate future seemed so dark and deadly was my tiredness. At other times, however, my cool political judgement recorded accurately that the end of the world was coming in the next few days or weeks.

As I say, when the Germans invaded I was far too tired to fight for my own life. The cat had caught me again, and this time for good. And out there, on Margit Boulevard, where every morning left-wingers and fugitives were being hanged and shot dead, I familiarised myself with the thought that I was living in a world and an age in which people like me would be killed by somebody for this or that, in one way or another, sooner or later. If I had been seriously ill I might have rushed to a doctor and obtained treatment. But to make a special effort now—pass myself off as a member of the gentry or the Greek Orthodox Church, lie low, travel, walk, bribe, beg, tell lies, play a role, only to be finally shot, battered to death or hanged—I was no longer prepared to do all that. I thought I would go to the ghetto with these twenty-five thousand doomed Jews, drift with them, let whatever happened to them happen to me, and so avoid on the road to certain death the personal and political troubles that were tailor-made for my real identity. I thought the Vásárosnamény businessman Samu Hirschler wouldn't have to make any special effort to be allowed to give up the ghost. Samu Hirschler would just be shovelled into the wagon with the other Jews and thrown on the fire somewhere in Poland along with the rest of them.

The gramophone has been blaring in the brewery since morning, playing recordings of the radio's request programme, so that the screams can't be heard outside. The civilian detectives are busy beating people—rumour has it, the richest taxpayers and property owners. The ordinary people, the small-timers, heave a sigh of relief. The expressions on their faces almost manage to suggest indifference and nonchalance, and some even say, with a mixture of pity and smugness: 'What was the point of being bad and riding roughshod over everybody for a life-time—now it's all gone.' The poor devils are saying it *pour la galerie*, hoping that the civilian detectives may somehow hear it or be told about it and not hurt them, or even—seeing how sincere, open-minded and disinterested they are for all their poverty—let them out of the ghetto. This lack of concern isn't the result of class difference or class hatred, for almost all of them belong to the same middle class. Rather, the less successful, the less fortunate now believe that for the first time in their lives they are better off than those who were successful in every respect outside. And there is something else . . . Just as the poor devils, kicked halfway to death by the gendarmes, have eaten their own excrement to be spared any more pain, they would, for the same reason, even eat each other.

In their eyes I could see their icy determination to do anything for one-thousandth of a chance of saving their own lives. I had heard from eye witnesses about people escaping from a burning theatre or a sinking ship, trampling over each other. Here they weren't visibly trampling over each other, because the gendarmes wouldn't have put up with such a riot, but mentally everybody had already sacrificed his neighbour and perhaps even his close relatives. So far they had actually sacrificed only the richest and grandest—and, indeed, at about half past eight the hospital saw the arrival, one by one, of the bloody parcels that had once been bankers with aristocratic pretensions, feather wholesalers impersonating American executives, patrician property owners, and the proud proprietors of jewellery shops founded at the time of the 1867 Compromise.* Their heads were like watermelons slashed in all directions, but all of them had received the worst injuries in the lower parts of their bodies. The prehistoric beast, awakened by the times, had given free rein to its fury in castration. These shattered people weren't even whimpering any more. The doctors stood helpless in front of their mattresses, as if they had to reassemble a broken cup. Now there was total silence in the ward and even the dying seemed afraid to give a loud rattle. The small-timers, who only a short while before had feigned indifference, nonchalance and gloating matter-of-factness, were

* Agreement granting Hungary a measure of independence within the Austrian Empire.

jolted and, somewhat guiltily, stared in front of them: no, this really was a bit too much . . . Even though they hadn't returned the ordinary Jews' greetings . . . even though they had been quick to sue and to auction their debtors' possessions . . . even though they had thought that the lord lieutenant and the canon were their friends—this was a bit too much . . . It was a bit too much and . . . suddenly they began to worry that it was by no means certain that the detectives wouldn't beat up the whole ghetto if they ran out of rich people. Now that they could see so graphically what happened to people when they were summoned to the brewery, a certain solidarity with the tortured VIPs awoke in them. Then they heard that so far everybody had confessed everything under torture and the detectives had already gone out into the town to dig up the gold and the jewellery. In other words, nobody could stand the beating of the soles, the small metal sticks and the electric shocks for long. And the small-timers became even more alarmed because of course they too had hidden something, just like the rich—some junk that had been treated in the family for decades as an item of value, or rather as a symbol of value and wealth: if nothing else, at least a vase bought in the market and, masquerading as fine porcelain, given pride of place in a display cabinet, or an old rug bought, according to family legend, by the grandparents from an Afghan in Vienna.

By hiding such valuables they revealed an ignorant optimism: they believed that once this madness had passed they would retrieve what they had hidden and have something to start again with. But it is certain that, behind the conscious practical purpose of these desperate and hopeless attempts to hold on to their objects, there was something else: the desire that these possessions, which were theirs, shouldn't fall into the hands of others, even when they were no longer of any use to them. It was probably for the same reason that primitive peoples had themselves buried with their jewellery and archaeologists have found so much gold in graves from the time of the great migrations. These middle-class people, who, despite their optimism sometimes suspected that they were finished, couldn't be buried with their bracelets, earrings, solitaires, pearl necklaces, Persian carpets and bank deposit books—but at least they could dig special graves for them. Of course the gendarmes soon made them exhume these graves, and it was only when the last objects had been taken away from them that they finally gave up hope. In the bourgeois mythology which guided them these objects had not merely material value but represented security, confidence, rank, the gold cover of life. And the more valuable these objects were, the safer and the more special and important they felt than those who had less. The objects were divinities, and now that they had finally lost the objects they felt abandoned by God.

Objects are the gods of the bourgeois, and if the objects are taken away from them, neither Jehovah nor Jesus Christ can help them—it's the end of the world. And were it really the end of the world, they wouldn't care: with their crazed eyes fixed on the lost objects they would neither notice nor acknowledge it. I mentioned earlier that in August 1939, a week before the outbreak of the Second World War, my wife packed all our objects into nine suitcases, which we were to take to Paris. On my travels all over the world I always packed what I absolutely had to in a small suitcase, and even that I sent on as registered luggage in order to feel free. I never travelled on a train together with my wife, who had a mania for having more suitcases than necessary. She used to pack for every possible weather, natural disaster, social eventuality and also, without any reason whatsoever, for the possibility that we might not return. Now that we were trying to emigrate to escape from the fascist war, my wife insisted on taking the nine suitcases, and so I left Budapest for Paris, without any luggage, two days before her. I arrived on 26 August. On the morning of 28 August I went out to the Gare de l'Est to meet her. Mobilisation had already transformed the city, and the station was teeming with conscripted soldiers and their alarmed relatives. The express from the east also disgorged masses of soldiers joining up. It was with difficulty that I found my wife, deathly pale and sobbing. There was nothing out of the ordinary about a weeping woman, and as she clung to me in panic people thought that I too was setting out for the Maginot Line.

What had happened was that in Budapest my wife had taken the nine suitcases into her compartment, not only to economise, but also because she didn't want to be separated from the objects. They occupied almost the entire luggage rack, until a pedantic German train guard came along in Salzburg and harshly ordered her to send the five largest ones, which contained our clothes, to the luggage van. She begged and cried, but the other passengers also turned against her and the guard showed no mercy. At the German border station in Kehl, receipt in hand, she went to look for the suitcases. They were nowhere to be found. The railwayman informed her that they had been left in Munich as the van was being reloaded. She wailed and raged, while the passengers either half-heartedly encouraged her or tried to cheer her up by philosophically declaring that in any case tomorrow the war would break out and a lot more would be lost than a few suitcases. This finally drove her to despair. On the Rhine bridge between Kehl and Strasbourg both the Germans and the French had already erected barbed-wire barricades, leaving only a corridor as wide as a carriage. Despite this, the German railwayman took pity on her. If only to give her something to hope for, he asked for her Paris address and promised to send the suitcases on after her, cash on delivery, if the war hadn't started by the time the next train arrived, and if they were on it. In disbelief, my wife wrote her name on a piece of paper and continued to wail and rage until she got to Paris.

I could understand her despair, as she stood in front of me on the platform in the only dress, underwear and shoes she had left. But while I was trying to comfort and calm her in the taxi home, I was thinking: *tant de bruit*, a lot of clothes and other stuff have been lost ten minutes before the war—so we'd get new ones. I had money, American royalties in dollars, and the dollar had risen at the news of the approaching war, while prices remained unchanged. When she had tired of her tantrums I risked the remark that, with the few thousand francs difference that we had automatically earned on the dollar, we could easily buy the most important things at the Galeries Lafayette.

'That's not what I want,' she screamed. 'I want my red coat! And my shoes! And the boxes! Grandmother's pearls! Everything was in the boxes!'

She had to have *that* red coat, *those* shoes and *only* those half-

34

finished Japanese beads, promoted to grandmother's pearls, that they had been selling for a few hundred lire in the streets of Rimini when we were there. And whatever else was in the boxes: clips, brooches, artificial flowers, handbags, manicure sets, photos— knick-knacks and jumble. All right, so losing our clothes was a serious blow. But we didn't have to go naked, and while I, like prehistoric man, only wanted clothes to protect me from the rigours of the weather, she could, after all, buy herself some elegant, fashionable Parisian clothes for the difference in value of the dollar.

'This is your money-launderer's mentality!' she yelled. 'I want *my own things*! And if I hadn't had to travel without a man . . .'

To my relief the *patronne*, *Veuve* Duverger came in at this point, bringing the blue paper to cover the window. I thought this blue paper might divert her attention from the red coat to the war. Blackout, air raids—perhaps she would wake up to what else was being lost here in a matter of minutes. But Madame Duverger already knew the suitcase tragedy inside out, and she too, the French bourgeoise with her overdeveloped sense of property, was much more upset by the lost objects than by the probability of war. '*O pauvre Madame*,' she said, wringing her hands and even weeping with her. What would *she* do if the *Boches* were at the gates of Paris? She would pack her suitcases and carry them right to the bitter end, if necessary even dying in their shade. They were members of the same sect, worshippers of the Object-God, and I, sacrilegious unbeliever seated in the armchair, felt as guilty as if I had stolen the suitcases.

She called me 'money-launderer' a few more times, although it was she who had taken control of the money from the very first day of our marriage. She had made me believe that she alone was able to manage our finances, because she knew how to, and because I was an infantile spendthrift. And, indeed, I didn't even know what a real dollar looked like. As the money had been arriving from America she had paid it into a bank account under her own name, where it was out of my reach, but now she wouldn't hear of touching it. She wanted the suitcases and the red coat, or nothing. Eventually I began to feel sorry for her, as if she were in genuine mourning over a relative I disliked, and I tried to comfort her all night. Without any conviction I swore that the German railwayman had undoubtedly sent the suitcases on. They would arrive by the morning and we would go out to the Gare de l'Est to collect them.

In the morning, on 29 August, we went to the Gare de l'Est and called on the station master. Within five minutes I could tell that the French would lose the war. In a strong foreign accent I related the suitcase tragedy to this fellow, who responded with understanding and even sympathy. He immediately allowed us to examine the luggage stores in the basement. If by any chance I had been a fascist agent I could have committed the decade's greatest act of sabotage one day before the outbreak of the war: nothing would have been simpler than setting fire to the Gare de l'Est with one match and thereby dealing an immeasurable blow to French mobilisation. Of course we didn't find the suitcases—we felt that they would never be found again—but the good station master didn't accept this as easily as I did. Without my asking him, he scribbled a letter of recommendation to the chief of the Gare Pajol, the express-goods station, asking him to let us rummage in the stores there. As we searched and again failed to find the suitcases, I muttered that it wasn't possible to win every world war with improvisations that might or might not work out at the last moment, such as the battle on the Marne. I brooded over this on the way home, while mechanically trying to comfort my wife by assuring her that *Paris Soir* wasn't telling the truth when it reported that there were no more trains coming from Germany.

Meanwhile in the Rue Linné, near our hotel, word had got around about our suitcase tragedy. The compassionate gaze of greengrocers' wives, bakers' wives and bistro waitresses overcome by emotion followed us from the car to the front door of the hotel. The mourning was becoming unbearable. Local women we knew, and even some we didn't know, came to present their condolences. I tried a few more times to persuade my wife to go to the Lafayette and Louvre department stores or to Lanvin and Paquin, but without success. Finally in the afternoon I decided to take her just once more to the station, where the last train from Germany had indeed arrived. I thought that if I could conclusively prove that there was no hope left she would agree to some reasonable solution. The station master was first to notice us across the steel helmets of the soldiers joining up. His face was shining with enthusiasm: 'Madame,' he shouted. 'Congratulations! The bridge may have been blown up by now, but your suitcases arrived on the last train!'

The German railwayman really had loaded the suitcases onto the last train. The French and Germans might have been ready to start bombing each other by the evening, but the German railwayman, automatically and with professional honesty, had forwarded the five 'items'. He was probably a member of the National Socialist Party but he also belonged to the International Sect of the Object-God, whose cult gives so much pleasure to its followers, although there are some fateful situations in which the divinity mercilessly demands their sacrifices.

Take one example. If that honest German railwayman hadn't sent those suitcases after us, our luggage would have been small enough for the Riviera express or the train to Madrid and Lisbon. Then I might not have come home in order to have one eye knocked out in the Ukraine or to end up here with the chassidim. On the other hand I might have died of fish poisoning in Madrid, like my friend Asbóth, who got as far as that city from the Rue Linné. Or perhaps I too would have boarded the one clipper in a hundred that crashed on its way from Lisbon to America, carrying El Melik, the Arab professor of mathematics, who had likewise set out from this hotel. All right, let's not rack our brains about what might have been, if . . . But all the same, to suffer for objects, to die for a fetish, is indisputably primitive behaviour. All these gangsters who have pounced on us here are also the Object-God's sectarians, turned into fanatical inquisitors. They pretend to hate us as a pretext for taking our objects away, and they pretend that we obtained those objects by criminal means, in order to establish their moral right to appropriate them in front of their deity. They are killing us for the sake of objects.

Seven

Everybody turned pale green when the gramophone music started again in the brewery. The original optimism of the small-timers had evaporated: why had the detectives, for example, beaten to death the grocer Klein from Pável Street who had only debts and five ugly daughters? The noose is growing ever tighter. With all attention concentrated on the brewery, the constant shunting of the railwaymen on the industrial siding in the ghetto has been overlooked. The unoiled brakes squeal, the skidding wheels wail like the midnight storm in a theatrical melodrama. Yes, there's a lot of movement on the siding. It's Thursday morning. The first transport is leaving on Saturday. Perhaps one will manage to drag it out till Saturday—it would be better to leave with the transport than be beaten again . . .

The nurse with the squint stops at the mattresses and bends down, saying:

'Daddy's all right. Thank God, they skipped his name in the Bs.'

Has she come here to let me know that she had done what the gendarme wanted? I look up at her, slightly sickened. I'm not surprised—after all, I've just been saying what people are capable of, how everybody would devour his own filth and his own child in order to escape. But on the one hand I had psychologically decided against the matter, and on the other hand—why has she come to me, why do I need to know? What business is it of mine?

'So, it has happened?' I ask roughly.

'What are you thinking of? Of course not,' she denies in embarrassment and her face flushes a dark red. 'He's a very nice boy. He's helped Daddy and he'll go on helping him. And he said that if there are a few decent people he's prepared to help them too. When he's on duty at the gate something can be done. I thought an important person like you . . .'

'I wouldn't dream of it. What will be will be.'

'I saw your wife upstairs,' the girl goes on in a whisper. 'She said I should speak to you. She's in a very bad way, poor woman. Of course something will have to be sacrificed. Your wife says you have resources outside the ghetto. But we shouldn't be talking now, I'll be on duty in the evening, then . . .' and, having been called to the third mattress, she leaves.

It's certain that last night the girl went to bed with the friendly gendarme, who had perhaps been softened and intoxicated a little by this beautiful Jewish girl and become slightly philo-Semitic. And when he saw all the Jewish loot in the brewery, the silver dishes and spoons, the rings and the wads of banknotes, he thought why shouldn't he help these honest Jews, who are being treated worse than animals and to whom he had suddenly taken such a liking? And why shouldn't he get some of this abandoned wealth, enough to buy a cow for the old people at home or a motor-bike for himself?

I'll have a word with the girl this evening. I'm somewhat surprised that my wife should be interested in this opportunity. So far she has been apathetic, and we talked about all this when we decided not to escape. We weren't glad that life was over. We could have had a few more good years living together, but we were both far too tired to face the discomforts of an adventure for the sake of survival. And apart from that, she's now lying upstairs, in the maternity ward, with her unhealed wound. She too has been hidden by the doctors under a false name, so that the gendarmes wouldn't know whose wife she is. Previously she had only been able to see her parents and her daughter from a first marriage surreptitiously because they were living here in Nagyvárad, where everybody knew who they were and how they were related to me. If she had been meeting them overtly it might have given the gendarmes a lead to me. But perhaps the poor woman now wants to live and wants me to live too. Just as in Paris, when she brought me home with the nine suitcases, she's forcing me into something again. All right, then, let me once more play the gentleman.

I'll have a word with the girl this evening. Meanwhile I listen to the squealing brakes, the wailing wheels and the gramophone music. And of course I hear many whispered rumours: the Russians are already below Kolozsvár, the Americans have landed in Portugal . . .

But even I got a thrill when I suddenly heard shouts:

'Down with the ghetto! Release the Jews . . . release our worker comrades and our employers!'

No, I didn't believe for one moment that the revolution had started out there. But these shouts were the first Hungarian voices since 19 March in which I recognised a human note. Up to now I had heard only the cowardly, perfidious whimpering of the friends of yesterday—Go away, I'm under surveillance too, don't ruin my family—and the foul abuse, the voice of mockery and vicious laughter, when we were being marched to the ghetto. They stood on the pavement, the respectable gentlemen twirling their walking sticks like magicians, and the blonde bitch of a school teacher gripping her tennis racket. They either laughed into our faces or looked over our heads with wrinkled noses as if the dustcarts were passing, bearing away all the town's rubbish. On the café terraces journalists, actors and prostitutes with their admirers and patrons sat sipping soft drinks through straws or drinking beer, noisily clinking their glasses. A Catholic priest with a gentle face, fair curls and the appearance of a pederast, like a scoutmaster who goes around with little boys outside school, was standing at the corner, with five brats in clean shirts, plus-fours and crew cuts. Pointing his tassle at the seventy-nine-year-old tailor Grünzweig, he boomed: 'Look at the Jew, he looks just like a monkey.' At the corner a syphilitic newspaper-seller with a hoarse voice yelled the headline of the official journal of the Catholic Bishop of Nagyvárad: 'The Jews have received their proper punishment! Christian Nagyvárad no longer a dream!'

We had been marching along the High Street, the stamping ground of the irredeemably corrupt bullies and toadies of the petty nobility, the vainglorious officer corps in all its stupidity and cruelty, the arrogant and thieving civil servants who had sworn loyalty to everybody and betrayed everybody, the patrician merchants who jeered at the loose business morals of the Jews, and the respectable middle-class ladies taking their promenade. These ladies were the most foul-mouthed. When they saw the few Jewish women who had been accustomed to buying their clothes in Budapest, travelling to foreign spas, reading English books, and having lovers—women who had given them a painful complex in the small town, whom they had tried to despise and look down on from the height of their own imagined sense of racial, official and military status, and whom they had envied, not so much for their wealth and elegance, but rather for their ability to enjoy life—they emptied over them the washing-up bowls of their souls, which were filled to the brim with decades of joyless marriage. These would-be sophisticated Jewish women of Nagyvárad were in fact notorious among the town's many headscarfed poor Jewesses—shopkeepers' wives, tradeswomen and workers—for their colourful way of life. But when they were abused in the High Street by the respectable ladies—who had turned into dragons while living on family income supplement in homes smelling of stale bedclothes, beside their dissolute, maid-chasing, apoplectically obese or drink-shrivelled husbands—they played their parts with such unmoving marble features, such staggering dignity, as if they were the martyrs of some cause and had deliberately asked for the abuse.

Since the unforgettable din of this infernal procession there had only been silence, broken by the gendarmes' orders and curses. Now for the first time in months the *vox humana*, the *vox populi*, rang out—the voice of the people, of the workers, who surely knew that their shouting was useless against the gendarmes' guns and tanks, but who at least signalled that there were still a few in this town who remembered the faded lessons, the forbidden and defiled ideas which had been taught by Nagyvárad's finest in the past fifty years. In the High Street it was the example and teaching of the great landowners, the gentry and the priests that made an impact, in the suburbs that of the scholars and poets. And now the voice of the suburbs rang out, even though it couldn't have come from more than five hundred throats—but immediately the weapons of the gendarmes also rang out.

While the shooting goes on the ghetto lies low, afraid that the guns, once they have finished outside, will immediately turn inward. Then follows a tense uneventfulness for hours. There's no news. Then the gramophone starts blaring, playing 'Lili Marlene' till evening. And they are again bringing in people on stretchers, the men to the ground floor, with their heads broken and their testicles crushed, with open hernias, and bleeding mouths that have swallowed their teeth, and the women to the upper floor, with blue bruised breasts and singed groins. And by evening all this has become as common as the death on the next mattress and in the morgue.

Then late at night the girl with the squint appears with her face turned green and her eyes tiny from crying. The friendly gendarme, who had saved her father in the morning from being beaten and who had offered to save a few decent Jews for some lolly, had completely changed. When the girl tried to discuss things with him he reached for his rifle and roared: 'Get off, you Jewish cow, I'll show you how to save Jews!' The girl didn't understand this change, particularly because during the night the gendarme had obviously been kind to her. She didn't understand why he had suddenly grown so angry and belatedly had her father dragged to the brewery, to be beaten until he admitted what he had hidden. They beat him and when he was dying they brought him in here and now he was lying among the other bloody wrecks. 'Daddy's the one in the blue shirt,' she pointed at him, sobbing. She didn't understand. All she had heard was that the friendly gendarme had been on guard duty at the gate during the socialists' demonstration. At first he hadn't known what to do, but then the lieutenant came running with other gendarmes and yelled at him: 'Why aren't you shooting, you moron!' The moron shot while his ammunition lasted. Of the six who died he had killed two. Obviously that was the first time he had used his weapon against humans: he hadn't been on the front line, he was a young gendarme on probation and hadn't killed a human being before. Now he had killed for the first time and discovered what a magnificent feeling it is for a man to kill another man. That was what had driven him wild, and the fact that he had tasted the intoxication of violence, the lust of cruelty. In the pride of his sudden rapture he wanted to shake off the dimly nagging memories of his manly tenderness, his small corrupt humanity, and to make amends to himself for caressing the girl with the squint on the previous night and thinking of saving people, when it was also possible to kill them.

The girl with the squint nursed her father all night, but the Jew with the letter B and the high blood pressure, who had hidden, all in all, one silver pocket watch and enough Czech material for one suit, died from his beating before morning.

During the night there were several air raids but again no bombing. The cattle wagons had been screeching since dawn, and during the morning it was announced that the ghetto would be divided into districts and the people taken away from one district at a time. 'Where?' a naive, desperate voice asked. 'To Siófok* for a summer holiday,' the gendarmerie lieutenant answered—and was almost offended, like a facetious teacher whose class fails to respond to his joke with resounding sycophantic laughter.

---

* A well-known holiday resort on Lake Balaton.

Eight

Surprisingly, the majority of the people believed the rumour, spread by the ghetto command with calculated malice, that we would be taken to a labour camp near Lake Balaton to drain swamps and help with the harvest. Very few here knew where we were really going. I, for my part, had heard a special messenger from London speak of a town called Oswiecim in 1942, but had forgotten all about it till now. Now that our deportation, which so far only a few had believed in, had become a certainty, a strange optimism suddenly filled the ghetto. 'One can survive anything! We're going to work, we're going to hoe and mow! If others have survived, we'll survive too!' So ran the slogans. People were invigorated and heartened by the mere hope of being taken away from this town, where their neighbours, their good friends, their colleagues, their bridge partners and even their lovers had so disgracefully betrayed them, away from the brewery, where by now the inmates of one building after another were being beaten to within an inch of their lives, regardless of their wealth, age or sex.

The typical bourgeois obsessions promptly appeared. Those who carried authority, nature's organisers, began to compose and choose groups, deciding with whom they were and were not prepared to travel in the wagons. Members of the same class and rank joined together, freezing out those whom in the outside world they wouldn't have invited to their houses and with whom they wouldn't have been seen in public, the ugly, the unpopular and the dull. The *première juiverie*, with the fastidiousness of the rich left without a penny, rejected not only the poor but also the dubious speculators and newly rich: and indeed there were some hopeless outsiders, some parvenus, who had never been accepted and who longed to redeem themselves, at least

44

here, by making their way into society and 'arriving' among the notorious but beautiful bankers' and industrialists' wives, their sour, genteel husbands, and their insolvent, sophisticated and amusing lovers.

Another kind of fastidiousness also made its appearance. The progressive, European-looking Jews refused to admit the Jews with sidelocks to their circles. 'These people are always causing trouble!' they were heard to say. 'These people are the reason why we're here, these people give you lice and scabies.' Meanwhile the Jews with sidelocks watched them sombrely from behind their shaggy beards, without batting an eyelid, full of distaste and scorn for these tantrums and these strange emotional ups and downs. They just stood there in groups, their hands deep in the pockets of their dirty caftans, and fell silent whenever a Jew in a suit passed by. They stood there, looking mysterious and determined, as if they had a plan and were prepared for whatever was coming. They owed this composure mainly to their faith: they were convinced that Jehovah would help. The wonder-rabbi had promised a miracle from the start. Admittedly, so far he had only worked a miracle for himself, having decamped with his family the night before, but if the first half of the miracle had worked, so would the second.

And then, these people with sidelocks were no beginners: this wasn't the first time they found themselves in such a predicament. They had escaped from the czar in Gomel, from Petliura* in Berdichev, from the Lithuanians in Kovno, from the Poles in Warsaw, from the Ukrainian White Guards in Lemberg, and all the way to Máramarossziget in Transylvania, from where they had not been escaping but bringing goods for sale to Nagyvárad. Even if, of the hundreds of thousands in a constant state of flight, tens of thousands were killed by bullets, bludgeons, epidemics, or simply froze to death by the roadside, the remaining mass would still find its way to some place or another. They were replete with Japanese fanaticism and ancient Turkish fatalism, although they had no martial virtues, fearing or despising nothing

* Symon Petliura (1879–1926), Ukrainian politician, responsible for the massacre of thousands of Jews.

so much as soldiers. They trusted in their God and they trusted at least as much in their gold, which they hadn't buried or given to Aryan friends for safe keeping outside, but had brought into the ghetto, God knows how. They too were beaten up in the brewery, but only because of their sidelocks. The civilian detectives never even thought of seriously interrogating them about any loot. These knock-kneed figures in shoes that were three sizes too large and turned up at the toes, threadbare shirts and dirty long stockings, obviously had nothing but lice. The detectives used them mainly for practice, to sharpen their own wit and to entertain each other. In any case, they couldn't be made to talk because they refused to understand Hungarian, German or Romanian and kept silent, like idiots, staring out of their bulging eyes with seeming humility, but in fact with infinite superiority and disgust—at the dirty animals, pork-eaters, ignoramuses who had never read the holy and secret books—and they gloated as they imagined the seven plagues their God would inflict on these sinners.

They also regarded me as an impure pork-eater and an ignoramus, but rather than hating me they only pitied me for failing to recognise the truth of the teaching and submit to the law. Through their mysterious intelligence channels they had been the first to discover who I was and, having heard that I had often attacked the enemies of the persecuted and of the Jews in my writings, they treated me with some forbearance. I asked one of them, who lay three mattresses away from me, how he explained the fact that the British Jews, who had deserted the faith, were leading relatively free and safe lives, while those in the East, who were most faithful to God and literally obeyed His commands, were being wiped out in their millions. He answered: 'He knows what He is doing. When things are bad in the East, they are good in the West, and vice versa. Now it's our turn. But tomorrow it will be a new moon, and things may change.' They believed in change and in the gold they had with them, which they had managed to save from the gendarmes, the detectives and the searches that continued daily even in the ghetto. They alone knew how. This was something else that a sharpened instinct for self-preservation, like that of animals on the run for centuries, had taught them.

They are as alien to me as Filippinos. I hate myself for saying so, but I have more in common even with the friendly gendarme who went berserk than with them. As a child, I had just such a peasant as a playmate. I sat next to him in primary school, and later I went to the front with him in the First World War. According to my own idea of morality, these chassidim with their sidelocks, their refined but one-sided and narrow-minded intellect, their physical uncleanliness, and their primitive ceremonies, are immoral. Nor do I feel the slightest racial solidarity with them. But now I'm nevertheless drawn to them, because they are resisting through their obstinacy, because they are defending themselves through their patient, resourceful passivity, and because they have fled a hundred times as far as I have and are still not tired. I'm drawn to them like the weak to the strong. I envy their fanaticism and their ability to hate somebody more bitterly for eating pork than I can hate Hitler and these bandits even at this juncture. I envy the toughness behind their soft masks, a toughness springing from their narrow-mindedness and, perhaps, from their amoral belief, which has now been proved morally legitimate, that they have the right to defend themselves by any means, however reprehensible and vile, against those who have persecuted them for centuries. Primarily, of course, by means of gold, the dirty metal that has turned out to be the most effective against the bludgeon, the gun, the stake, the laws of the state, and even the mob. They certainly love gold, but they are hoarding it, above all, as protection from the guns.

These are the people with whom the beauties, the bankers and the intellectuals don't wish to travel. It would take a Thomas Cook to group the passengers for this package tour to the gas chambers with the necessary tact. What do most of them know about the cattle wagon? I myself got off it only a few weeks ago. The cattle wagon is really the means of transport tailor-made for my generation, even though I allowed myself to be deceived for a time by the international express trains and *trains bleus* in which I travelled, not under duress from nine suitcases, but motivated by pretentious hedonism and the urge to show off. I rushed through countries by night in sleeping cars, drawing the curtains back in the morning to find that we were in Bologna or Amiens and it was time to get dressed. I travelled by luxury liner to the Canaries, by car around Switzerland, Austria and Germany, and by mountain railway to Jungfraujoch. I made the crossing to Copenhagen in a train carried on a ferry, and landed three times by seaplane in the port of Venice.

These conveyances made me temporarily forget that my first serious trip abroad had been by cattle wagon. I was nineteen and had previously only travelled the short distance between Komárom and Budapest. Now I was jolted with forty others for six days in a wagon decorated with ribbons and green twigs, amid the dreadful stench of rifle grease and infantrymen, towards the Russian border. As a poet and aesthete I was a pacifist and hated war, but this was my first proper journey and I was elated. Sitting on the steps all the way, I at last got to know my homeland. I saw the Tisza river for the first time at Szolnok, looked for the mirage* at Debrecen and, eventually, made out the Carpathian mountains in the blue distance, those glorious peaks of which I was so proud because they were the highest in Eastern Europe. Then we crawled over the Uzsoki Pass, which was a staggering experience, even though I had caught a nasty gastric flu, because it was the first time I had crossed the border of my homeland: we reached Austria, and Austria to me, the Hungarian, was more abroad even than Russia. Then we stopped for twenty-four hours in Stary Sambor, and although I hated war, with the soldier's or warrior's privilege I immediately went in search of a woman. Then back into the wagon, which stank like a cage at the zoo but which couldn't touch my youth, even though every part of me was aching from crouching on the naked floorboards. Then we went to the front line, and eleven months later I was put back in the wagon: a big shell splinter had hit me in the face, flattening my nose and making me swallow my teeth, and although I was conscious I was unable to speak for twenty-three days. They put me back into the wagon, laid me down on the mucky straw and deposited a row of dishevelled and bearded soldiers, covered in congealed blood

* Formerly a famous atmospheric phenomenon in the great Hungarian Plain near the town of Debrecen.

and as yellow as Chinamen, like logs beside me. The one nearest to me had been hit in the stomach and was squirming like a chicken with its throat cut and thrown into the garden by the cook. And they kept on loading the wounded into the wagon, while the engine puffed and whistled and shunted all night, as if being pushed to and fro by playing children, but showed no intention of starting. At sunrise the man with the stomach wound next to me stopped squirming and died. I tried to tell the orderlies, who would hardly want to take a dead man home with us. But I could say nothing because I was dumb with my own wound. The wagon door was closed. When it was full daylight we left. That was how I travelled back to Sátoraljaújhely in Hungary with a dead man as my companion.

No, I'm not a beginner, I'm not lying among dead bodies for the first time, here in the synagogue of the wonder-rabbi. That was how my youth started, and I'm an expert cattle-wagon traveller. All my other journeys were merely a shuttle service between two cattle wagons. In 1942 there I was again, on the way towards the Russian border. This time I was in my own civilian clothes, which I had worn in cafés and editorial offices—except for a soldier's hat and boots, which belonged to the Treasury, and a yellow armband, which I had also been given by my homeland. My homeland had sent me out to the front line, not in order to protect it, but in order to test my loyalty and my vitality by forced labour, stigmatisation, cruelty, and by soldiers trained to behave like wolves, until I either died or began to loathe it enough to betray it. I did almost die, but I didn't betray my homeland, because I'm incapable of betraying anybody or anything. I don't even really loathe it, but I am in a terrible conflict with it, as if my mother had vilely rejected me, pouring poison into my soup and spending my inheritance on drunken kept lovers. Even so, I haven't been able to exchange it for another, even in theory, while these Jews here are still dreaming of Palestine, the new homeland—admittedly a purely theoretical matter at this point. But if my homeland has brought me to this chassidic synagogue and is sending me to the gas chamber then I don't want it any more. Nor do I want the other that's on offer, simply because I'm not interested in any other homeland.

And now I'm about to be taken away from my homeland for the third time in a cattle wagon. The wheel comes full circle, as superstitious people say. Things are becoming serious, the engine is already shunting on the industrial siding—we are leaving! Where are we going? What was written on the German tourist poster in Paris? Weeks after the outbreak of the war I could still read on the walls of Metro stations: *Visitez l'Allemagne joyeuse!* Visit merry Germany!

Nine

At ten o'clock in the morning Kelepecz, the registrar, came to
the ghetto to record the deaths. He had hardly got through the
gate when a gendarmerie colonel protested:

'Why do you bother, registrar? You can simply cross out all
the twenty thousand in your book. We're not going to waste any
paper on this lot!'

The registrar was a hairless old man with a limp and a pear-
shaped head, the spitting image of Voltaire. Wearing the same
faded green redingote with a sash in the national colours, he
had married couples and kept the record of births and deaths
among the population of Nagyvárad for forty years. He was
unmarried and had been drinking for decades at the Blue Cat
in the company of other bachelors and widowers at the regulars' table. He would sit there, gloomy and lethargic, surrounded
by merry and cantankerous Christians and Jews, philistine professionals and pretentious tradesmen, who gathered at the same
table with the red tablecloth every night under the pretext of
an interest in children's education and town planning, washing
down their sausages with a glass or two of what they fancied,
and arguing about local politics, tenders for public transport,
thefts and frauds, and the desirability of women with large hips.
The registrar, like all chronic alcoholics who drink at a steady
slow rate, was always slightly under the influence, but no more
so at the regulars' table than during the day in the office. He
was neither a good man nor a bad one but, even in his permanent alcoholic haze, an accurate and pedantic machine. If he was
disturbed in his official automatism he became cross. Now he
had come to the ghetto, with an NCO in a policeman's hat
carrying his register of births and deaths after him, and he wanted
to clear the backlog. A dead person's place was in the register—

that was what the law demanded—and for forty years even the unknown bodies found by the roadside had had to be entered. As the gendarmerie colonel tried to prevent him from doing his job, he said in a hard, official tone:

'Colonel, I must warn you. I'm in the process of fulfilling my official function. If anybody tries to stop me it's my duty to report him to my superiors.'

The colonel persisted: 'In the territory of the ghetto I'm the superior authority and I order you . . .'

'I only take orders from the mayor and the town council.'

A heated argument broke out between the two. The Jews hiding behind the window heard them, and within minutes the rumour spread that the registrar had defied the gendarmerie colonel and given him a piece of his mind. At last there was one human being among those villains in the town hall, who only a little while ago had been kissing the hands of Jewish women and accepting money for dirty schemes, and who were now the meanest and most wicked thieves. It was recalled that this registrar had actually always been quite decent: he had married the whole town and cordially shaken hands with every bride and groom. Within minutes he had become a great man, a great humanitarian, the determined enemy of the Germans and the champion of the persecuted, although in reality all that had happened was that the obsessive bureaucrat had tried to assert his authority, the professional machine had demanded its raw material for processing, admittedly outside the office but nevertheless during office hours. He would have done the same if the Angel of Death himself had arrived: he would have followed him with his register. Whoever is not in the register is neither dead nor alive. The blanks must be filled with particulars of the parents and, more recently, of the grandparents and great-grandparents, with religion, occupation and the cause of death. On the other hand, the gendarmerie colonel's view was that Jews had only one particular: they were Jews. The rest was not interesting.

'This liberal, bureaucratic trifling is over, registrar,' the gendarmerie colonel explained. 'Leave the territory of the ghetto!'

For a while the registrar continued the heroic fight for his entries and, like the correct civil servant that he was, didn't give in until his real superior, the mayor, instructed him by telephone to carry out the order without any objection. 'We're in a military communication zone,' the mayor shouted into the telephone. 'Refusal to obey a military order amounts to mutiny.' The mayor was right. The registrar was the only member of the middle class to resist, even if he only did so for the sake of his entries. To him the entry was a symbol of a nation and a society following lawful and civilised guidelines. But this rebellion also failed, like that of the old women, and he crept back to the town hall, with the NCO lugging the register after him. Nevertheless, his batty resistance was not only blown up to a heroic deed by the Jews, but his obstinacy was also being watched by the military and civilian authorities with suspicion, and one of the newspapers that had been smuggled into the ghetto took him to task: did he only want to make a fuss or was he planning to supply details to the Russians if they came? Of course, they wouldn't come—but this registrar with the pear-shaped head had always had Jewish friends . . .

Ten

The dead were not only left out of the register but also out of the earth. As the cool and rainy night was followed by stifling heat, the stench of the bodies became unbearable. The ghetto hardly noticed it—we had become amazingly used to the characteristic odour produced by the decomposing dead, the disgusting latrines, the overflowing drains and the sweet reek of the nearby molasses warehouse. But the town beyond the fence had a more sensitive nose. Soon after the registrar's ignominious retreat the hospital saw the arrival of the chief medical officer, a cross between a Swabian and a Romanian, the town's worst physician and worst chess player, with whom his colleagues would only sit down for a game, during the doctors' afternoon gatherings in the Elite Café, out of pity.

Now he summoned his most forebearing chess partners, the Jewish doctors of the ghetto, in an affected military rattle. He ordered them to make immediate arrangements to dispose of the bodies. It was a strange psychological phenomenon that since the arrival of the Germans every overbearing official or civilian from outside who had any dealings with us pretended to be a soldier. It would have been understandable if they had been trying to share the prestige and aura of a victorious army by assuming its behaviour. But I had actually seen our Hungarian soldiers fleeing two thousand kilometres together with the Germans, when I was forced to flee with them willy-nilly. Normally these lackeys didn't associate themselves with a lost cause even unconsciously. Idiots—did they still not realise that they were beaten? Then I began to understand the purpose of their military make-believe: on the one hand they hoped to neutralise old personal associations, friendships and professional relationships that had become uncomfortable, by adopting a cold, tough formality that precluded any discussion; on the other hand they copied the soldier's and gendarme's fierce behaviour to make themselves appear more frightening, in case it still occurred to somebody to doubt their right to carry out arbitrary and capricious acts of despotism or individual thefts. Outside, the civilians were still restricted, to some extent, by the remnants of the law, while in here it was the soldier or gendarme who both enacted and executed the law.

Dr Németi explained to the chief medical officer that up to now the ghetto commander hadn't allowed the dead to be buried. The chief medical officer, staring fixedly at the star of David on the Ark of the Covenant, continued in a didactic and reproachful tone, as if he hadn't heard him: 'You're doctors, you must know what a dangerous threat this is to the town. I don't suppose you want to let loose a plague, which . . .'

I would have liked to ask him what was meant to follow that 'which'. But there was a new moon and apparently the tide had turned. The synagogue was shaken by a huge explosion: on the cue 'which' the first bomb had fallen on Nagyvárad without any warning. The soldierly chief medical officer's knees buckled and he turned green. Revolving on his own axis, with only the whites of his pale blue eyes showing like puddles of whey, he almost begged Dr Németi in a stammer: 'My dear colleague, where is the shelter?'

'There is no shelter, chief medical officer,' Dr Németi answered gleefully. 'When things like this happen we don't go anywhere.'

It was only now that the siren began to howl, although the bombs were already pouring down. The people jumped up from their mattresses to watch the destruction with eagerness, curiosity and alarm. Through the large window the wedge of white planes could clearly be seen, gaining and losing height, separating and rejoining each other. Walls crumbled and trembled, glass shattered and tinkled incessantly. The town from which they had dragged us here, with its unfeeling church towers, its corrupt county hall, its thieving town hall, its domed extortionist banks and its prison-coloured barracks, was enfolded in smoke and flames. We thought that within minutes nothing would be left of it. We were happy that the usurpers were being smoked out of the houses which had been ours and from which they had driven us, and that everything they had stolen from us—the furniture, the clothes, the children's toys, the family pictures, the laundry tub, the bicycle, the shop, in a word, the objects—was turning to ashes before the robbers could enjoy it. Now we were all overcome by a savage Old Testament fervour: if Jehovah's unfathomable will was not to reward merit on this earth, then at least He should wreak vengeance. Now these women, young louts and malignant old men, who so far had only encountered the unarmed enemy within their borders, would learn that it is not possible to wage a one-sided war for ever, that the other side also uses weapons. There's always a reckoning. We're finished, but so is the town.

Of course the town wasn't finished. The air raid produced a lot of smoke and noise, but the church towers and domes remained unscathed. The bombs had only hit the general hospital and a workers' estate near the station—perhaps the homes of the very same people who had yesterday demonstrated on our behalf and of whom six had been shot dead by the gendarmes. It hadn't worked, the bad magic persisted: it seemed that the sufferers must still be those who didn't deserve it. The smoke had dispersed: the evil High Street's tile and slate roofs, gleaming in the sun, were grinning at us.

However, the ghetto, in its excited optimism, was inventing false rumours. A thousand dead, ten thousand wounded. Such and such no longer exists. The station has been burnt down to the ground, the deportation can't start. No doubt this optimism was also nourished by the fact that the auxiliary gendarmes, experiencing an air raid for the first time, had become confused, indecisive and less aggressive. Since no bomb happened to have landed near the ghetto they believed that the Jews were a good cover against air raids. This put them in a gentler mood. They even engaged in conversation with the Jews: how had it been, who had first heard or seen it, had it come from the direction of Fugyi or Debrecen, had it lasted ten minutes or half an hour, etc.

The emotion of the air raid marked the whole day. The Jews

became somewhat more confident, as if, even without the unfaithful God, they had some allies on high. Then the evening brought a clear sky and a new moon. Thirty wagons were shunted to the middle of the ghetto. The engine was uncoupled and left all thirty behind. The blue lamp had already been lit in the ward when the order came that in the morning fifty Jews were to go out to the cemetery to bury the dead.

Eleven

At six o'clock in the morning the gravediggers, the younger male relatives of the dead, reported for work. Before leaving for the cemetery they were ordered by a gendarme to load all the bodies into two small vans the colour of smoke. The bodies had to be literally squashed in. Although this seemed downright impossible with the last three, the gendarme's orders to hurry were so threatening that the frightened gravediggers managed it by folding them in two and, amazingly, were able to bolt the door on them.

This was the only exciting event of the stiflingly hot day that preceded the departure of the first train with the first section of the ghetto, although it may also be worth mentioning that around noon the inmates of the first section were ordered to collect the keys to the front doors, rooms and cupboards in each building, and hand them over to the gendarmes in one bunch. This order had no practical purpose whatsoever. To this day I don't know what it was meant to achieve. The Germans had probably sent printed general instructions for deportations, broken down into points, one of which could have referred to the confiscation of keys. They wouldn't have given such an order without any reason, and it might have been necessary in other circumstances. But the Hungarians copied it stupidly, blindly, uncomprehendingly, out of admiration for German thoroughness and efficiency, like a precept of Holy Writ. With their cheap historical imagination they may have regarded the surrender of keys as some kind of symbolic action: the Jews were capitulating, symbolically abandoning their houses to the victors, like the lord of a castle giving up the key to the castle gate. Or perhaps they were trying literally and figuratively to reproduce the Hungarian saying 'handing in the key', which corresponds roughly to 'kicking the bucket'.

One other thing that happened was that they stopped giving us beans, which had until then been our exclusive diet, like a mocking reminder of the traditional Jewish Saturday dish. The thick-set gendarmerie colonel, the son of a small-time crafts-man, and the town's director of food supplies, the illegitimate son of a priest's housekeeper, who may both have acquired their sense of humour from a clerical calendar when they were chil-dren, obviously thought it a good joke to feed beans to these 'itzigs' and 'jordans', including babies and old people with stomach cancer—let them stuff themselves with sholet before they bite the dust. But now it had transpired that beans formed too significant a part of the national resources to be wasted on a ritual joke. 'Beans are required by our heroic soldiers,' the director of food supplies explained to the president of the Jewish community. 'Yesterday the government requisitioned all the beans for the front line by special edict. For you non-combatants turnips will do.'

The news that the beans would be taken from the ghetto to the front line aroused no interest, let alone excitement. The ghetto didn't care what muck was cooked in the Jewish kitchens set up by the town—the ghetto simply didn't eat. The mouthfuls stuck in people's throats, and the longer they starved the less hungry they became. I myself don't remember eating anything for days after those dry, rancid biscuits of the first night—from then on it had never even occurred to me that I should eat. We were kept in extreme emotional tension—by the fear of being beaten and recognised, by the agonised question of where we had gone wrong and of how all this could have been avoided, and—despite the hopelessness of the situation—by the stubborn belief that something miraculous must happen at the last moment. Some were waiting for the intervention of God, others for the inter-vention of twentieth-century civilisation, or at least the inevitable action of Aryan relatives or influential Christian friends. We were concentrating so hard on a single point that our physical needs ceased to be heard and our reflexes were almost entirely switched off. One man announced, face aglow, that under Romanian rule he had been an irredentist and constantly bribed civil servants who hadn't sworn an oath of allegiance to the occupiers.* Another had fought the communists in 1919 and expected a telegram about his exemption from the anti-Jewish laws to be delivered at the office of the ghetto commander. A wispy teacher of religion had sent three urgent telegrams to the department that awarded honours to deserving ex-servicemen, before he was taken to the ghetto: in 1918 he had fought the Czechs at Nagybiccse, he had all the necessary documents, and the reply, the exemption, must be on its way, since he was 'appreciated in the Honours Department'. Meanwhile the bloody parcels still kept arriving from the brewery, and by now it was certain that nobody would be spared. The rich and educated were being beaten up, and the gramophone was playing all day.

Who cared about beans here? Those who weren't waiting for exemptions put their trust in their Aryan wives, who were surely doing all they could outside, or in their mixed-race sons, who were riding motor-cycles on the front line. Others, who had no connections, waited for the miracle of Russian or Anglo-Saxon paratroopers landing at the last moment, occupying the town and letting the Jews go home. Those less hopeful and optimistic waited for the white planes to return and finally bomb the town to pieces, if necessary with them in it. And those who had talked politics for half an hour in the afternoons while drinking their coffee in one of the four cafés in Brémer Square waited for the government to fall as a result of this nonsense—somebody had read in a newspaper smuggled into the ghetto that Imrédy was going to be prime minister again, and Imrédy, being a financial genius, knew what it meant for the country if the Jews were prevented from making their contribution to trade and industry.† Everybody was waiting for something. Who cared about beans and turnips?

The children, particularly those below the age of fourteen, were of course hungry day and night, and caused a lot of trouble.

---

* From 1919 to 1940 parts of Transylvania which formerly belonged to the Austro-Hungarian Empire were under Romanian rule.
† Béla Imrédy (1891–1946) was prime minister of Hungary in 1938–9, when in fact various atrocities against Jews took place.

They whined, howled, threw tantrums and made demands, letting slip dangerous remarks about politics, not least about British radio. Their mothers gave them the swill from the public kitchens with the statutory 100 grams of bread together with their own rations, and they managed to find some hidden jam, cheese, sausage or cake at the bottom of their bundles; but the children were insatiable. Having got up, according to orders, at five o'clock like the adults, they were out and about in the courtyards of the ghetto, constantly on the move and playing all kinds of tricks thanks to the great freedom that had been thrust on them— particularly the well-off middle-class ones, who in the outside world had been under stricter supervision by schools and parents. The adults, wrapped up in their anxiety, their longing for mira- cles, and their thirst for news, only took notice of them when they came with their relentless demands for something to eat, like creditors who aren't interested in what *force majeur* prevents their debtors from fulfilling their obligations. They had hardly eaten when they were hungry again. Then the parents desper- ately scraped together something for them to gobble, and if they had nothing, they begged, borrowed or swapped a piece of bread for their last rags to disarm the threatening gaze of the children calling them to account.

The children were very wicked indeed. At lunchtime the adults, who couldn't satisfy their hunger, were more afraid of them than of the gendarmes. With their aggressive urge to live, which vociferously and accusingly demanded its rights, these children were holding them responsible for everything that was happening. Near the station, a textile manufacturer's lanky, elderly faced twelve-year-old daughter, who had been educated by nuns in the convent of Notre Dame de Sion, shrieked at her mother, as she tore out her own hair: 'Why are you Jews? Why? And if you are Jews, how did you dare to make me?' But even in less extreme cases it could be felt that these precocious, spoilt, messed- up, neurotic Jewish children regarded their parents as criminals because, after all, only criminals could be punished so cruelly. The parents, cornered and helpless, were unable to defend them- selves against the inquisition: what have we done to be locked up in here without our clothes and our toys and without food, when outside the fence other children are going to the beach, licking ice-cream cones and cycling in the park—and all that because of the sins of our fathers! The least the children could do to take revenge was to scream and stamp when everybody dreaded the smallest noise and movement, to neglect washing and combing their hair, and—with early puberty bursting its dams—to hide in the bushes, climb into attics and go into the toilets, boys and girls together, while grown-up women were missing their periods and grown-up men acting as if they had been castrated. The parents, numb with fear, at times intervened mechanically and distractedly, but soon abandoned these attempts in order to run to the gate: somebody was coming with news— apparently they were going to vaccinate us, which meant that we wouldn't be killed after all, because the dead need no vaccination for typhus, cholera, dysentery and diphtheria.

So the children would complain about the beans, but they would also gobble up the beets and turnips. And if the beets and turnips ran out we wouldn't need to worry, because they would soon gobble up us old people. A separate book should be written about the children in the ghetto—the *Giovinezza*,[*] who here too were the most cruel, the unhappy *balilli*[†] of the gas chambers, who were constantly holding the adults at bay. Of course there were also good, gentle, sad and sick children, but they weren't typical. Then there were the blind, deaf-mute and crippled children, who had been pulled out of their institutions on the orders of the government and piled into the other synagogue, which was being used as a store and collecting point. And there were the little idiots, who had been brought in from the mental hospitals.

But there were also blind, deaf-mute, crippled and insane adults. The insane talked and gesticulated a lot but caused no trouble: they behaved as if what was happening were the most normal thing in the world—the world had simply joined them in their madness. Although they were insane and Jewish, there were three Hitlers among them, but not one Einstein, Bergson

[*] The Italian Fascist party's youth organisation.
[†] Members of the Italian Fascist party's children's organisation.

or Marx. The Jewish convicts, too, had been brought in from the prisons—three of them managed to escape during the first night. A theological student, classified as a Jew, had been brought in from a Catholic seminary—he was a rabid anti-Semite who refused to talk to anybody and who prayed all day in a loud voice for a German victory. And two Jewish prostitutes had been brought in from the VD department of the general hospital, when it was discovered that they had had the entry relating to their religion in their medical card forged by the vice squad for a fee of fifty pengős.

Twelve

In the evening the gravediggers returned to the ghetto. Their weary faces were engraved with depression and anger, as if they couldn't come to terms with having missed an opportunity— perhaps the best and the last. This is what had happened.

They were trudging behind the vans along the long road towards the cemetery, with their shovels on their shoulders. Coming out from behind the fence for the first time, they were assailed by fear, the pain of their memories, their shame and their helplessness, and a sense of vulnerability that outweighed any forlorn hope raised by being in the open. Now they realised that the fence was not only a wall of confinement but also one of protection. Inside the fence, they shared the fate of the crowd, and if they were the captives of a cruel enemy, at least the enemy was in uniform, recognisable from afar, and not in evidence everywhere and all the time. Outside the fence, everybody was an enemy—the whole town, the whole world. They didn't dare to look either right or left: like criminals afraid of eye witnesses who might recognise and denounce them, they were afraid of being seen by people they knew. Once more they had to bear the worst abuse from the women, while the children pelted them not only with coarse insults but also with stones, trailing along close behind as if following a brass band or a circus. Even when the gendarme snapped at them, the children tagged along for a long time at a distance. When the procession crossed the market place some of the peasant men and women, who had come to the town for the weekly market and were perched on their carts or asleep in the shade, glanced at them out of the corners of their eyes without much curiosity: these gravediggers were neither here nor there, didn't really concern them, weren't their responsibility, and they weren't going to interfere. What the nobs and gendarmes were doing was of course somewhat distasteful, but on the other hand these people were townies in suits and, on top of it, Jews who had crucified our Lord Jesus Christ and who had money even under their skin, while the poor people were being harassed to death by the bailiff. It was the Germans' and nobs' business, not theirs. And, after all, their own sons were also dying in the war. They shrugged their shoulders.

Only at the other end of the market place, in front of the hardware shop, did something encouraging happen. A worker, scarcely twenty years old, was standing there, in rags, determined, with his hands in his pockets. 'Patience, Mr Friedländer, it won't last much longer,' he whispered. 'Budapest got another dose last night, the Russians are at Rahó.' Perhaps it was possible. The race was still open. The Russians, or the invasion, could still win by a nose. Or the government could still come to its senses and realise that it mustn't debit its account so brutishly at the end of the war. They walked on towards the cemetery in speculative and hopeful mood.

They laid out forty-nine bodies—which were in an appalling condition and exuded a ghastly smell—in the dirty, weed-infested grass. It seemed as if all the blowflies in the world had gathered in the cemetery of Várad-Velence in anticipation of a grand feast, but the news of the mass burial also brought out the five regular gravediggers of the Jewish cemetery from the local taverns. These men had long known the posh amateur gravediggers, most of whom had at some time or other accompanied a parent or relative out here. The gendarme, who had barked his orders at the Jews while they were loading the vans in the ghetto, had changed on the way out. He had turned strangely, suspiciously quiet and had startled them—heartening some and increasing the misgivings of others—by shooing away the mocking and stone-throwing children with a jerk of his rifle. When he noticed the professional gravediggers he said to them:

'Listen to me, you lot. You're experts. Help them.'

The pros got to work, measuring out the mass grave in a craftsmanlike manner, and once they had produced their well-used spades from the tool shed the pit rapidly grew deeper. The Jews were also digging, and at first there was a small commotion whenever one of them recognised a body he knew, but then they continued in dreary silence, sweating and toiling, and squinting back at the gendarme from time to time with timid obsequiousness. They were lawyers, teachers, civil servants, but most of them knew how to dig, because in the last few years almost all had been called up to construct military roads, to build fortifications against the Russians in the Carpathians or bunkers on the Don, or simply to burrow in the earth, as a way of removing them from their homes and their own jobs so that they were no longer able to compete with the Aryans. But though they knew how to dig, the grave wouldn't have been finished even by the next morning, had the pros not helped them. Now it became clear how weak these people from the ghetto had become as a result of hunger, thirst, sleeplessness and nervous tension, not to mention those among them who had been beaten up in the brewery. They dropped out one after the other. The gendarme watched them without saying a word before he turned away to take a walk between the graves. Nor did he say anything when the professional gravediggers' wives arrived with cans of water and when former employees, superficial acquaintances, neighbours, customers—outsiders with whom they hadn't had a close relationship, but who had got wind of the fifty Jews working in the cemetery—brought food parcels, cigarettes and newspapers. It was they—and not the friends, the debtors, the brother freemasons and the drinking companions—who turned up and, seeing that the gendarme didn't object, ventured further in. Eventually they were sitting on the old graves together with the Jews, taking down instructions and messages in their notebooks, cycling into the town and returning after carrying out some urgent commissions. The Jews were unable to tip the gravediggers. Yet the gravediggers arranged for brandy and bacon to be brought to them. Then a few elderly maidservants came walking out to the cemetery, having heard that their former employers were digging graves. They cried with them for a while, scraped some food together for them and, with trembling lips, inquired about the children.

That was how the day passed, and the grave progressed steadily. The gendarme left the cemetery and for a long time gazed from the perimeter at the vineyard with its red-roofed villas, its white-washed hut housing the wine presses, and its red-domed calvary. He was from a different region, from the plain, and he was intrigued by this new scenery at the edge of Transylvania, where the hills began their journey towards their final destination, the snow-capped mountains. When he slowly returned, the men sitting on the graves jumped up and stood nervously to attention, but he said:

'Never mind that. Who owns these vineyards?'

There were four among the fifty who owned vineyards, with pretty holiday homes, on the hillside. At the end of the school term the families used to move up here, and in the evenings, when the shops or offices closed, the fathers used to walk up or, in bad weather, shared a taxi to join them. The air was excellent up here and, imagine, fifty kilometres away the mountains were already a thousand metres high. And the wine was good too—they explained like toadying experts to the gendarme, whom they took for a tippler—it had the rich bouquet of a wine grown on sand and on a hillside. One of them even told him the alcohol content of the wine.

The gendarme listened to them seriously, calmly, with interest, before he left again and didn't return for half an hour. He might have been about forty, with an intelligent Tartar face, a red moustache and greying hair. He gazed at them as if he had something at the tip of his tongue, but changed his mind about saying it. By four o'clock in the afternoon only the professional gravediggers were still working. The fathers, brothers, friends and children had been put in the grave, one after the other. There was not much left to do: they had only to throw the earth on the bodies and build up the mound.

The gendarme pointed at Friedländer: 'You, with the blond moustache, come here.' In a normal voice, as if talking to an equal human being, he said: 'Listen, please . . . tell these people . . . if they want to disappear they should go . . . Nobody has counted you. There's no register. You're now like hay. The cart doesn't stop if some falls off. But only smart people should go, because if you're caught you've had it.'

'Are you serious, sergeant?'

'It's only five kilometres to the Romanian border. If anybody has the nerve he should try.'

Friedländer reeled back to the others and, stuttering, told them what the gendarme had suggested. They stood up, but were unable to move, as if their feet had been rooted to the spot. They conferred in wary whispers. What if he was trying to trick them—they would start and he would shoot them. And even if he meant well . . . where on earth could they go from this cemetery? Where could they go? The road was full of soldiers and gendarmes, or somebody might come along who knew them . . . They would be caught after ten steps. From behind every fence in the vineyard, vintners, holiday-makers from the town and malignant women were watching them. Even if they got as far as the border, which was indeed only five kilometres away, how would they steer clear of the border guards? And even if they managed to slip through the Hungarian border, who could say that they wouldn't be polished off by the first Romanian? On the other side there were also Germans, the Iron Guard and Antonescu,* and Jews were being deported to the Dniester . . . And if they weren't polished off by the Romanians, what would happen to their families in the ghetto? They couldn't leave their families, parents, children, wives behind without a man. Of course they could do nothing to help at the moment, but all these dependants would be lost if they were taken away somewhere without the men. And even if it was true that families would be split up and sent to separate camps for men and women, what would the family in the ghetto say if the husband or father escaped alone?

Only one gravedigger, the red-haired Grosz, said that he was going to escape. Grosz had only recently returned from the Ukraine. While he was being chewed up out there by the lice, his wife had got involved with an Aryan deputy notary and gambled away all his money on rummy. Grosz didn't care: the worst that could happen was that the gendarme shot him. He tore off his yellow star behind the bushes and stepped out on to the road. He walked down the road, at first rather unsteadily,

* Ion Antonescu (1882–1945), fascist dictator of Romania.

then more confidently, slowly, then faster and faster until he was almost running. The gendarme turned his back on him, the Jews watched him spellbound. Grosz disappeared round the corner in a cloud of dust. Meanwhile the mass grave had been finished, with a mound half a metre high. The professional gravediggers patted it for a few more minutes with the backs of their spades to make it smooth.

'Fall in, men!' the gendarme ordered in a harsh voice. Then he again beckoned Friedländer and said to him: 'What a bunch of cowards you are. What can one do with you? I know that my family will be exterminated in six months because of what the gendarmerie is doing here. But if any of you stay alive, remember this: Gendarmerie Corporal Sándor Torma from Kaposmérő tried to help you. Shoulder spades!' he roared and the gravediggers from the ghetto stood in line. The dust, sparkling red in the sunset, lit them up like Bengal fire.

The town was wrapped in a dirty, stifling heat that seemed to make people too drained even to hate. Now it appeared as if nobody had noticed them—men in shirtsleeves were reading newspapers at their windows without so much as looking up, and scantily dressed women watering flowers hid their faces in the pots. The radios were blaring, vilifying the Russians, the British, the gangsters in the sky—they were constantly blaring because of the air raids. Nobody standing at the tram stops or in the doorways of shops glanced at them. They might as well have been invisible.

At the Oroszlán pharmacy, near the ghetto, they were alarmed by sudden footfalls. Venturing a backward glance, they saw Grosz trotting after them, white with dust. Even his bare red head was white. The gendarme also turned round sharply. He stopped, stamped his foot, and spat. Grosz slunk back into the ranks, mingling with the rest and marching in step as if he had never left them.

After his escape Grosz had walked and then run a bit, until he met a peasant cart. The peasants paid no attention to him. A car full of officers and women tore past and nobody took any notice of him. A hundred steps later he met a gendarme on a bicycle. 'Now I've had it,' he thought, but the gendarme on the bicycle only asked him: 'What's the time, brother?' 'I haven't got a watch, but I think it's about a quarter past five.' As he walked on, cold with fright, he met people coming in the opposite direction and was overtaken by carriages, cars and lorries, but he wasn't asked by a single soul what he was doing on the road. When he had reached the forest, only three kilometres from the Romanian border, he suddenly felt his nerves giving way. He could no longer bear it. He met a man with a green hat, a grey moustache and an evil face, who looked like an Arrow Cross party boss. The man inspected Grosz and said: 'Keep going, my friend. Cut across to the baths, walk round the pool and turn left'—the Romanian border was close to the park in the beautiful spa of Püspökfürdő. 'He has recognised me,' Grosz thought shivering, 'and now he'll report me.'

Two elderly militiamen appeared from the bushes. They were doing up their belts, probably after answering a call of nature. Grosz, having been taught the drill while he was a forced labourer, clicked his heels and saluted:

'Officers, I've escaped from the ghetto. Please take me back.'

'Go to hell. Escape where you like, for all I care,' one of them said, and they walked on in disgust.

He just stood in the middle of the road, rooted on the spot, waiting to be captured. People continued to come and go, but nobody wanted him. He set off again and once more took refuge in the forest—all right, but who could he turn to in Romania? He knew nobody, had no addresses, neither in Arad nor in Belényes. He didn't have a penny . . . and he didn't have a change of underwear . . . This was no good. A thing like this had to be arranged in advance with a smuggler . . . He couldn't forge ahead blindly, it was certain death.

And then he suddenly turned round and started running. If somebody had tried to stop his escape he might have fought back, knocked the person down, and flee as far as he could see. But, as it was, having done nothing to break the law, he was already asking the authorities, the powers that be, to forgive him. After all, he had only strayed a little, only stayed a little behind the others. That didn't deserve a great deal of punishment, and in any case . . . It was also the gendarme's fault . . . the gendarme had as good as tricked him . . . the gendarme wasn't going to report the matter, he would be only too glad to hush it up . . . And he ran and ran, like a dog following a cart, and his only fear was that he might be stopped by somebody as he was 'escaping back', and be prevented from catching up with the gravediggers before they reached the ghetto. He was afraid of having to ask to be let in on his own. He ran and even clambered on to a truck carrying soda water, where he gave the driver his last cigarette, extracted from his jacket lining. At the Oroszlán pharmacy he managed to catch up with the gravediggers and, sneaking into their line, with a huge sigh of relief, he released the steam of fear and tension that had almost blown him apart. His face bore the rueful expression of one who recognises that he has disobeyed orders but has immediately put his mistake right. His imploring, obsequious gaze pleaded with the gendarme: you see, sergeant, I'm here, I'm not causing any trouble.

The gendarme, having watched him with contempt out of the corner of his eye, roared: 'Get a move on, damn you, you rotten Jews!' He briskly saluted a passing lieutenant-colonel, who graciously acknowledged the greeting.

The gates of the ghetto were opened wide in front of the gravediggers. Grosz, pushing his way to the front, slipped in almost in ecstasy, like a mesmerised rodent into the python's throat.

Thirteen

Friedländer told me all this, sitting on the edge of my mattress. I wasn't surprised to hear that the red-haired Grosz had tried to escape and then sneaked back. How many times had I seen the same in the Ukraine. A young man who had been worked to exhaustion in the extreme heat or made to roll and crawl in the snow till he was frozen stiff decided to stand for it no longer. 'I've had enough. I'm going to do a bunk tomorrow.' At dawn or dusk he really did do a bunk during the march alongside the edge of the forest. He slipped between the trees and set out east, where the Russians were and the forest was full of partisans. He trudged for an hour or two through the firs, the shrubs, the thistles and the snow drifts, stumbling over stumps, getting stuck in marshes, stepping into huge anthills or gullies hidden by snow—the whole area was nothing but traps. He heard rustles. There were footsteps, murmurs, voices and echoes, distant shooting. Every tree trunk and every wrecked tank assumed the human shape of an armed guard or a field gendarme. Then the path that had run steadily through the deep moss turned out to be going nowhere. The sun or moon that had been shining through the trees in front of him was suddenly behind him. He was all on his own, without a map, without a compass and without real, unwavering determination, and with only a little bread and jam in his haversack. How could he have embarked on this madness? And the evening, the weird Russian evening. Here the sun didn't set as it did at home. When it reached the horizon it suddenly dropped, as if it had been hanging on a string that somebody had cut with a penknife. The thick, pitch-black darkness came abruptly, followed by complete silence, as if everything that had a voice had been frightened to death. The insects and birds were still. The wild animals had either been killed by the war or had fled to some place in the east where they weren't threatened by human beings. The fugitive felt as if he had fallen into a deep well, where no sounds from above could penetrate and even the sky was invisible.

Standing bewildered at the bottom of the well, in the dark and the silence, he made a desperate effort to claw his way out. He had to get out by hook or by crook, find the road, and slink back into the most hideous servitude—where he might or might not be beaten to death, but where he would at least be among the other prisoners with their humble and sly hatred, and would no longer have to face the objects, the shadows and the noises, would no longer have to find his own way—for everything was easier to bear if it happened to everybody. That was how most of the fugitives returned, escaping from the horror of freedom back to the doomed community of slaves. A dog will flee to the forest if it's thrashed by its master, but it won't stay there, despite being descended from a wolf. It creeps back home and can hardly wait to be beaten, chained up again, and given its bone.

Admittedly, a few of us showed occasional flashes of the wolf's nature. These flashes were miraculous, because after the First World War all these young men had attended fascist schools, where they were taught to hate revolution and any other kind of freedom. Then, only a few years ago, the overwhelming majority of them had served as conscripts in Horthy's* army, where it was drummed into them that they must hate, and if necessary oppose, anything to do with freedom—liberalism, democracy, Western civilisation and Bolshevism, and even despise themselves for being Jews. In that counter-revolutionary army of Horthy's, which was really the white guard of the white terror, these sons of the petty bourgeoisie had gone out of their way to prove that they were more fervent patriots and better, tougher and more obedient soldiers than the Hungarian gentiles. Pre-fascism had left a corner where loyal and politic Jews could do business, so long as none of those in power coveted and took the business away from them. It had even allowed them to enjoy life in their own way. They hadn't regarded it as an insult to their dignity

* Miklós Horthy (1868–1957), regent of Hungary, 1920–44.

that their sons were forbidden to attend Hungarian universities and they had sent them instead to Prague, Brno, Paris or, preferably, to Bologna, Genoa or Rome, because they liked Italian fascism and admired Mussolini, who had tidied up Italy and built motorways, which the Jews of Budapest knew down to the last bend, almost as well as the road from Budapest to Siófok on Lake Balaton. In Budapest there had been anti-Semitism, but honeymooners had still gone to Venice to have their photos taken at the foot of St Mark's flagpole, just as their parents had done in the age of liberalism. And on their return home they had reported in transports of enthusiasm that the military commander of Rome was a Jew, there were no beggars, the black-shirted militia were polite and—of course—the trains were on time.

This was the background from which they had joined the counter-revolutionary army, feeling honoured by the fact that the anti-Semitic regime gave Jews a chance of being soldiers and even receiving a commission. They had wholeheartedly supported the power of the state and kept even stricter discipline than the regular officers. At the same time they were deeply distressed by being Jews. They were like Monsieur Georges, the black lawyer from Dakar, who joined the French army as a lieutenant at the outbreak of the war. We met him when he came to our hotel to say farewell to his blonde, white girlfriend, who had the room next to ours. The black man explained to us that he believed in the Nürnberg racial laws and hated Daladier, Blum, Cachin and, most of all, Diagne,* the deputy president of the National Assembly, who was a debauched, corrupt democrat like the whole gang that was now plunging France into ruin.

'But, Monsieur Georges,' I objected indignantly, 'if it weren't for these gentlemen you would still be an item for sale on the slave market in the port of Dakar.'

'And it would be quite right, too,' he said. 'I know the negroes, they don't deserve any better.'

---

* Léon Blum (1872–1950), Jewish Social Democrat and prime minister of France for short periods. Marcel Cachin (1869–1958), French Communist leader. Blaise Diagne (1872–1934), first black member of the French National Assembly, representing Senegal.

Such was the template imposed on large sections of the young Hungarian Jewish bourgeoisie by virtue of education and coercion in the first quarter of the century. And when they were suddenly stripped of their uniform, when they had the yellow stigma sewn on them, when they found themselves relegated to the lowest level of human existence, many of them were still unable to forget that although they were Jews they had once been allowed to share the power of their anti-Semitic homeland. These proud memories kept them going in the middle of unimaginable ordeals and gave them the strength to bear being trodden on by any Hungarian private. 'Last year this miserable bastard stood to attention, as stiff as a post, when I walked past him,' last year's lieutenants and cadets hissed as they crawled on the ground, ragged, dirty, louse-ridden, with their noses in the dust. They were still expecting to be rehabilitated by this homeland, this system that had become their executioner. Meanwhile those who hadn't been officers or soldiers remembered that over the past quarter of a century they had been able to make a reasonable living by a little opportunism, corruption and cleverness, so long as they weren't revolutionaries or 'bolshies', and didn't open their mouths too wide. Jews should steer clear of politics. Politics was not the business of the Jews but of the gentiles, who were the majority. Jews should look after their families and make money.

They only realised that German Nazism was a threat to them personally when Hitler invaded Austria. But as the Germans were winning one victory after the other in Europe, they had, with shocking optimism, assured each other that when Hitler won the war he would abandon anti-Semitism, because he would no longer need it. Even out in the Ukraine, in thirty-five degrees of frost or in scorching heat, they were still finding reasons and mitigating circumstances for the cruelty that was being perpetrated on them: 'Let's face it, it's quite understandable,' they would tell each other. 'If they're calling up the Christians they can't let the Jews kick their heels at home. That would only create bad blood and more anti-Semitism.' Or, in another version: 'The Germans demanded Jews from the Hungarians. The Hungarians have brought us here to the Ukraine to avoid turning us over. We're still in Hungarian hands. The important thing is to remain alive till the relief comes.'

Even when it was obvious that they had been brought here to die, and their vile company commanders told them as much with an evil grin, they still believed that the military rules and favours applied to them. In six months' time the 'relief' would arrive, and they would travel home in the wagons, to be discharged from the barracks and have the Ukraine massaged out of them in the Rudas thermal baths. For a week they wouldn't work but spend their days in the cafés and their nights in the bars, then they would see what they could do for a living. Although they often contemplated taking fearsome revenge on their torturers, most of the time they were only able to plan small individual actions. Once the guard had become a conductor on the trams or the railways, an office messenger, or a caretaker at a technical college, they would sort him out: they would ambush him in the street on his way home and give him a thorough hiding. Their feelings were ambivalent. They hated the guards, but at the same time it was their ambition to be addressed by them in a friendly tone. They were pleased when a guard honoured them with a crude joke or some personal request. Most of them toiled really hard, competing at the exhausting tasks, which were almost always pointless, and priding themselves on being good workers. They laughed at the clumsy ones who were singled out for the guards' cruel humour, and they bullied the pathetic weak ones who didn't know how to handle a pickaxe and who collapsed under a sack of oats weighing a ton.

I was the oldest and—because of my age as well as my officer's rank in the First World War, rather than my occupation at home—they tended to treat me with consideration and courtesy and to help me when the work I had to do was too hard for my physical strength.

In the depths of the Pripiaty swamps, in a hail of bombs and shells, they showed true personal courage by testifying in my favour when I was hauled before a court-martial in a wooden hut by the commander who, having failed to get me summarily beaten to death by his soldiers, tried to have me shot in due legal form on the pretext of mutiny. As I said before, at difficult moments they were capable of solidarity, bravery and, towards me, even of some affection, but it could also happen that they tired of being tactful and considerate, and one or other of them would shout at me: 'Remember you're a shitty Jew, just like me.' I wasn't offended because I knew that if Einstein himself had been here he would sooner or later have received the same treatment. Petty-bourgeois Jews are proud if another Jew rises above them, but they won't let him dwell on the difference, particularly when he is with them. If a Jew's way of being a Jew is not exactly like their own they will consider him pretentious, affected, or even a renegade. Perhaps I was no better, but when the Russian offensive started and I was feverishly listening to the thunder of the approaching guns it still shocked me to hear one of them say in despair: 'This is terrible, now we'll be lumbered with the Russians. The others can win the war in the west, for all I care, but I don't want these here to give an inch. What's going to happen if we retreat? They'll do us all in.'

In their wallets they kept photos of their wives and children, which they would produce, show off and kiss, and they judged the military and political news mainly by whether it brought them closer to returning home. As they laboured, marched, fetched and carried, their only thought was of going home.

There were some magnificent chaps, some intelligent, educated and talented men of admirable character among them, but most were exactly what the botched mass production of human beings almost everywhere between the two world wars had made them. It was not their fault: they had been churned out by the factory of the age.

I myself, having lived in my own literary, political and intellectual circles, was surprised and saddened by the dismal educational level of the Jewish petty bourgeoisie. It was of course the schools and the *numerus clausus* at the universities that had from 1920 prevented this teachable class from being educated and acquiring more dependable tastes. Nevertheless, I was deeply ashamed when I heard them rave, lying on their straw pallets in the dark after a day of horrendous labour, about the plays and films that had come into vogue after the expulsion of Jewish directors, writers and actors from the theatre and the cinema. I had always regarded it an exaggeration to attribute a special political significance to the theatre, but these expelled artists had made political statements through their work every day, until some Arrow Cross clown had proclaimed in the papers that the Jews, the British and the French must be driven from the stage. A jumped-up bassoonist had banished Meyerbeer, Mendelssohn, Offenbach, Halévy and even Bizet (because of his Jewish wife) from opera and concert hall. In the past the petty-bourgeois Jews in particular were very sensitive about such things, and I had thought that they would never set foot in a theatre again. Now I heard them discuss, before they fell asleep, operettas and films glorifying irredentists and soldiers, and enthuse over films, actors and actresses whose names I had never even heard. Admittedly, I hadn't been going regularly to the theatre, even before the actors had begun to call the audience bloody Jews every day. But these chaps had still been going when they were called up for forced labour, and right to the end were unable to break free from the petty-bourgeois magic to which the theatre had been degraded by the previous age. They had still been going to the theatre to guffaw and blubber when it had become an official instrument for inciting political hatred against them. They remained addicted heart and soul to the petty-bourgeois theatre. Their very tastes and pleasures bound them closely to the system that would inevitably lead them here among the chassids, to the gas chamber, or into the Danube. No wonder they were unable to tear themselves away and escape from this system, even when it had become a mortal danger to them, partly because they feared a cruel punishment and partly because they felt most at home in it.

At that time I was away from these companions, having been 'detailed' to Unieca to search for mines, together with the bad workers and a few peacetime Jewish thieves and burglars, the scum of the company, in the expectation that within days we would be blown to bits. But we were laughing up our sleeves, because we had never had it so good: our commander was a decent, middle-aged sapper officer, and the sappers, all of whom had families, treated us quite gently. As everywhere, the forest was full of partisans and we could only fell trees at the edge.

From Jelonka it was reported that the guards were drunk all

day, demanded impossible amounts of work, tied up everybody, stole the food and perpetrated extraordinary acts of malice against the labourers. In contrast to larger garrisons they didn't need to worry that a staff or medical officer might occasionally take notice when their inhumanity went beyond what everybody took for granted. On their own with the labourers, they could do anything they dreamt up, undisturbed by any supervision and any physical or moral impediment.

After observing this madness for a week from the forest, the partisans took action one Sunday morning: they surprised the guards and shot two of them, while the rest ran away. 'Well, Jews, you're free. Follow us,' the partisans shouted in Russian, Hungarian and Yiddish. They gave the forced labourers as many horses as they could find, fed them bacon and bread, and escorted them through the forest until, after a long trek, they reached the partisan camp. There the commander asked which of them wanted to have a gun and to fight. An alarmed silence followed. Then one of them said that they knew nothing about weapons and would rather work. The commander answered that the partisans had no need of forced labour as they could fell trees and build bunkers themselves. The labourers started explaining that they were physically and emotionally finished, after living in inhuman conditions and not seeing their families for a year and a half. The commander answered that the partisans were also living in great discomfort and some hadn't seen their wives and children for three years, let alone a year and a half. They went on arguing, without getting anywhere. Then suddenly the Germans opened fire on the forest, and it started raining heavily. The partisans left the labourers behind. They could go where they liked. So, from a distance of about fifty kilometres, they trickled back to their company's quarters, just as the red-haired Grosz had slipped back behind the fence of the Nagyvárad ghetto.

Of course, some of them would have liked to fight, but in the mood created by the majority any independent action was impossible. And really, what could they have done? What could I have done if I had been there? As I say, I was no better. I had also been reduced to a hysterical skeleton in a year and a half, and it's certain that I too would have shrunk, if not from fighting, at least from the ordeal of a nomadic life in the forest. I have often thought that my vanity might have saved me from sneaking back from an exhausting and risky freedom to an exhausting, disgraceful and no less risky servitude. I believe that if I had stayed away I would have done so mainly because I couldn't face being told by everybody for the rest of my life that all I had scribbled so far had been nothing but lies and chitchat. But what do I know? Perhaps I would have gone back with the others.

In fact there were about a dozen among them who revealed a heroic or adventurous disposition when the time came, but even they had to be captured by the Russians, or left behind during the disintegrating Hungarian army's retreat, to jolt them into action. However much they longed to exchange their servitude for freedom under the enemy, they needed an external force to break the threads binding them to the past and to the community of their fellows before they dared, and were able, to fulfil their longings. It isn't the suffering, the accumulated hatred, that makes revolutionaries out of the masses, but the revolution itself.

Fourteen

Friedländer is still sitting on the edge of my mattress. The blue lamp casts thick grey shadows on his face, making it look like the speckled face of a cadaver. With his elbows on his knees and his chin pressed to his fist, he is breathing heavily, with an occasional gurgle. He volunteered as a gravedigger to bury his son. He doesn't mention him, and neither do I. There's nothing to say. The lad, a mechanical engineer, was twenty-seven when he caught galloping consumption in a labour camp in the Carpathians. As he was dying in the sanatorium near the Nagyvárad vineyards, the order came for everybody, including the dying, to be taken to the ghetto. He was taken to the ghetto and died within three hours.

'I'll volunteer again tomorrow,' Friedländer says. 'I'll take my other son with me, perhaps he'll manage . . .'

He no longer mourns his dead son, whose grave he will use to help the other escape. But will there be any burials tomorrow? Will there be enough bodies? Indeed, there will be more than enough, because every ten minutes a suicide is arriving on a stretcher. The false hope that galvanised the ghetto at the news of the impending departure soon collapsed. Not because people suspected that where they were going they would be killed, but rather because the tired, the indolent, the sensitive, the fastidious, and those who could concretely visualise what would happen to them tomorrow, changed their minds and took cyanide. They could imagine, precisely and in every detail, being squeezed into the wagons with seventy others; seeing their own grey face, and those of the rest, reflected in the others' eyes that had suddenly grown much bigger and brighter in their deep hollows; standing packed together and pushing and shoving for a better place, nearer the window, nearer the air. And nearer the water, which would be gone after a quarter of an hour because the stronger and more aggressive would have drunk it or somebody would have knocked the canister over. Parents using their children to blackmail the others for space, air, water. No water—that was the worst. One's tongue sticking to one's palate. Then fighting one's way to relieve oneself into the bucket—which would fill up to overflowing within minutes—and arguing, or actually coming to blows, with somebody who, even here, would loudly invoke the principle of equality and declare that everybody was nothing but a shitty Jew like everybody else. Being unable to move, with stubbly chin, itching unbearably and breathing in the stench, the dreadful body odour, of the others. Some would die, too suddenly to clutch their hearts, and wouldn't even fall down, because there wasn't enough room. Some would go mad. Some women would give birth prematurely. At night the train would stop in a siding, in Szajol or Csap, and in the strange acoustics of a nocturnal station railwaymen would be heard blowing their whistles at regular intervals or chatting during breaks in the shunting: 'The wife got a goat from the Kelemen farm, but it only gives so much milk,' one voice would narrate, and another interrupt him officiously: 'The three hundred and forty has been delayed, track three is free.' That was how they would be talking in their arcane jargon, knocking back two large spritzers at the station bar, with their red flags under their arms.

Before the war, the traveller often heard such conversations when he woke up with a start in the night on the slow train home to Nagyvárad. At the Eastern Station in Budapest he bought the evening papers, gobbled down a ham sandwich, took off his collar and tie, went to the WC and looked into every compartment to see if there was anybody sitting there whom he knew. He read a little, before his lids became heavy with the jolting, and by the time the train reached the first station, Rákosrendező, he was asleep. Roused by the conversation of two railwaymen, he became thirsty. In Szolnok and Ladány he got off briefly to buy a green bottle of chilled mineral water and a paper cup . . .

No, we're not going, the suicides decided. They were suddenly gripped by a burning thirst and, for one last time, filled their glasses to the brim with Nagyvárad tap water, before unpicking their jacket lining and producing the tiny medicine bottles with the brownish grey powder. The bottles were hermetically sealed with corks, their necks wrapped in gauze. They removed the gauze and levered the cork out with their penknives. Recoiling from the smell that hit them, they hesitated. Then they took a grip on themselves. No, even if everything were to turn out all right in the end, it wasn't worth putting up with all that for the sake of what would be left of their lives. They poured the brownish grey powder into the water . . . the smell was dreadful, but it had no taste, and soon there would be no smell either. Without delay, their neighbours informed a gendarme. The gendarme, exasperated, ordered them to put the bodies on stretchers and take them to the hospital. In the dark ghetto, by the scanty light of the new moon, men were lugging stretchers everywhere. It was like the nocturnal processions in plague-stricken Florence, except that the men weren't wearing cowls and no plague bells were ringing . . .

Friedländer will have something to bury tomorrow and he will try to help his son escape. The ghetto has been divided into six sections, and the first section is leaving tomorrow. The hospital, which is the last section, will leave on the sixth day. In six days anything may happen. One may escape or one may die, and even those waiting for a miracle may turn out to be right.

Just as the wispy teacher of religion turns out to be right.

A gendarme pushes the door open, looking for Jakab Leuchtturm, born in the village of Felsővisó in 1879. Leuchtturm crawls out of the cluster of mattresses occupied by patients from the poorhouse at the far end of the room. In the blue light even his reddish goatee is blue and he is incredibly skinny, like some character in a South German fairy tale. The gendarme says in a soldierly but encouraging tone:

'Your exemption has arrived at the commander's office. Get dressed at once, you may leave the territory of the ghetto.'

For a second the teacher of religion doesn't move. Then he sways and doesn't fall only because he isn't heavy enough for gravity to pull him to the floor. Suddenly an unbelievably mighty voice bursts out of his small body. It's neither the voice of unbridled joy, nor the voice of inarticulate bliss, nor even a hallelujah to his God for working this miracle for him, but the voice of ecstatic boasting:

'Didn't I tell you!' he blares like a foghorn, laughing and crying. 'Didn't I tell you that they appreciate me at the Honours Office? You didn't believe it, did you? But I fought against the Czechs at Nagybiccse, officer. I've always been the greatest Hungarian patriot, officer. The greatest!' he blusters, pounding his breast with his red, freckled fists.

Everybody rises from the mattresses and listens to him, pale with amazement, envy and silent hatred. As he jumps up and down like a grasshopper in his awkward haste to get ready, I too hate his triumphant, gloating face and the smug, contemptuous look he gives us inferior beings he is leaving behind to meet their doom.

The people of Nagyvárad—as they now explain—have never been able to stand him. He had come from somewhere in Ruthenia fifteen years ago to teach religion, which he had done badly, because the children hadn't even learnt the Hebrew alphabet from him. He had always been preoccupied with his own affairs, a devious, obsequious fellow, and a constant burden to the community. The money for his wife's funeral and his young children's school fees had been raised by the community, and his elder son and daughter, whom he had sent to university in France, had of course also been kept by the wealthier Jews. There had always been something wrong with his house: first the roof had leaked, then the stove had needed relining, and he had incessantly demanded a cellar, because his potatoes were rotting. He had constantly pestered the community leaders with his begging. Having been brushed off one day, he had always come back the next to continue his obstinate, importunate, truculent begging, and he had nagged everybody until he got everything he wanted, only so he would go away. At such times he had gushed with repulsively fulsome declarations of gratitude, but this hadn't prevented him beating his pupils black and blue whenever they had played some time-honoured tricks on him during religious instruction. The parents had urged the president of the community to fire him, but in the evenings he had turned up on the doorstep of the beaten child's father, tearfully apologising and noisily denouncing himself for not being able to control his evil temper. He had never spoken to anybody about his heroic exploits at Nagybiccse, but now it was obvious that he had been taking out his own repressed aggression on the children he had so viciously beaten. In biblical times Leuchtturm might have become a famous general, but the Jews watching the scene from their mattresses would have loved to spit in his face and give him a good hiding. They could have killed him, at least with their looks.

When he had finished dressing, he struck his forehead: 'Excuse me, officer,' he said, 'I had a stick.' Stretching his arm behind him, he called out over his shoulder to his former neighbours on the mattresses, the patients from the poorhouse. When they didn't respond he turned his whole body towards them and demanded in an insolent and accusing tone: 'Where's my stick? My stick must be here.' He fumbled between the mattresses, and the patients, alarmed by his imperious tone, went down on all fours to look for the stick in the interstices.

'Get a move on,' the gendarme chivvied him. 'You aren't lame, you can walk without a stick.'

'Excuse me. I've had that stick for twenty years. I brought it with me to Nagyvárad. Every child knows that stick,' he said with a bloodthirsty swagger and continued rooting and rummaging until it turned up in some corner.

'Come on, or I'll leave you here,' the gendarme threatened.

The teacher of religion had already set out towards the door with large steps, tapping the floor with his stick in a staccato rhythm. The tapping could still be heard when he had reached the entrance hall and then the concrete pavement outside the synagogue, and even when it could no longer be heard, the people sitting on their mattresses and staring at the door that had slammed shut behind him could follow it in their minds. Now he was tapping the ground at the ghetto gate . . . tapping steadily . . . and nobody stopped him . . . Now he was tapping the uneven cobbles of the great market place, now the granite pavement of Kapucinus Street, now the tarmac of the little market place. Then he was tapping the streets, large and small, that led directly to his home . . . The people sitting on the mattresses knew every square inch, every dent and bump, every crack and patch in the streets of Nagyvárad that he tapped with his stick . . . He could tap to his heart's content, because no policeman or gendarme had the power to stop him . . . and when he got to his house in Szacsvay Street he could tear off the official seal that the authorities had placed on his front door . . . The neighbours couldn't call the police, and if they wrote anonymous letters it would do them no good, although they would certainly write some. This nobody, this beggar, this good-for-nothing who had been a millstone round the community's neck and who didn't even know the holy book properly—hissed and moaned those who remained captive—was going home to live, while they, who had worked hard all their lives, created something, brought up their children, served in the army, and paid the state huge taxes, would go to the wagons. They, too, were good Hungarian patriots, they had taken part in the First World War and disliked the Czechs, the Romanians and the Bolsheviks—but who could prove that? Who would have thought that one day they would need to prove it?

There was a strange silence outside, that night. The gramophone in the brewery wasn't playing and the thirty wagons that had been shunted in weren't to move till morning. There weren't even any incursions by enemy aircraft. In the silence the stick continued for a long time to tap against our eardrums, like the loud beating of a feverish pulse.

Somebody said: 'What nerve! Anyone else would have been only too happy to leave as quickly as possible, but he kept on looking for his stick for a quarter of an hour.' A second voice joined in: 'I don't envy him out there, alone, with them all around him. He won't be able to set foot outside his house.' A third added: 'He'll starve to death. He won't be able to stuff his face in a restaurant and if he goes to the market nobody will sell him anything. He hasn't got a cellar, and they won't let him go to the shelters with them.'

That was how they cheered themselves up, sentencing him to death by starvation and bombing. Then they fell back exhausted on their mattresses and almost died of helpless envy and hatred.

Fifteen

Some others were also freed that evening. Dr Németi reported that the two prostitutes had been released.

Towards evening a tall, pear-shaped lady in a puritanically dark dress had appeared at the gate. Apart from the red dye in her hair she looked exactly like the ladies in the altar societies, the women's clubs and the associations for providing clothes to children in need. She was known to everybody in the town, particularly the better class of gentlemen, who had frequented her salon for almost two generations. She owned the largest and prettiest brothel in Vitéz Street, where the houses with red lights stood in a row. Her establishment had the largest number of mirrors and the largest staff. For a four-month period it had even included a black girl, which was unique for a small Hungarian town. In recent years it had acquired a political character: since the Hungarians had repossessed Nagyvárad from the Romanians and anti-Semitism was growing more virulent by the day, it had become the meeting place of army officers and civil servants, who got rid of any Jews who had ventured in, first by staring them out, then by harassing them, and eventually by simply ejecting them. Finally the porter refused to let them in. At that time cafés and shops had adopted the fashion of displaying notices such as 'Christian business' or 'We do not serve Jews', and it was common knowledge in the town that Mrs Szilassy's house was also such an 'Aryan house'. The lady herself, although the 'y' in her name identified her as a rightful member of the historic middle class, had no particular objection to Jews, especially since the law had taken away their trading licences in order to ensure the economic success of the gentiles against their competition. However, her clients were high officers and leading figures of the municipal, regional and fiscal administration, 'bigwigs' who would have eaten a Jew for breakfast in the morning, let alone in her salon at night when they were drunk. In addition, the medical officer, who examined the girls twice a week and on whom so much depended, had also gone mad, put on a green shirt, joined the Arrow Cross party and begun to curse the Jews during his visits, even before he had put down his tweezers.

The gentlemen spent much of their time in the salon telling dirty jokes or talking politics, and every political discussion developed into violent invectives against the Jews. The lady wasn't bothered by this, because, as it happened, her establishment had never done better than since it had become an Aryan house, and the Jewish guests had in any case ceased to be an asset when they stayed away as a result of the bullying. But she didn't care whether somebody was Jewish or Greek Orthodox, and two members of her staff, Vilcsi and Sárika, one from Beregszász and the other from Beszterce, were Jewish. Both were attractive and nice girls, who produced a good turnover, and she alone knew that they were Jewish, while neither the other girls nor the guests suspected anything. The fat and forceful Vilcsi was more popular with young businessmen, and Sárika, who had the gift of the gab and who was as thin and flat as a boy, with the old men, the journalists and the officers from the capital.

After the German invasion the lady failed to report that the girls were Jewish, but then she became too frightened to continue hiding them. With the help of a hundred-pengő note she arranged for a nurse to smuggle them into the venereal department of the general hospital—surely, those thickheads who had nothing better to do with their time wouldn't look for them there. In short, the idea was to gain time. For two fifty-pengő notes, she also got the police clerk, the morphine addict Danci Kovács, to amend the girls' religion on their medical cards. God knows how his superior, the head of the vice squad, found out. The beast started an investigation and discovered the girls hiding in the venereal department. The day before yesterday he had sent them to the ghetto.

Of course neither Danci nor Mrs Szilassy got into trouble over this prank. The Aryans are never the real culprits, they are only tricked into such things by the Jews with their money and their vile deceptions—and in any case Mrs Szilassy had been paying a regular monthly salary to the head of the vice squad since his transfer to the town eighteen months ago. In fact he immediately regretted picking a fight with the lady. But what else could he have done? He had been seized by fury when he heard the story—what did the two Jewish whores think they were doing, polluting the good Hungarian air, now that the country was finally being cleaned up?

When Mrs Szilassy called him to account in a threatening tone he abjectly apologised: what am I to do, it's too late, I can't get them out, if anybody can get them out it's you, Ma. Mrs Szilassy left the police station and hurried straight to the ghetto, where she snapped at the police guard at the gate: 'Go and tell the gendarmerie colonel that Mrs Szilassy's here.' She knew the colonel well, because he patronised her salon at least twice a week. He liked the large Magda, who always said that he wasn't a bad bloke apart from thinking that a gendarme must always scare people, even in bed. 'Well, he doesn't scare me,' Mrs Szilassy told herself reassuringly, and when the colonel appeared at the other side of the gate with the wire lattice, she pulled herself up to her full height and faced him pugnaciously.

The colonel's brutal face brightened. He assumed a nonchalant, jovial and chivalrous posture and said in a pretentious voice, which attempted to be both pally and flirtatious:

'I say, Ma, what brings you here?'

'I must speak to you urgently, colonel.'

'Right you are, Ma. Step in. Let the lady in,' he said, winking at the guard, who grinned back at him, humbly but with manly complicity.

'Out with it, Ma. What's the matter?'

'Have you gentlemen gone barmy?' she shouted with a playful kind of aggressiveness. 'Are you trying to take away my best girls, Vilcsi and Sárika?'

'Who the hell are they?'

'You've brought the girls in from the venereal department. What do you want from them?'

'Are they ill?'

'The devil they are.'

89

'Are they Jews?' the colonel asked more seriously, frowning.

'Jews, Jews!' Mrs Szilassy crowed. 'They're whores. Whores aren't a race. A whore is a whore.'

Meanwhile two lower gendarmerie officers had appeared, a captain and a lieutenant. Uncertain as to what was happening, and not daring to laugh, they watched the colonel's face. When they saw him shake with coarse guffaws they joined in.

'A whore is a whore. But the law is the law.'

'The law,' Ma waved her hand. 'The number of times you lot break the law! Every time you were drinking at my place during the prohibition. And married men aren't supposed to make love outside their own homes, it's even forbidden by religion, but you're still doing it!'

More guffaws.

'Well, I ask you, gentlemen,' the colonel turned to the officers. 'What do you think of that?'

Ma felt that she was gaining ground.

'What good will it do you if you take them away with the others? The Germans aren't going to miss them,' she begged the colonel. 'Come on, boys, don't be like that. Let the two whores come home with me. I'll make it worth your while. Hitler isn't going to declare war on you if you do.'

The gentlemen at the gate were having a great time. Their laughter whistled through the ghetto which, having heard no laughter for a long time, trembled with fear. If these people laughed, the inmates had all the more reason to cry. But Ma had won.

'All right then, where are these . . .' the colonel barked at the gendarme on duty standing rigidly at attention.

'They're in the big synagogue, sir.'

'All right then, bring the two Jewish whores here.'

The girls were brought at once. They were tired, pale and dirty, but they immediately assumed a professional manner. They hadn't lost their slinky walk and their inviting glances even in the big synagogue. When they saw Mrs Szilassy they ran to embrace her, squealing:

'Ma, you're here, Ma. I said Ma wouldn't abandon us.'

The gendarmerie officers stood by, enjoying themselves, with their feet wide apart and their hands in their pockets. Grinning superciliously, they looked the girls up and down as they would horses at a market. They felt as if they were doing something generous and good, and perhaps they were even softened a little by being treated to this spectacle of 'mother love'. They continued to exchange good-natured obscenities with Ma and the girls for another quarter of an hour, before the colonel remembered that next morning the first transport had to be dispatched, with seventy Jewish fathers, mothers and children in every wagon. He couldn't spend all his precious time on such idylls. With friendly robustness he growled at the lady:

'Off you go, Ma, take your girls.'

The gate was opened, and Ma and her girls left. Back to business, to the Aryan house. Yes, Ma was a brave woman. She had come back for her girls, while the reverend sisters hadn't come back for the little girls they had brought up as Christians at Notre Dame de Sion and the Premonstratensian priests in their white habits hadn't come back for their pupils either. Doubtless Ma was above all else a businesswoman, but it wasn't merely out of greed that she had decided to fetch her girls back. Her salon would have survived without Vilcsi and Sárika, particularly now, in wartime. After all, a soldier doesn't care who he goes to bed with, so long as it's a woman.

Sixteen

As I was saying, the silence that night was unimaginably complete. It was an intangible silence, as if the night itself were holding its breath. It was a silence that provokes prayer or blasphemy. It was a treacherous silence that pretends to be gentle and safe, as if a showy theatrical production had banned the slightest noise, down to the humming heard in a shell, in order to give, at the appropriate moment, an even more sensational effect to the sudden screams of the chorus in an unprecedented and unparalleled tragedy of fate. Tomorrow morning a scene that was unique in civilisation would begin. White people with fixed addresses, carrying documents of domicile and nationality, and wearing European clothes, would be crammed into cattle wagons—as many as the wagons would take—and transported to some region inhabited by other white people where, not long ago, if somebody was hit by a tram, voluntary ambulancemen sped through the streets, sirens blaring, in cars marked with red crosses and financed through the contributions of good people, and where the government awarded a medal to anyone who rescued a ragged travelling journeyman caught in a current while bathing in the Bug or the Vistula. They would be taken to some place in Europe, where at every hundred steps along the road there were notices of the International Automobile Club warning about gradients and bends and fast trains, and where nature tamed by civilisation had long since banished pumas, hyenas and poisonous snakes from the forest. They would be herded into a barbed-wire enclosure, where their hair would be shaved and collected in sacks, and their clothes stripped off them, sorted and deposited in warehouses with rows of tidy compartments like those used in pharmacies—not one part of them would be wasted, not even their nails, flesh and bones. They would be given towels and shoved into a hut that looked like a bathhouse, appreciatively mumbling about German hygiene in their stubborn Jewish Germanophilia. Then the door would be locked and gas poured over them. And when they had been suffocated by the gas, thick fingers with pale nails, grown soft with foul idleness and covered, like those of a *nouveau riche*, with rings stolen from corpses, would prize their jaws apart and burrow in their blue-rimmed mouths until they found the gold or platinum teeth. The teeth would be pulled out expertly and collected in paper bags specially manufactured for the purpose. On the paper bags would be printed: '*Metallabfallsammelstelle No 17. Auschwitz. Gewicht:* ——, *Packung I*'.*

I had seen a photocopy of such a bag in the spring of 1942 in a Swedish magazine, which reported that SS soldiers were using them to collect the gold teeth of Austrian, Polish, Slovak and Yugoslav Jews. Before the First World War the National Chief Inspectorate of Silkworm Breeding had sent bags of a similar shape and with a similar text to the children in the villages, who were to collect the silkworm eggs in them. I, too, had collected eggs, and I remember that I didn't have to stick stamps on the bags because they were forwarded free of charge. I handed them in at the post-office window provocatively, taking malicious pleasure in the idea that the rude postmaster was obliged to send them free of charge to Szekszárd, which at that time was the silkworm centre. Now, in this perfidiously orchestrated, treacherous silence, with my eyes closed, I could see thousands of millions of silk cocoons bobbing in the the boiling water of the cauldrons of the silk factory in Komárom, where millions of silkworms had been killed in order to supply the ladies with rustling petticoats for the balls at the beginning of the century.

But let's not get sentimental or philosophical, let's not lose ourselves in Franciscan clichés for the prevention of cruelty to animals: silkworms die, worse luck. For I also remember the bazaar at the Trinité in Paris where, as late as 1925, it was possible to buy fancy goods made of the skin of Congolese natives for a few francs. Through the good offices of King Leopold and

* Waste metal collection point, No. 17. Auschwitz. Weight: ——, Pack I.

French and Belgian big business, volumes of love poetry and portfolios of obscene etchings to go with bibliophile editions of Rabelais, Choderlos de Laclos or Balzac's *Contes drolatiques* were on offer, bound in the tanned skin of negro women's bosoms, and, for particular connoisseurs, there were even enticing purses, crafted from the genitals of negro girls, on which the artist, for the sake of authenticity and entertainment, had even left the wiry pubic hair. The bazaar remained open all night, so that we wouldn't be at a loss on our way to or from Montmartre, whether at midnight or daybreak, if we suddenly thought of how exciting it would be to give a woman we had picked up during dinner at the Café Weber a very special souvenir on the morning after, when she would be repairing her make-up in front of the mirror in our hotel room, prior to being dismissed from our life for ever.

No, what is happening to us isn't really comparable to the case of the Congolese natives, and doesn't diminish the bizarre horror of what was done to them. But I still ask myself how many nights' sleep I lost over the hairy purses from the bazaar near the Trinité. Was I any less engrossed in Giraudoux's *Amphitryon* at the Comédie des Champs Elysées after skimming, in the interval, an eight-line notice in the evening paper about the six million flood victims on the Yangtse river? In China people may be reading eight-line notices about how we are being gassed, but can I therefore expect the mandarins and coolies to toss and turn restlessly on their rush mats? Even when refugees told me personally that Slovak Jews and anti-fascists—my next-door neighbours in my early youth, when Hungary and Slovakia were still the same country—were being taken to Poland to be gassed, did I enjoy my fatted chicken, bought on the wartime black market for my dinner, any the less? And the day Ossietzky* died in an internment camp, didn't I order the waiter to search heaven and earth for some pure coffee, because coffee made with chicory wasn't good enough for a dog?

That was precisely why I didn't expect any miracle—those

---

* Carl von Ossietzky (1889–1938), German journalist and pacifist, winner of the Nobel Peace Prize.

who are themselves not far from destruction, but have not yet confronted it eye to eye, try hard to regard those who are already prepared for meeting their fate with pathological indifference. This is not simply because we are in a state of euphoria—not simply because, at times like this, life is only bearable, even for a few hours, if we don't visualise the reality until we are finally forced to do so—but because we have slipped back into a pre-biblical religious frame of mind; accepting the rite of human sacrifice, which is rooted in the notion that the man-eating demons and demiurges who demand my life can be satisfied and pacified only through the sacrifice of another life. So that I may live, somebody else must die—and since 1933 the whole of Western Europe, the whole civilised world outside the German sphere, has become a priest and devotee of this rite. So that the world of Western civilisation may continue to live in its own way, let the East European Jews, the socialists, the scholars and the poets be gassed, burned at the stake, eaten alive. So that a Christian in London, Paris, Boston and Sydney might remain a Christian in Christ, it is necessary, with the passive help of these Christians, to reinstate in the East the divinity of the Cretan bull, the perverse Egyptian gods, the fellah and African idols who devour babies and drink the blood of virgins.

Well, things haven't worked out the way my proud and sober 'integral pacifist' friends imagined in Paris. Perhaps, in the camps of Maison Laffitte, Drancy and Argelès, or out there in the Ukraine, they have learnt by now that they weren't entirely right when they replied to my complaints and accusations: 'Forgive me, this is very sad, but we can't risk the whole of civilisation for the Jews of Eastern Europe.' Perhaps those left in Paris know by now, and perhaps it even occurs to somebody or other in the air-raid shelters of London, that they haven't been able to save themselves through the wholesale human sacrifices demanded by prehistoric ritual: the idols haven't satisfied their appetite with the East Europeans, but are now crunching bones further afield.

Of course, all this doesn't make it any easier to bear the singularly stubborn silence before the departure of tomorrow's transport. I rage against the weather—if at least I could hear a little wind blowing, or rain knocking against the window. Or wagons

95

shunting, or planes flying past, or just the gendarmes banging about. Any sound would do, but everybody and everything thwarts me, even the patients refuse to wriggle, the dying to rattle, and the nurses to giggle with nervous tension. The silence is like those moments between the lighting of a fuse and the terrifying explosion.

Is this silence orchestrated by God because He has a vile desire to create a sensational effect, or because He is helpless and can't think of any excuse or defence? Is that the reason for this dreadful pause? Is it God who directs this whole devilish play? This silence invites blasphemy—perhaps one should open the Ark of the Covenant to see whether Titus wasn't right after all when he destroyed Jerusalem, suspecting the Jews of worshipping a god with a donkey's head. This God really is suspect. With all kinds of mysterious prehistoric threats, demands and other cruelties He has terrorised a group of people for five thousand years into clinging—intellectually, morally, physically and socially—to something that makes them different from others, something that arouses suspicion and revulsion in others—to formalities, ceremonies, gimmicks by which the murderer instantly recognises the Jew—for instance by circumcising the men's genitals in order to help the dimmest murderer identify immediately who is to be butchered.

What was the big idea in allowing the Jews to make Christianity, which turned out to be the greatest and most coldly calculating power in the world, and then excluding the Jews, of all people, from Christianity and from that power? What was the big idea in letting the Jews remake Christianity in the nineteenth century in a more humane and more practicable revised edition—i.e. socialism—and then excluding the Jews, of all people, from socialism, because by the time socialism comes—although it will come soon—the Jews will be extinct? What's the big idea, you great almighty God—*du grosser allmächtiger Gott*, as the Jews often wail in German—in bringing destruction to a largely insignificant and dull group of commercially minded people, who work or hustle hard to earn a living and who live and die like everybody else, just because a fraction of them cling to some primeval obsessions, to some ideas which leave the majority cold but which, once they have been accepted and have solidified into a system of power and business, improve the lives of precisely those who have destroyed the Jews?

The profits of Christianity weren't reaped by the down-and-out disciples who remained faithful right up to the descent from the cross, but by Roman imperialism with its pogroms. What stupid God is this who, in the face of all these experiences, expects His followers to remain faithful to the metaphysics of a naive epic and a plethora of laws, customs and superstitions picked up from the nomadic tribes of the time? That this gave rise to monotheism—should I be proud of that, should I rave about that, here in the Nagyvárad ghetto? Now, if ever, it has been proved that one God is worth nothing. Even a thousand gods, a million gods, wouldn't be enough, there would have to be at least as many gods as there are gendarmes. There would have to be a god to every single human being to imprint on him a fraction of something that resembles, not God, but at least a human being of the time before 1914—not a prophet, priest, rabbi, scholar or poet, just a nineteenth-century pimp or murderer. In those days a pimp blushed if he was confronted with the obscene fact of allowing himself to be kept by the work of others, and a murderer, even if he felt no remorse, knew very well that killing people wasn't a normal, regular occupation, that the jurors and the spectators at his trial didn't go in for murder, that murder wasn't a public service or patriotic communal project.

Having railed against God with such flagrant presumption and shamelessness, I suddenly became frightened. Frightened of Him—because death was too close and I also felt that God was too close, as if He were sitting on the edge of my bed, like a fanatical party leader whose stubborn sectarian determination is impervious to any argument, or like an obsessively pragmatic politician, who is unable to relent and modify his course because he believes that the idea can be served even by things that are bad for everybody. The French, the British, the Americans and all the rest eat, drink, make love, write books, or work in their factories and laboratories, without ever thinking that they have been marked out and chosen for anything in particular as they go about their smaller or larger affairs. But the condition of the

Jews was illustrated in a magnificently revolting way by a scene I witnessed during the First World War. An old man in his eighties, with sidelocks and a stick in his hand, was giving instruction in the Bible, the Talmud, the Doctrine, to some boys aged four or five in the ruins of a village that had been totally shot to pieces. It was daybreak, and when the children nodded off during the lesson the old sage whacked them with his stick, saying: '*Sag' schön!*'* Then the sleepy, bleary-eyed four-year-olds continued to recite the Doctrine, the Idea, in the midst of the ruins at daybreak. To hell with doctrines, ideas and objectives! When the French accomplished their great revolution all they wanted was to improve their own lot; they wanted to eat more, pay less in tithes and taxes, suffer less harassment from the nobles and officials— and, thanks to this ruthless selfishness, not only did the material conditions of life improve over the next century and a half, but the intellect and the arts flourished, and the social existence of humanity, which had always been coarse to the point of brutishness, was tempered by such a degree of gentleness and tolerance as had probably never been experienced before. This wasn't the result of doctrines, ideas and idealism, but of logical, sensible, base selfishness. To hell with ideas—if people always did what, on careful consideration, was in their most selfish interest, there would be nothing wrong with the world. Who wants to die and starve? Nobody. If people weren't driven crazy by ideas and by their God, nobody would, for instance, go to war in order to starve and to die a beastly death.

* Say it nicely!

Seventeen

That was how I railed against God in the silence that had become not just unbearably tense but thoroughly frustrating, as I waited in vain for the explosion that didn't come, the reversal that didn't take place. But although the silence continued unabated I had at last succeeded in chasing God away with my blasphemies. I don't know whether or not He forgave me but, by God, I had really and truly told Him what I thought of Him before He finally abandoned me. Now only Friedländer was left perching on the edge of my mattress. His face was a bluish red, and his head drooped to one side, like the head of a hanged partisan in the Ukraine. I could no longer stand the silence without saying something. I sat up and nudged the sleeping man:

'Wouldn't it be more sensible to lie down somewhere for a while?' I asked with false tenderness.

Friedländer opened his bloodshot blue eyes with an effort. Staring at me in embarrassment, he apologised:

'I dropped off. I thought I'd never sleep again after everything that's happened,' he explained, as if I had called him to account. He was ashamed of having fallen asleep after burying his son in the afternoon.

'How deep did you dig the grave?' I asked matter-of-factly.

He was surprised by my question.

'I don't know. It wasn't us who did it. One metre seventy, I think.'

'We used to dig one metre ninety out there,' I explained. 'The earth was damned hard. In winter it froze down to one metre fifty.'

'Did you use pickaxes?' Friedländer asked.

'They gave us rotten pickaxes. The guard said: Dig, Jews, dig with your nails or any other part of you. That was precisely the point. We had to work without proper tools and if the grave wasn't ready for the burial the priest himself kicked us.'

We were silent. We pondered the craft of gravedigging—I as the professional who had been in the business for three-quarters of a year and he as a man who had only begun that day but had already acquired the basics.

I certainly know how to dig graves, and if I were obliged to fill in a police registration form accurately at this moment I would have to write 'gravedigger' in the blank space for my occupation.

At least that was my last occupation. I had completed my training in three-quarters of a year and hadn't resumed my previous profession since. After being brought back from Russia I was immediately imprisoned, and after my release the doctors did all they could to repair me, but within a few days the Germans arrived. In any case I felt as if I could never write a single sentence again. Nor did I want to write. What had happened to me was indescribable—and, what was more, I resisted my own experiences with elementary force, like a man who tries to overcome a malignant tumour that pokes conspicuously through his skin by not looking at it while he is dressing and undressing, by not touching it with his finger, and above all by not allowing it to be touched with a knife, even though he knows that it is lethal. Better to die of it than have the operation: better not to write, or even talk, about it. And, in any case, after what I had seen in the Ukraine, I had come to the conclusion that writing, as a weapon or as a method of demonstration, had become totally outmoded and useless. How could one hope to stop or change anything or anybody by writing, when writing could no longer even convey what was actually happening? No chronicler, no novelist, no newspaper reporter or radio broadcaster who cared about his credibility and who knew how to put things across would write down absurdities, even if the absurd had become the real. Reality had become improbable, and any writer trying to picture it faithfully would have been regarded as a vulgar, bluffing sensationalist. If I wanted to be believed I would have to organise the incredible events with a fake economy, and project falsely human traits on the people I had met. Otherwise the reader would ask: does this sadistic teller of fairy tales or madman think that I believe in hell and the devil? Indeed, I would have to twist the hell in which I lived for more than a year and a half into the form of some institution or enterprise accessible to the average imagination, and the devil into a monster of a kind that really exists. But I maintain that neither hell nor the devil resembles Virgil or Dante's mythical moral vision, which is in fact a bearable, feasible hell of human proportions. And even the human and animal monsters of Gothic art are mere domestic animals pretending to be horrors, compared with a German field gendarme or a guard from the Hungarian village of Nagykáta, who is hidden inside a normal human skin and equipped with a brain and heart in the right anatomical place. Hitler spoke of *eine einmalige Erscheinung** and I also believe that it will take another thousand years before man can again play the satanic part in which I have seen, and still see, him appear. This miracle is an even greater miracle than the miracles of mythological fairy tales or the miracles of Christ. What is the miracle in a fairy tale—that the giant has seven-league boots and the prince marries Cinderella? Well, the British pilot who bombed Nagyvárad the day before yesterday was having tea with his woman in a tea shop in Jermyn Street that same afternoon, and isn't there a Swedish prince every three months who marries a poor and perhaps even plain reporter or a boatswain's daughter who looks like Greta Garbo? And what is so special about Jesus raising the daughter of Jairus from the dead? By now Russian scientists have advanced beyond adrenalin, which keeps the heart going even after the head has been cut off. As for the whole complex of miracles surrounding Jesus Christ—how much greater a miracle than the Cana wedding is the fact that we forced labourers didn't starve to death when the guards were stealing practically all our food over a period of a year and a half. And isn't it a greater miracle still that Europe under blockade has not yet perished of starvation? The real miracle is that man is capable of shocking even those who have always despised and loathed him as a counterfeit animal whose instincts have been lost and whose

* A unique phenomenon.

mind and soul have proved to be a cheap *Ersatz* that failed the first severe test. The misanthropists, the pessimistic philosophers, the Utopian believers in man's corruptibility—they all got it wrong: man is capable of even greater things in the field of wickedness. The miracle is that the guard from Nagykáta, after regularly attending school and church in his home village, tortured Mannstein, the forced labourer, in the most ingenious way until he was half dead, then threw him out under the eaves, naked in thirty-five degrees of frost, and finally urinated on him, so that his dead body froze in the devil's excretions.

Or who would believe the following story?

When I was trundling home from the Ukraine, prison-bound and sitting in the wagon on a backless bench between the gendarmes' bayonets, a group of German field gendarmes suddenly appeared on the open track and, having stopped the train by waving their white handkerchiefs, yelled:

'Alles aussteigen!'*

We all got out, men on leave, convalescents, Russian civilians, gendarmes, and I, the only Jewish forced labourer. Everybody was afraid—why had these field gendarmes stopped the train on the open track? We were forty-five kilometres from Minsk. They lined us up in threes, and we set out on foot between the rails. We walked twelve kilometres to the nearest village. Two dead men were hanging from the raised gates of the level crossing, one on each side of the station. Their ragged peasant clothes were bloody, and we could see the bloody and sooty holes in their chests, where they had been shot before being hanged. They were without their trousers, and lumps of clotted blood, still dripping, hung from their crotches, while German-shepherd dogs scuffled over the scraps of their castrated parts. At the head of his unit a well-dressed, slim officer with an expressionless face was issuing orders in a clipped Prussian voice. The *Obergefreiter*,[†] standing at attention, was hanging on his every word.

'Die Leute musst du an den Brunnenrand aufstellen!'

'Jawohl!' the NCO barked.

---

* Everybody out!
[†] Lance-corporal

'Die Leute sollen warten. Rauchen erlaubt.'[*]

The NCO took immediate action. He led us away about a hundred and fifty paces, to where the clearing broadened into a pasture with a pole-well in the middle. We stopped and were allowed to light up. We weren't allowed to sit down, because the NCO hadn't received any orders to that effect.

I hardly dare to describe exactly what I saw—if anybody read it in New York he would think that I was a bad writer, even at the level of pulp fiction. Did it really happen? And is it believable that what is happening to us in the ghetto now is happening?

Anyway, as we watched the Germans from beside the well we were naturally worried about what they might want from us, why they had taken us off the train, why they had brought us here, what they were going to do to us. At first we only saw a lot of coming and going, then, about a quarter of an hour later, four men of the Todt organisation produced a number of spades— exactly as many as we were—and each of us was given one. Perhaps we would be digging bunkers or air-raid shelters—hardly our own graves: after all, I was the only Jew and the others were Aryans. The Germans who had brought the spades immediately returned to the square in front of the station, where the twenty Todt and ten SS members had meanwhile positioned themselves in a row. The Todt men all held identical oil cans. The officer, with his feet spread wide apart and his hands on his hips, said something to the soldiers. At a stroke the Todt men put the cans down in front of them, in a line as straight as an arrow. Then some White Ukrainian militiamen arrived in the square and formed another row about fifteen paces behind the Germans. The Ukrainian *politsai* weren't as brisk as the Todt and the SS. There was something slightly reluctant about them, but they moved in a fairly soldierly way in response to their orders. The German officer spoke to them through an interpreter, and they dispersed in twos through the village. None of the villagers, apart from the two hanged men, could be seen. The White Ukrainians

[*] 'Line the people up at the edge of the well!' 'Yes, sir!' 'Tell them to wait. Smoking permitted.'

disappeared into the houses and a little later began to drive cows, *panje* horses,* pigs and goats out into the street. When each militiaman had collected five or six animals they started herding them towards the pasture, where we were.

The first bunch has just arrived. The *Obergefreiter*, who has joined us, orders:

'Ten men come here! Take charge of the animals!'

Ten of us jump forward and, with outstretched arms, try to herd the animals along. The horses understand nothing, they kick and break out. We grab sticks and thrash them. The cattle, the goats and the pigs, the petty bourgeois among domestic animals who are interested only in feeding, immediately start gobbling the grass and rooting in the earth. A bull even turns randy. Within an hour and twelve minutes—by the watch of the sergeant next to me, formerly a musician—all the livestock of the village has been assembled on the pasture. What is going to happen now? Like a theatrical chorus, twenty men of the German territorial army—Prussian grandfathers with grey moustaches—appear on the scene, wearing official and officious expressions on their faces, to take delivery of the animals. Five of them fill in forms divided into sections for the different kinds of animal, and the others dictate the numbers to them—so many horses, cows, goats, pigs, and one sheep. Then, shouting directions in German, they drive the motley herd towards the main road. So they're requisitioning animals, I think, and this assumption isn't contradicted by the bodies of the two men hanging on the railway gates. According to German custom, they were probably shot and hanged for trying to prevent or obstruct the requisitions. But why, if we have finished our work, are we still standing at this well?

Now the Todt men fan out in the square with almost graceful movements. As they separate with tripping steps, leaving regular distances between them and holding all the oil cans at the same height, they remind me of a ballet in a variety theatre. I always knew that most of what Hitler had learnt in the way of propaganda and ceremony had come from Barnum's circus

* A robust East European breed of horse.

and Hollywood movies—this particular scene had been plagia-
rised from musicals set in New York, London and Paris. But the
ballet, a typical pederastic fantasy, turns into reality and breaks
up, albeit still with harmonious artistry. Each of the Todt men
climbs on to one of the thatched roofs and pours the contents
of his can on it. Another half-hour passes. Then they reassemble
in the square and, fanning out once more, set fire to every
thatched roof. In the smoke and flames Russians are seen for
the first time—not so much particular human forms and faces
but rather gestures of mortal fear. As they flee from the smoke
and flames, the machine guns strike up. The stage management
falters, the rhythm becomes irregular, the machine guns cease to
rattle in unison. And the *stariks*, the *dyadyas*, the *kloptsis, matkas*
and *barishnyas,** also unsynchronised, tumble all over the ground,
into the glowing ashes. My nostrils inflate with the smell of
burning flesh. And what is this? Now I know why in folklore
the symbol of conflagration is the red rooster. On the road a
golden red rooster with burning feathers flutters towards us. He
has quite forgotten how to crow and clucks miserably before
dropping like a sick old hen. It would have been pointless, and
technically difficult, to take away the poultry. If any fowl left in
the houses were burnt to death it was their bad luck. Those that
escape are chased by the Germans—and by the evening transformed into chicken soup for the soldiers.

The dogs hadn't been taken away either—they had immediately run out, howling, into the street, but the machine guns had
mowed them down too. One or two might have escaped
wounded into the trees, but most were left lying in the ashes
with their masters, the charred Ruskis.

It was only when the machine guns had fallen silent that we
realised what our job would be. We had been given the spades
to bury the five hundred and twenty-seven villagers. When we
set out to dig the grave we weren't as brisk and graceful as the
Todt men, and the *Obergefreiter* ticked us off for not holding the
spades in a straight line on our backs and stepping out firmly
enough. When we had reached the other side of the village, he

* Village elders, uncles, kiddies, little old women, farmers' wives.

indicated, with undeniable good taste and flair, the highest point of the edge of the forest as the place of the mass grave. In Berlin, as in Budapest, a special department of the Ministry of War is responsible for ensuring that graves near the front line obey the aesthetics of piety, both in terms of their position and of their architecture. The cemetery must be in a beautiful location and mustn't spoil the scenery. One shouldn't forget that Hitler was once a landscape painter. On three sides the straight trunks of the silver firs formed a wall—and, as for detailed instructions, the *Obergefreiter* could tell me nothing new. I had worked in the trade for three-quarters of a year. I was an old hand and knew that the German and Hungarian regulations for gravediggers had been brought into line: a mass grave must be dug one metre ninety in depth and there must be a gap of twenty-five centimetres between the bodies. And I also knew that gravedigging was an unpleasant variety of forced labour and a bad 'racket', because the guard or the SS man constantly checked from the edge of the grave that you were leaving twenty-five centimetres between the bodies and that you had laid the bodies parallel to each other. If one body wasn't completely parallel to the rest the guard kicked the gravedigger—which was dangerous because the gravedigger's head was level with the guard's lace-up boots.

The others were bunglers and beginners, but I knew all this because, as I say, the two armies followed the same principles. The only thing that I didn't know was the procedure with regard to dogs. I hadn't come across the corpses of dogs earlier in my occupation, and my professional perfectionism induced me to ask the *Obergefreiter.*

'Sir, may I ask what's to be done with the dogs?'

'The bloody Jew wants to bury the dogs with the people,' he bawled at me indignantly, giving me a whack with his whale-skin whip.

It took us all night to dig the grave. It was a phenomenal night. In the moonlight the silver firs with their white trunks recalled the magic garden in *Parsifal.* In the distance guns thundered and, closer by, mines exploded left, right and centre. The partisans were also working. In fact this village had been destroyed by the Germans because the partisans had blown up the rail tracks on its outskirts. That night they would again blow up tracks, either in front of us or behind us, and other villages would die, with the aesthetes from Berlin indicating other locations for mass graves at the most delightful points of the landscape. The unburied dogs would be devoured by the countless Russian crows or torn to pieces by vultures. The surviving ones would slink back to the cold and empty site of their former village, squat on their haunches, turn their faces towards the sky and mourn the dead of their species, howling in the moonlight. The wretches would be hungry, because even their masters had had hardly anything to eat in two years of servitude—but dog doesn't eat dog.

Eighteen

As I say, my dear friend Friedländer, I was thoroughly trained in gravedigging out there. On 12 November 1942, at eight o'clock in the evening, it was still a warm and misty autumn, but by midnight the snow had started falling and wouldn't melt again till March, with the temperature sinking to twenty-seven degrees of frost and set to remain below minus twenty for four months. At daybreak the duty sergeant pulled me out of the line— together with a surgeon and a hawker—because the heroes' cemetery had requested assistants for the two old Jewish grave-diggers, who could no longer cope with the work.

In the last few days the weather had been foggy and the number of mine victims had increased. The typhus epidemic had also arrived, and from the bases nearby one suspect after another was brought in with forty-two degrees of fever, unstoppable diar-rhoea, louse bites, and a rash on their stomachs. The reason why more were being killed by mines was that the fog made it diffi-cult to see where the soil had been loosened and squares of turf replaced by the crafty partisans. While the good weather lasted, the mine-seekers had been more or less able to recognise these telltale signs, or to feel instinctively when they were close to danger, but later on, the fog and drizzle had covered all the traces with mud, and when the snow finally arrived their nerves became so numbed by the leaden grey sky and dreary white steppe that they could no longer sense the approaching disaster. With the mine-seekers disabled, more and more men trod on or drove over mines and were blown up in the fog and snow. The typhus epidemic, for its part, had been gaining momentum because the men had hardly washed themselves or their underwear since the onset of the extreme cold. They were full of lice—we too, friend Friedländer—actually we Jews in particular, because we were not only chivvied from dawn to dusk, but were even harassed in our quarters at night, so that we never had time to clean up. Nor did we have the energy to do so. We were too worn out, too dismayed and disheartened, abandoned, as we were, in mid-winter and in our summer clothes—not to mention how, on being ordered out of the wagons in Kiev, we had literally been plundered by counter-intelligence officers and soldiers and left with scarcely a change of underwear.

Naturally the first case of typhus occurred among us, in Seredina-Buda, one of the bases in the Bransk forest, which housed the headquarters of the Hungarian partisan-hunters' command for four and a half months. That was where we worked and where I dug graves, friend Friedländer. As soon as the first case of Jewish typhus was reported, the blood libel spread among the soldiers. It was said that we had created the disease in order to weaken the Hungarian army. The first man to die of typhus in the garrison was also a Jew, and the divisional command didn't permit a Jew to be buried in the heroes' cemetery. We had to volunteer to bury him in a shallow grave in the Ukrainian cemetery on the outskirts of the town, beyond the stream, at half past three in the morning, half an hour before the official reveille. The local Ukrainians hadn't liked us very much until now, because the Germans had revived some of the anti-Semitism of czarist times, which had been almost eradicated by the Soviets. But the Hungarian command, with its deep flair for propaganda, had united Ukrainians and Jews. With our graves in the same plot, the Ukrainians realised that we shared not only a common cemetery but also a common enemy. That started the psychological complicity which, during the four months we spent in Seredina-Buda, grew into human solidarity and political alliance.

The construction of the heroes' cemetery had been started by the Germans in accordance with a plan issued by the Ministry of War in Berlin. The Germans had requisitioned the main square of the town, where the public buildings, the theatre, the largest church and the department stores were situated, and where the young liked to promenade. All the important streets of the town led to this square and had now been turned into culs-de-sac by the birch fence of the cemetery. By positioning the cemetery in the main square, the Germans not only intended to annoy the Russians but had deliberately disrupted the town in order to make their constant presence felt through the traffic diversions. Moreover, the cemetery followed the principle of Gessler's hat,* for in accordance with German rules the identical wooden crosses had the dead heroes' steel helmets placed on them, and every Russian was obliged to raise his hat as he was passing. To avoid having to do this, the Russians preferred to take different routes, involving long detours round the straggling town. When the Germans had handed the town over to the Hungarian occupying troops, there were only ninety-one steel-helmeted bodies in the cemetery. Within six months the number had increased to three hundred and one, and all the new arrivals were Hungarians belonging to the older age group. They included men who had been brought to the local hospital to die after being wounded in battles with the partisans, who had trodden on mines but managed to live a few hours longer, or who had died of some illness. Those who had died in the forest were unceremoniously deposited in the earth somewhere under the trees.

As I was saying, friend Friedländer, the plan for the cemetery had originally been concocted in the Berlin Ministry of War, but by the time we took the town over, the Hungarian Ministry of War had revised it. The outstanding feature of the Hungarian plan was a national flag, twenty-five metres high, planted in the middle of the cemetery. Wherever Hungarian troops stopped in Russia for a few weeks they immediately erected the Hungarian national flag as a symbol, no longer of the recovery of old possessions, but of new conquests. The soldiers were convinced that we would take equal shares of Russia with Hitler. They were saying so to each other, and the more good-natured and talkative among them condescendingly assured us: 'You see now, you Jews, you can say what you like, but the Germans . . . We aren't leaving this place, the Germans have given us this territory for ever, and the land here will be distributed to those who haven't been able to get any at home.' The plan of the cemetery had been worked out in

* According to Swiss legend, the tyrannical Austrian governor Gessler had placed his hat on a pole in the main square of Altdorf and ordered all passers-by to bow to it.

such detail and with such finality as if it had been, say, a blue-print produced by the town-planning department for a new National Theatre designed to last for centuries. The mad field chaplain constantly carried it about in his pocket and if the ground we had broken for a new grave was a centimetre out of line he immediately beat us with his whip, shouting:

'You stinking swine, you should be buried alive!'

The steppe wind was blowing mercilessly when we began to dig the grave for my first corpse, private Ferenc Császár from the village of Zalaszentgrót. Our tools were atrocious, the snow and earth as solid as a rock—but Veinberger, the printer and expert gravedigger of long standing, taught us the tricks of the trade, and we were all ready and determined to learn. It was desperately hard work—a bad 'racket'—but it had the great advantage that the guard wasn't constantly standing behind us. Only the field chaplain turned up unexpectedly several times a day on horseback to strike us with his whip or kick our heads for no apparent reason. We were already prepared for this and waited to get it over with, so that we could have some peace for another hour or two. A further advantage was that the deeper we got into the ground the less we could feel the cruel steppe wind that seemed to throw a million razor blades at us. The grave sheltered us from the cold. In the evenings, when we 'returned from the grave' to our quarters, we used to say that the best place to be in the Ukraine was 'in the grave'. When a grave was more or less finished we would crouch down and chat. The surgeon-gravedigger had been the assistant of the famous consultant Professor Ádám. Until now his task had been to flay dead horses for the officers who ran a legitimate business selling the skins. 'Well, professor, operate,' he used to be told by the staff major, who had personally detailed him to flaying. Now he was satisfied with his new position because at least he no longer had to burrow in the bloody innards of horses all day long. The hawker-gravedigger was an orthodox Jew, who had held a semi-official position in the religious community, acting as an occasional sexton and deputy prayer leader at a synagogue. He was constantly turning east in his grave and mumbling the prayers designated for the time of day. The printer was the smartest and most public-spirited. Slipping out of his grave from time to time, he used to beg for bread and potatoes on our behalf in the neighbouring Russian houses. We were always hungry and the Russians always gave us some food. And all the while we were digging the graves of Hungarian private Ferenc Császár and his companions. We had indeed become the gravediggers of the Hungarian people, although not quite the 'gravediggers of the Hungarian nation' of the chaplain's harangues.

By now, Friedländer, you also know how quickly such an occupation ceases to seem strange or horrifying. At daybreak, on our way to the cemetery with our atrocious tools, we used to call at the hospital to ask how many had died overnight. After a few days we no longer thought of Hungarians or human beings or, rather, of Hungarian human beings, torn to shreds, lying in the ungainly wooden boxes. We weren't like the gravediggers in *Hamlet* with their deliberately macabre and philosophical humour. We would talk seriously, sombrely and sometimes with bitter merriment about anything that came into our heads but— apart from the immediate details of gravedigging—never mentioned our raw material, death. The evil field chaplain—who kept a traitorous whore somewhere in the town—was often in a great hurry. He would turn up on his horse, rattle off the liturgy and jump back in the saddle, leaving us to bury the coffin or do whatever we liked with it. As soon as he disappeared round the corner we, for our part, would decide that there was no need to hurry, for the forced labourer is apt to slack if he isn't chivvied. We would sit down on the coffin, light a cigarette, eat if there was anything to eat, discuss the news of the war and show each other the letters from home that had been smuggled out to us. When it was nearly time to go back to our quarters somebody would sigh: 'Come on, men, let's do some work.' And we would do some work, because in spite of everything the coffin had to be lowered into the grave, the mound built, and the regulation cross stuck into the ground at the head.

We were billeted in Russian houses, which were our 'quarters' when we weren't at work. The Russians were silent, deceptively bad-tempered, good people. Only the village elder, a grandfather aged seventy, disliked us. Under the czar he had been a prosperous horse dealer and he preferred the Germans and Hungarians to the communists because they let him do business again. But the old woman, his wife, was as kind to me as a mother—she put compresses on my septic foot, brewed tea when I coughed and gave me milk because my thinness made her cry. She was a pious woman and because gravedigging was somehow related to God and heaven and hell, her tenderness was also addressed to my ecclesiastical function. The boy, aged seventeen, and the girl, aged fifteen, were communists. One day, early in December, I walked into the kitchen, looking for some milk. The boy was sitting at the table in his ragged jacket, his nose running, his hands blue with cold, engrossed in reading by the faint light of an oil lamp. Having learnt five or six hundred words in Russian, I asked him what he was reading. He gabbled the title so fast that I was unable to understand. I took the book out of his hand. In brackets under the Russian title I saw: *L'Éducation sentimentale*. He had borrowed the book from the municipal library, which had been hidden in the potato clamps when the Germans came and from which books could still be borrowed surreptitiously. Of course the boy used to spit on the floor, like the other peasants. My dear Friedländer, Russia is a country of extremes: Flaubert along-side the roughest, most primitive manners. But Flaubert and company have already taken root there and it isn't they who will disappear but the ancient neglect of manners. The girl recited Mayakovsky and Pushkin for us—the year before last was Pushkin's centenary. She wanted to be a teacher, although since the beginning of the occupation she hadn't been able to attend school herself. Now, with a Hungarian permit, she was working as an assistant teacher in a nearby village but, as we knew, she also used to go out into the forest to deliver and bring back messages for the Jewish chaps from Budapest, who had long since established friendly relations with the partisans.

The 'partis' provided us with a lot of work, killing many soldiers. One morning, when the weather was even harsher than usual and we got to the cemetery in forty-one degrees of frost, we found an old Hungarian sapper with a red moustache sitting by a fire in the space cleared for the graves. He had all kinds of tools—a hatchet, a saw, a drill and nails of various sizes. 'Good morning, folks,' he greeted us in a friendly manner. 'I'm building a birch chapel for the bodies to be laid out in state.' The mad chaplain had angrily demanded such a chapel from the divisional command, saying that it was inhumane to leave the dead heroes' coffins on the bare snow like so many discarded crates. When the command asked who could build a birch chapel the sapper had volunteered. He had driven a milk cart on the estate of Tihany Abbey, but he was also a handyman. His name was Gergely Kovács and he was married with two young sons. He had a foul mouth, swore a lot and cursed the priests for letting his wife and children starve while he was already spending his thirteenth month on the front line, but he was an old-fashioned, clear-headed peasant. 'Who the hell wanted this war?' he would ask. 'What the hell are we doing here, two thousand kilometres from home? This isn't even helping the toffs because after the war the poor people will demand what's due to them.'

He talked to us in this open manner from the very first day, when he gave us some of the potatoes he was baking, before saying: 'But now you'd better get working, folks, before an officer comes. I shouldn't really be talking to you. We've been given orders not to have anything to do with you Jews because we'd catch lice and typhus from you. And because you spread false rumours. But I've got enough lice of my own without you and I know everything even if I don't talk.'

That was how we met Uncle Kovács. Every morning he lit a large fire and squatted down next to it. Soon both he and we stopped worrying about the orders that were supposed to keep us apart, and when the coast was clear we sidled up to the fire to warm ourselves a little. Meanwhile he drilled, carved, sawed, nailed, and within a fortnight the birch chapel began to take shape. Before long the walls were standing, with the fire on the inside. When there was a blizzard and we knew that the chaplain with his whip wouldn't venture out, we moved into the chapel and sat round the fire, mostly on the coffins. Uncle Kovács also sat on a coffin, baking potatoes. By now he was bringing us something every day, for instance some sardines issued to the sappers as a supplement to their rations, which he simply couldn't get down himself. When he was in the process of making the altarpiece—a really beautiful work of folk art which would have delighted any ethnologist or folklorist—he cursed the saints in his foul language every time he missed the right spot or hit his finger with his hatchet. It would take a writer like Anatole France to do justice to this godless, humane peasant, who swore and shared his food with us while he was piecing the holy objects together.

We continued to dig graves, in increasing numbers every day, all according to the plan of the Ministry of War. We had resigned ourselves to some or all of us being kicked or whipped by the chaplain, and we liked going to the cemetery because of Uncle Kovács, with whom we openly talked politics. Uncle Kovács hated the Germans. He wanted them to be beaten by the Russians and was delighted to know that they were actually being beaten. He could hardly wait to 'bugger off' home, he to Tihany and we to Budapest. 'My brother-in-law's a miller in Arács,' he told us. 'After the Commune of 1919 he was in nick for seven months. He'll be a big shot in Arács one day.'

On 24 December 1942 there should have been four funerals, but we had been unable to dig the graves in time. We had come up against the foundations of a destroyed building under the crust of ice and frozen soil, off which our pickaxes rebounded as if they had hit a steel plate, and we couldn't move the bricks. The only way to deal with this was by blasting, as we established with our expert knowledge. By three o'clock we had got nowhere. The whole garrison had been drinking continuously since morning, and we had also been drinking because Uncle Kovács had treated us to some of his Christmas ration of rum. The chaplain was angrier and more drunk than ever. He had never beaten us so badly as he did that Christmas Eve afternoon, and one of my eyes was swimming in blood after being hit by his whip. Realising that it was impossible to dig the graves with pickaxes, he postponed the funerals till after the festival. However, as a punishment, he forbade us to leave for our billet before nine o'clock, so we had to huddle in the unfinished graves. It was a cold but clear evening, with large stars. The quarter-moon looked like a Cyrillic letter. Uncle Kovács had knocked off at five, leaving his bacon, bread and rum behind to save us from freezing to death. It was getting colder by the minute, but the town became all the merrier. The officers were also drunk by now. There had been some reception at the divisional command, and they were coming back past the cemetery, shouting, laughing and visibly tight. Four of them climbed over the birch fence and headed straight towards us. The chaplain was with them.

'Which of you is that Jewish scribbler?' a middle-aged officer with a hooked nose, a clipped moustache and a fur jacket asked.

The chaplain pointed to me. 'That one. Why don't you answer if the colonel asks?'

I stood to attention in silence.

'Did you write those traitorous articles? You didn't expect to end up like this as a gravedigger, did you?'

'The gravedigger of the nation,' the chaplain promptly added.

'Carry on, then,' the drunken colonel continued. 'Or ring up your friend Roosevelt and tell him to stop this war, he's made enough money already. Do you understand?'

'Yes, sir,' I said dutifully.

As they left, heehawing with glee, their gestures reflected their sense of having scored a vast intellectual victory. All right, I would call Roosevelt. But meanwhile the whole town was roaring in Hungarian, drunk with Christmas rum—just like Sunday evenings at home, with the same sort of din coming on all sides from the village taverns and dance halls before the knife fights began.

Nineteen

It was Christmas Eve, Friedländer—I'm not sure what that means to you. To me it had been a great night ever since I first became conscious of it. The Christmas tree had been part of my festive flora since I was baby. As late as 1941, before I was taken to Russia, we put up a Christmas tree. We always had a lavish meal, with fir logs crackling in the stove as prescribed by the English book of fairy tales I had as a child. The weather was always Christmassy, with a snowy landscape and very large stars in a clear sky. If there was ever any unseasonal Christmas weather I have forgotten it. There was also an exceptional silence, a silence like tonight. My parents had inherited Christmas from their parents as a folk custom. They disregarded its religious meaning but kept to the festive etiquette: on that night there was never a family quarrel and the various embattled branches engaged in great reconciliations. Relatives treated each other with almost formal courtesy, enjoying not so much the presents but rather the pleasure of giving presents.

Naturally we didn't expect the little Lord Jesus to visit us. He only called in the kitchen where the Christian maids kept singing 'Angels from Heaven' until he came down to them. At least that was what they told me the morning after, showing off the brown knitwear headscarves and two shifts' length of Rumburg linen he had brought them. 'Why doesn't he come to us?' I asked. 'Why should he come to you? You crucified him,' the cook said. When I asked my mother about the crucifixion of Christ—my poor mother, who has been burnt since—she reprimanded the cook: 'Julis, is this your gratitude for the nice headscarf I bought you at Schlesinger's?' Julis cried, threw tantrums, knocked things about, ruined the festive lunch, and on New Year's Day gave notice with effect from 15 January, insisting all the while that we had crucified Jesus. That's the reason—one reason—why we're here, Friedländer, because Julis couldn't be fobbed off with a headscarf.

I began to ask about details, and my poor mother, driven into a corner, desperately defended herself, as if she had been responsible. She insisted that the Romans had crucified Jesus and it had nothing to do with us. Nor was it Jesus's fault, he was a good man. It was just the priests who were putting crazy ideas into the maids' heads—like the local vicar, who would have been better employed stopping his two teenage sons constantly breaking windows. And the postmaster, who had embezzled all the money and set fire to the post office before an audit so that his crime wouldn't come to light. These people would have eaten the Jews alive. But for all my mother's efforts to set my mind at rest, when I went to bed at night I was assailed by doubts: perhaps we really had done it and the adults were keeping it from me, as they did with so many other secrets. All year long I waited for next Christmas, when I would go out into the kitchen when He came to the maids and tell Him that it wasn't us and He must believe that it was the Romans. Then I learnt the story of Jesus— it was a very exciting and moving story for a child of five—and I placed him side by side with Rákóczi,* Kossuth,† and the thirteen martyrs of Arad‡ whom I particularly admired at the time. To this day I feel some of the attraction and magic, although of course I have never been a follower of Christ.

In any case, religious feeling isn't my strong suit: I'm like a man who would like to enjoy music, but has no ear for it. Often when, like now, I need to believe in the unbelievable, I'm driven to despair by being unable to strike one spark of belief out of myself. Nevertheless, I'm constantly troubled by that cycle of legends, as if impelled all my life by the guilty conscience of my childhood to prove that I wasn't an accomplice to the crucifixion, that I hate every kind of injustice and violence. And if I don't believe in him as God, or even as a prophet—I don't

---

* Ferenc Rákóczi II (1676–1735), Transylvanian prince, leader of the Hungarian struggle against the Austrian Empire.
† Lajos Kossuth (1802–94), Hungarian revolutionary leader.
‡ Hungarian revolutionary generals, executed in 1848.

worship the sun like the Persians either, but I still love its light and heat. Believe me, Friedländer, I've never denied my Jewishness, not only out of solidarity and tradition, but also out of bloody-mindedness. I never wanted to shake it off, like many others, who can't resign themselves to it as long as they live and who become neurotic because they're constantly trying to shed it. But all the same, I must say here, at this final point, that I've always felt a godless and profane but deep and genuine sympathy for Jesus and for what the gospels reveal about his moral and social objectives. I'm closer to him than these Christian gendarmes and the church-going females we saw grinning at the edge of the pavement as we were being marched to the ghetto. Or the priests . . . his priests, including your Bishop of Nagyvárad, who assisted in our clearout . . . And that mad field chaplain, who made us crouch in the half-finished grave till nine o'clock on Christmas Eve 1942.

At nine we returned to our quarters in the Russians' house. On the way home we were abused and laughed at by drunken soldiers. An ensign, tottering with rum, even shot after us with his revolver. According to the orthodox calendar, the Russians celebrated Christmas thirteen days later. In the kitchen there was still a light, although normally the house was dark soon after sunset, when the family went to bed. They had no petrol, and dry wood and turf were a rarity. But now the reddish-green light of the oil lamp filtered from the kitchen on to the snow. As we stamped our feet in the porch to shake the snow off, the door opened and the old woman stuck her head out:

'Come in,' she said. 'There's a little soup.'

We went in. The kitchen was warm, filled with the rank and bitter odour of the turf, but warm. The oil lamp was in the middle of the table and next to it, in a chipped gherkin jar, a fir branch. The girl was sitting on the oven ledge and the boy was balancing on a rickety water stand, reading. The old woman lifted the sooty earthenware pot out of the oven with a two-pronged fork. She had given us soup on other occasions when we returned frozen from the cemetery, and we had eaten it in our room, sitting in the hay with our legs crossed and holding our mess tins in our laps. This time, however, she put tin plates on the table and invited us to sit on the bench. The boy and the girl joined us at the table. We were having potato soup with small pieces of bacon floating in it. When everybody had his portion the old woman also sat down. We began to slurp the soup without a word.

The old woman had organised a *prasnik** for us, friend Friedländer, even though it was neither her festival nor ours. They were Pravoslavs, whose Christmas comes two weeks later. We were Jews, who have no Christmas. But the old woman made a Christmas for us with the warm kitchen, the one fir branch and the rancid, oversalted bacon that she had perhaps saved up since the German invasion. These Christians gave us all the good things they had. For a long time nobody said anything, we ate in silence, and after the soup the old woman brought potato pancakes.

In the officers' mess, four doors away, the divisional commander was giving a big Christmas dinner for the officer staff. All the musicians from the rank and file had been drafted in, including an accordionist and two Jews, a pianist and a viola player. From seven o'clock they had been playing jazz, dance music and the latest hits. Amid the banging and the clatter we could hear cheers and applause—perhaps they were drinking to Hitler and Horthy. Sometimes we could also hear the shouts of the drunks from the street—the privates had been given Christmas leave till midnight and an extra half litre of brandy with their supper. We sat there, wordless, with heads bent and eyes half closed. Even though we were Jews, each of us—including the orthodox prayer leader—was moved by powerful memories that Christmas night.

The old woman went out and returned with a green bottle that she put on the table.

'Don't be sad,' she said consolingly, but it was she who burst into tears. 'Drink a little vodka.'

We drank from the bottle, one after the other. At first we felt a bit dizzy, then we took heart. We were alive, no matter how, and that was something. We were the lowest of the low and our lives weren't worth the skin of a dead horse or the life of a louse

---

* festival

that any one of these drunken soldiers could have squashed with his thumb nail. But, all the same, who would have thought in early November, when seven out of twenty Jewish mine-seekers trod on a mine and a Jew went down with typhus every day, that we would live to see this Christmas?

We took another gulp or two of vodka. The boy and the girl also drank heartily, but the old woman barely licked the rim of the bottle.

When the officers' jazz was silent for a while, the old woman asked: 'Do you know any Christmas carols?'

I intoned 'Angels from Heaven'. The hawker-cum-part-time prayer leader initially shook his head in disapproval but, wanting the vodka more than any of us, suppressed his scruples about participating in this 'treason'. Then the surgeon, who had studied in Glasgow for two years because he had been refused admission to the University of Budapest, sang an English children's carol. When the old horse dealer heard the singing, he came shuffling out of the next room and stared at us with his piercing eyes. The old woman passed him the bottle. He took a large swig and sat down on the oven ledge, more willing to give us the benefit of the doubt but still not prepared to mingle with us. The old woman and the girl sang a Pravoslav Christmas carol. The boy didn't sing along with them. He rolled himself a cigarette with a piece of newspaper, lit it and, with his elbows on the table, gazed into the flame of the oil lamp. Then he continued to read, picking at the wick from time to time without looking up from his book. This indifference wasn't directed at us but at Christmas. The boy didn't believe in God.

Across the road in the mess the officers had begun to dance with each other or with the whores they had brought with them from Poland. In our house the oil lamp on the table was flickering, the turf fire in the oven was dying, and the vodka bottle was empty. It was nearly ten, time to make a move. Tomorrow we would have to dig graves again, although it was Christmas. We kissed the old woman on both cheeks, and finally even the horse dealer shook hands with us. The surgeon, who had got a bit tight on the vodka, kept hugging them before taking his leave of them in English:

'A happy Christmas.'

That was my last Christmas in a family circle, Friedländer. The Chistmas after would see me in military prison. I sat in the hay for a long time, with my elbows on my raised knees, listening to the accordion till dawn. On one side of me the drunken surgeon mumbled in English until he dropped off. On the other side the hawker cried himself into a snoring sleep. In the morning we went to dig graves.

Twenty

I don't know whether Friedländer was listening to what I was telling him and I don't know whether I was really telling him all that or only remembering it silently. I was trying to break the unbearable silence—and subconsciously perhaps to reassure myself that if all that had happened out there in the Ukraine had become a memory of something that I had survived, then perhaps again . . . ? But no. I didn't believe for a moment that I could survive this. It was already a miracle that I had lived to see my first Russian Christmas despite the mines and the typhus, and then another Christmas, what is more, in prison. That was a gift, or rather fate teasing me. This time we were not going to survive: the first transport would leave tomorrow morning and the people in the hospital six days later. Nothing could be done about it—and how many more times must I explain that I didn't even want to do anything. That nurse with the squint and the long legs hadn't been seen since she had slept with the gendarme who told her that he would help a few decent Jews. Had she been transferred or had the friendly gendarme taken his revenge by removing her from the hospital? If I remembered, I would try to find out tomorrow what had happened to her.

I must have told my gravedigger's memories aloud, because Friedländer opened his eyes apologetically the moment I stopped talking. There was total silence again, and that was what had startled him. After an immeasurably long interval the clock of the Capuchin church struck a quarter to twelve. Then no other sound could be heard again from outside for hours. In the ward, too, there seemed to be absolute silence, although it's possible that over four days I had got so used to the heavy breathing, moaning and snoring that I had ceased to be aware of it, like a railwayman who lives near the station and no longer hears the whistle of the engines. Perhaps I was concentrating exclusively on noises from outside, because after all any unexpected noise— any sign, any change—could only come from outside.

One thing that happened was that in the blue light I could see two white coats floating towards me. Dr Németi was swaying in one and a doctor I hadn't seen before in the other. The second doctor turned out to be in charge of the obstetric department upstairs, where my wife was hiding. I took a dislike to him as soon as his wavy, well-kept red hair flared up in the dim light and his cold, prying, pale blue eyes fell on me. He had a more striking face than the average provincial gynaecologist, and his general appearance was not provincial but rather sophisticated in an affected and histrionic way. He gave the impression of having risen from far below by clever and crooked means and having moved in classy circles ever since. Even here he was elegant, with his silk tie peeping through the opening of his white coat. Heavily scented, he was a typical neurologist in a sanatorium in some fashionable spa, or a psychoanalyst who uses the secrets he wheedles out in therapy to extort love, or preferably money, from his patients. With his eye on the solitaire sparkling on the aging millionairess's eiderdown, he will, if necessary, sleep with the lady and, if necessary, go through the whole *Ars Amatoria* with her, until by dawn he has coaxed her into renting a sanatorium for him. Once she has rented it, and has herself been admitted from time to time to have her stomach pumped after attempting to commit suicide, he'll push or freeze her out, within a few weeks, with the excuse that other patients need the space.

Such was the image I had formed of this doctor within minutes, and the reason why I am going into such detail is that this doctor saved my life and that of my wife.

I felt that his persuasiveness could not only disarm his opponents and enemies, but also make people with more intelligence and stronger nerves than himself agree to whatever he wanted. He was like a satanic commercial traveller who could sell a seeder to a doctor or an electrocardiograph to a farmer if he turned his mind to it. Now he was trying to flog my life to me. He wasn't the kind of person who would want to save my life purely

out of human solidarity or because he thought that I was somebody who might still be needed by the world. He must have
had some ulterior motive. If a man of this kind got involved in
saving a life then saving a life was a cover for some greater trick
or scam, which went even beyond saving his own life. Be that
as it may, from the first moment he spoke to me I felt that if
anybody could save me from the wagon and the gas it would
be this doctor with the red hair.

'I've been sent by your wife, master,' he said in an insolently
familiar manner. 'She tells me that you had typhus in the Ukraine.'

'Yes, I did,' I said. 'But does that matter now?'

'In Kolozsvár the deportation was stopped because of typhus,'
he explained. 'They had a genuine typhus epidemic there. We
haven't got an epidemic here, but we'll make one,' he said, smiling
mysteriously.

'How do you know that it was stopped in Kolozsvár?' I asked
doubtfully. 'This lot doesn't get frightened by a little epidemic.'

Dr Németi answered in his place: 'My colleague goes out into
the town. He heard it from the best sources. My colleague's the
only person with a permit that allows him to go in and out of
the ghetto. He goes to the general hospital, but meets many
other people besides.'

'He's allowed out?' I asked, but I wasn't at all surprised that
the red-haired doctor also had these naive provincial gendarmes
in his pocket.

'I'm the only person with a permit from the colonel,' the red-
haired doctor explained. 'I can go around without a star and
without an escort.'

As I say, I wasn't surprised that the satanic commercial traveller had been able to nobble that same colonel who hadn't
allowed the Jewish corpses to be buried, who had thrown out
the registrar when he tried to register the Jewish dead, who had
small children shot at if they stood by the window, and who
regarded the twenty-five thousand Jews here in the ghetto merely
as a stinking heap of manure, for which even being put into
wagons was too great an honour and which he would have been
most happy to set fire to. The red-haired Jew had been given a
laisser passer by this colonel, while the twenty-five thousand of

us remained crammed in here behind the fence. He could hang about the town on his own, without the stigma, and escape across the Romanian border if ever he felt like it. Obviously he hadn't escaped but kept coming back because he had a bigger plan. Now he wanted to fake a typhus epidemic and he needed me. Perhaps chiefly because typhus could be detected in the blood even a year later, and my illness would only be a year old in October. But he didn't need me in particular for this purpose, because the ghetto was full of former forced labourers who had contracted typhus in the Ukraine. So he had probably chosen me for this important part in the prank so that, when it was reported after the war, he could point out that he had saved a well-known political journalist from the capital. But, having realised all this, I still couldn't see his real objective, the catch, the big deal.

'Your wife', the red-haired doctor continued, 'would very much like this to work. She's finding life hard here. She cries a lot, I change her bandages, and she's still suffering badly. She keeps saying that there's no way she'll get into the wagon, and I agree that she shouldn't, because with her open wound she would die while still in the wagon. And even if she survived the wagon, the Germans would finish her off at the terminus. The Germans are liquidating all those who can't work immediately on arrival. Do you know where we're going?'

'Not for sure. At least . . .'

'To Auschwitz.'

'That's probably the same as Oświęcim. My friends wrote to me about it from London in 1941.'

'Oświęcim in Polish, Auschwitz in German. That's the gas and the fire, the crematorium. The Christians in the town know that that's where we're going. They even know the details. I can't say that they're very sorry for us.'

I was silent for a few moments, holding my breath.

'Well, how do you intend to make typhus here?' I asked, my interest aroused.

'That in itself wouldn't be difficult. The colonel eats out of my hand. Outside, in the town, it could also be arranged. The director of the general hospital is an old-fashioned liberal and a friend of mine. Of course, the thing would need money. The money wouldn't be for the director of the general hospital, the director is a humanitarian and he's on our side. The money is needed above all for the laboratory. The laboratory will say what it likes, whether or not there is typhus. And then some money's also needed for the town hall. For the mayor and the police. Your wife says you have left some money with Christian friends outside in the town.'

'I don't know. I think there is some. If my wife thinks it's a good idea . . .'

'It doesn't matter if there isn't. Your money doesn't make much difference here. But we've got to scrape together all the money that can be raised, mainly from the rich. If I can lay on the epidemic by tomorrow evening I guarantee that the second transport won't leave. Unfortunately I can't, of course, save the first transport in the morning.'

The plan wasn't entirely hopeless, assuming it was true that in Kolozsvár the deportation had been broken off because of typhus. And that probably was true, because this man could go out into the town without the star, read newspapers and listen to the radio every day, and be informed of everything. Now that he had given me a glimpse of the concrete possibility of rescue—with the deportation being postponed by the twenty-one days of the statutory quarantine—suddenly life no longer seemed so undesirable. After all, something had happened at the last moment in the great silence.

For a while I tried to persuade myself that my change of mood was due to my wife's experiences. Yes, the suitcases had also arrived in Paris on the last train just before the outbreak of the war, when all hope had faded and I had given up on them. Such things always happened to my wife: in a completely desperate situation, when all seemed lost, at the last moment, everything took a turn for the better. So at first I also tried, somewhat maliciously, to interpret this prospect of a change of fortune as a function of my wife's horoscope, because I wasn't prepared to admit to myself that at the first real hope of escape, greedily and selfishly, the longing for life, the feverish idea of freedom, had revived in me.

I tried to weigh up the position in objective political and military terms. Let's see. Well, twenty-one days today were really longer than six months had been a year ago, when we tried to dispel our fear of the ominous prospects by asking reassuringly where these Germans would be in six months' time. Now every minute really mattered and now it was actually possible—as I was explaining to myself like an expert to a layman—that within twenty-one days the Russians would be here on the western slopes of the Carpathian mountains and the British and Americans in Milan or Paris at least. Then perhaps this beastly, dumb government wouldn't have the courage to deport us at the eleventh hour.

So I tried to calculate and speculate with a cool head, while in reality I was already burning with hope. This red-haired doctor had pulled me out of my numb fatalism, which had kept me in a stupor like a patient under anaesthetic. I had been like a man in a permanently drugged state who knows and hears everything, but doesn't want to act and rejoices in not wanting or having to act. But now this soothing passivity had gone at one blow: with a sudden sharp pain I felt the horror of the whole situation, and of course my own situation above all. Now any way out would have been a good one: I would have accepted it from anybody, from the devil, from the Gestapo, like a drowning man who doesn't care whether the straw he is clutching at is smeared with tar or excrement. Now I no longer passed judgement on the teacher of religion who was appreciated at the Honours Office—now I envied him, as I also did the prostitutes whom Ma had rescued and who had no doubt been servicing the officer hangmen ever since. And, like a dying patient who holds on to anything he can in order to stop death dragging him over to the other side, I desperately grabbed the wrist of this demonic ponce of a doctor, whom I had received so sourly and whom I rightly suspected of every possible villainy.

Yes, now I panicked like a man who, looking back down a sheer mountain side, realises for the first time where he is.

'Do you think it's going to work?' I whispered cravenly.

'I believe so,' he said with a superior smile as if he sensed my cowardice. 'Of course it's also a question of money.'

A question of money—let the scoundrel take the money, all the money in the town. Let the people tell him where they had buried their treasures so that he can dig them all up, going around with his permit and without a star. Of course he was after the money. I had known from the first moment that he was after something big: he was trying to hold the ghetto to ransom on the threshold of the gas chamber. All right, let him hold it to ransom, he deserves the money if he can save us.

Yes, this was the turning-point. As soon as the possibility of escape flashed before my eyes I had begun to fight for life, agreed to any villainy, and become the accomplice of the villains. I was the resident expert on staging typhus epidemics, and I immediately sat down with the doctors to talk matters over. They had only learnt and read about typhus—I, having had it, knew its smallest actual details, expressions and gestures, all its authentic external signs. First of all it was necessary to collect a few louse-ridden people from among the chassids, the most ragged, the thinnest and the palest, which wasn't difficult because most of them looked shabby, grey, sickly and bent. The most important thing was the fever: we had to make a fever, because the main ingredients of typhus were lice and unconsciousness accompanied by a high temperature. And the third was diarrhoea. I explained that the isolation ward should be located in a cellar and the people laid down in their dirty underwear on stinking straw, so that the gendarmes and medical officers would shrink back on the doorstep and not dare to approach more closely. On the front line the officers had never dared to enter the typhus hospital. To make sure that it was they who died, those who had to work there were Jewish doctors and nurses selected from among the forced labourers and, in order to keep the bullying officers and army doctors at bay, they deliberately made things look even worse, although there were also genuine patients dying. As a result we were neither inspected nor harassed. Not one of our superiors set foot among us, particularly after a doctor holding the rank of major, who had been strutting about the hospital, giving orders and dealing out blows ever since it was opened, contracted typhus and died. The Germans in particular gave the typhus hospital a wide berth: of all nations they died most easily of typhus. In Seredina-Buda one out of ten Hungarians and two out of ten Jews died of typhus. Of the eight cases of German typhus we had at the time all eight were *kaputt* within ten days. They are lying under the regulation crosses with the steel helmets in the Main Square, the heroes' cemetery, if the Russians haven't since removed them.

Twenty-one

The doctors listened attentively to my instructions. Then the red-haired gynaecologist stood up from the edge of my mattress, shook hands with me like a man of the world, and with his other hand patted Friedländer on the shoulder, saying:

'Don't worry, Mr Friedländer. We'll be going to the Riviera together yet.'

Yes, the nimble, pleasure-seeking Jews of Nagyvárad at the end of the last century had learnt from the gentry how to gamble elegantly, and then the pupils had outdone their masters. Eventually they—the gentry and the Jews—joined in designing systems every year for breaking the bank at one or other of the world's great casinos, in Monte Carlo, Ostend or, at the time of the first great inflation, Sopot. The doctor probably also had a system, which was why he had been going to the Riviera—and now he behaved as if he were trying out his system for breaking the ghetto. But I didn't care how much extra money he made, so long as it worked.

'I'll call in during the day to keep you informed about developments,' he said as he left. 'Till then I must ask for your discretion. I have the colonel in the palm of my hand, but if he suspects anything he'll stand me up against a wall and the whole thing will come to nothing.'

The clock of the Capuchin church was striking a quarter to one when the doctors disappeared into the blue darkness. The excitement had roused my survival instinct to such an extent that I felt as if I had to do something immediately—as if every minute spent in inactivity constituted a dangerous omission. But Friedländer said in a sleepy voice:

'That doctor is the greatest fibber in town. I don't believe a word he says. I know what he wants.'

'What does he want?'

'He'll trick everybody out of their hidden money. He'll take everything the gendarmes haven't been able to beat out of us. Then he'll cross over to Romania with the money and leave us in the lurch.'

'It's possible, but the money won't be much good to us anyway if they gas us. On the other hand he may well fake that epidemic.'

'I'm not counting on it. In the morning I'll take my son with me to dig graves and if that gendarme from Somogy is on duty I'll definitely try to get him out of here.'

'But if they stopped the deportation in Kolozsvár, then here too . . .' I said, trying to boost my enthusiasm.

Friedländer waved his hand, then put his chin on his palm again. But I wasn't willing to let my own hope be dampened— and I couldn't have done so even if I had wanted to, because my will to live was now in charge.

'Listen, Friedländer, twenty-one days is a lot of time. And the only thing they're at all afraid of is typhus. They don't want to drag it all over the country and they don't like the idea of infecting the wagons they use to transport their army. When we were on the front line there was once a six-week quarantine because of typhus. Nobody in our garrison was allowed on leave, and nobody from another garrison was allowed to join us—they took it that seriously. Here, too, things are serious now, and the front line is nearer, on the threshold of Transylvania. If we got twenty-one days' respite now—that's how long the quarantine takes— then perhaps we'll have weathered it.'

Suddenly Friedländer raised his head, surprised, and with some hope.

'You really believe that?'

'I believe it a little.'

'You think we can still be saved?' he almost begged.

'It's not impossible. If I look at the military situation then . . .'

'If you, with your expertise, believe it . . .'

'I'm no more an expert than you,' I objected, but continued to explain feverishly that things could now change a lot, not within twenty-one days but within minutes.

Friedländer, listen to what happened out there, on the front line, on the morning of 18 February. We had three new coffins in the morgue. The chaplain was cursing and beating us as usual, chivvying us to finish the grave by two o'clock. Of course we already knew about Stalingrad and El Alamein, but for six weeks the papers had been held back so that the soldiers wouldn't see them, and we had no idea of the latest events of the war. For the last six and a half months we had been in the forest of Bransk near a remote railway siding. Even in more normal times the train was only scheduled to pass twice a week, but since the partisans had stepped up their work it sometimes took more than ten days to mend the lines blown up by them, and for ten days we had heard nothing, not even false reports or horror stories. Of course we knew that the Germans and Hungarians were retreating on the major fronts, but here we neither saw nor felt any movement. Naturally, we were told least of all what was happening in our immediate neighbourhood, in the hundred kilometres of impenetrable forest. We could hear the roaring of the guns and the explosions of the mines, but that had been the same ever since we had arrived there in the summer. 'We're fighting the partisans,' they explained, and for a long time this was true. Then for some weeks it had seemed as if the guns and the mines were roaring and exploding a little more frequently and perhaps somewhat closer. The officers said that a specially equipped unit of partisan-hunters had freshly arrived from Sevsk and was finally mopping up the 'rats' to clear the way for our departure to the Urals in the spring. The privates believed them— because in this war the privates believed everything the officers and the newspapers told them—and we Jewish forced labourers were confused, because we didn't know exactly where we were and couldn't locate our sector of the front on a mental map. Nor could we reconstruct our position in relation to the front line, as we never saw a real map. And to be honest, we didn't believe that the Russians could have pushed so far west that winter. We had heard that Kursk—which was the nearest large centre but still three hundred kilometres away—had fallen, but we didn't believe that the Russians could cover such a distance within a few weeks in winter.

Well, on the morning of 18 February, when we started digging

133

the three graves, everything was as usual in Seredina-Buda. The chaplain produced the Ministry of War plan, marked out the place for the graves in the snow with the heel of his lace-up boot, delivered his daily dose of swearing and abuse, and then rode away, with the snow thrown up by behind his horse's hooves sparkling as it always did. The duty doctors, the nurses and the first-aid men with their red crosses, their patient registers under their arms, were leading the invalids of the various formations to the hospital in succession. The sledges of the service corps were fetching food from the supply unit, and convoys of Russian peasant sleighs were taking wood to the military bakeries. Uncle Kovács, sitting on a coffin in the chapel and baking potatoes, as usual, said:

'We're going to scarper, folks. I can smell it in the air. We're going to leave soon. Maybe as soon as the start of next month, the sappers tell me. The officers say that we're going to be relieved. They even know that the men from Pécs are coming to take over. But I think the whole caboodle's going to scarper before long, folks.'

By then we had stopped believing that we would ever leave that place. Our intellect told us that the Russians would drive us out sooner or later, but we could simply no longer picture a day when our unrelieved misery would cease. Even the idea of our suffering somewhere else seemed like redemption. At ten o'clock in the morning I left Uncle Kovács' chapel to go on digging graves. At a quarter to eleven a corporal came jumping over the cemetery fence and running towards us. He roared:

'Back to your quarters, at once!'

'What are we to do about the coffins?' the printer-gravedigger asked.

'Shut up,' the corporal yelled, still running. 'Get back to your quarters at once and await further orders!'

Uncle Kovács emerged from the chapel and called after the corporal:

'Does that also apply to me?'

'Why, do you want to stay here? Of course, it also applies to you.'

'You see? We're scarpering!' Uncle Kovács bellowed with a grin.

We had scarcely returned to our quarters in the Russian farm-house when we received orders to report to company head-quarters with all our equipment within ten minutes. We had hardly enough time to say good-bye to our hosts. I could only kiss the old woman on both cheeks. As soon as the company had lined up at the headquarters we were ordered to depart. Strangely enough, all that time there had been no new signs of the war and even the continuous roar of the guns had almost stopped. There were only some planes circling very high above—in fact, whole squadrons of planes so far unknown to this region, where we had only seen Soviet Ratas ever since the day we arrived. Of course the guards, who watched the planes with their hands shading their eyes, claimed that they were German planes. And we immediately set out along the road at the double.

We set out, my friend—what am I saying, 'set out'?—we ran. There's never been such a happy run—in thirty-five degrees of frost, before us the howling blizzard, above our heads the planes, behind our backs the Russian tanks, whose rattle could clearly be heard. We were running, laughing, partly because what we had never believed would happen—that we'd ever get out of there—had happened, and partly because it was no longer a horror story, a false report, or a reckless Jewish and anti-fascist hope that the Germans were being beaten, that we were being beaten, my friend.

You can't imagine, Friedländer, how improbable it had seemed to us until this moment that this bunch would ever be on the run. And now they had caved in within minutes and were running as if they were out of their minds. And then, believe it or not, I witnessed something that any writer who wanted to debunk history would give his last penny to see.

Our divisional commander, Major-General Makay, was a dwarf with strikingly long hands, a sour face and a sickly appearance. He must have had some stomach trouble, because the chaps who had for the last few days been digging an air-raid shelter in the courtyard of the divisional command were laughing their heads off about how he ran every quarter of an hour to the com-mander's latrine that had also been built in the courtyard. Of course this latrine had also been built by us Jewish forced labourers and wasn't really a latrine, but—a luxury here in the half-destroyed town—a rural kind of outdoor privy. The Jews had even managed to liberate a red coconut mat for it and to decorate the walls with battle pictures from the *Hungarian Messenger* and the *Signal*. Naturally the locksmith who had made the key was also a forced labourer who wasn't really a locksmith but a chemical engineer, and it had turned out far too large and unwieldy. The major-general always kept it on his desk, lest it should occur to some inferior officer to usurp his lavatory.

Well, Friedländer, about noon I saw this major-general run without his coat and sword, carrying this enormous key. The whole company was laughing with glee when they recognised the key from a distance, and believe me, my friend, with this ludicrous sight before us we too found it easier to run, and would have even found it easier to die. The Russians had arrived so quickly that he had only been able to put on his hat and grab the key, which must have become his most important possession since the onset of his diarrhoea—more important than his sword and his maps. He couldn't get into a car, because the Russians had, within minutes, cut off the command from the part of the town where the garages were. So the dwarf with the red stripe on his trousers and the diarrhoea was running, with his adjutant running beside him, and waving the key in his long hand, until after about fifty steps they wrapped him in a common private's coat and he was able to let the key disappear into one of its pockets. We never saw him again.

Believe it or not, Friedländer, it happened literally like that— you see, such a thing can happen in no time at all. We were 'scarpering' in a matter of minutes. Although the division had probably expected the Russians, it must have been thought that they wouldn't arrive for days and that when they did come they would obey the division's own schedule and allow it to evacuate the town according to its own plans. This will show you that things aren't necessarily true just because people in a miserable plight, like the one we're in now, tend to believe them. It isn't true that these bastards with the knowing faces really know everything in advance because they're in touch with the supreme command or the government. As if a measly company commander, or our gendarmerie colonel, for example, could really be informed about the military situation and the political or diplomatic secrets! Stuff and nonsense. Maybe in half an hour even this gendarmerie colonel of ours will be running with his lavatory key.

So we ran cheerfully through the blizzard as far as the village of Chernovskoye, eight kilometres from the town. Here we were suddenly halted, given shovels and pickaxes, and lined up on the road at seven o'clock in the evening to move snow. We set to work with desperate laughter, almost certain that we'd freeze to death by the morning. They had never made us do such insanely pointless work before. As soon as we had shovelled away some of the snow the wind brought back a thousand times more. They even ordered us to level and flatten the snow to please the eye, and they warned us that the major-general with the key would come and hold an inspection. Was he the lunatic who had issued the order for us to clear and titivate the road for the troops retreating through the blizzard and the snowdrifts?

But where were the retreating troops by the morning? The Russians hadn't honoured the plans that the major-general with the lavatory key had prepared long in advance, designating this relatively wide and firmly built road as the route for 'evasive action'. The Russians hadn't allowed the troops to escape by this fairly comfortable road but had driven them into the forest directly from the town. Only a random few got away along this road, which we'd had to clear with shovels stolen from Russian peasants. First came the medical column's two trucks with the dangerously ill and the doctors, whom the Russians had probably deliberately allowed to slip out of the encirclement. Then, at long intervals, came an artillery carriage with four men on the box and no gun, and some cars with officers in them. From the direction of the town the tanks' guns roared continuously and the nocturnal forest crackled with submachine gunfire, but in vain, in vain: the battle noises didn't come any closer. We went on shovelling snow, a little cowed, and tense with expectation, waiting for the Russians.

We waited for the Russians, and when the tanks hadn't arrived by dawn we began to doubt and lose heart. Lance-Corporal

Bota, who had chivvied us all night with his rifle butt, taunted us with a grin:

'Well, you dirty Jews, can you hear them retreating? All your whispering and gloating were for nothing. We're beating the swine back.'

Of course the Russians weren't retreating, but it was half an hour before both Bota and we learnt that they'd got ahead of us and cut off the road a fair distance to the west. As a result we too were chased off the road and into the forest. Between the indifferent firs with their ice-covered trunks even the blood-thirsty guards were overcome by gloom as they slipped on the frozen snow, stumbled over protruding tree stumps, and sank up to their necks in unexpected hollows. They grew quieter and tried to catch our eyes on the sly, as if they were wondering whether it would be possible to make peace with us quickly at the last moment. Because, Friedländer, we now had a real prospect of becoming 'pheasants'—that is, prisoners of war—which was what we all longed for. Now these revolting guards were afraid that we would immediately tell the Russians everything that they had done to us and that the Russians might do them in at once. They no longer dared to say anything even when we fell out and crawled on ahead as best we could, or stayed behind, each as he pleased.

Why didn't we all stay behind to await the Russians? Partly because in all probability the German and Hungarian field gendarmes were behind us, ready to bump off any stragglers without warning. And partly because in the thirty-five degrees of frost it wasn't possible to hide in the forest without a proper plan—we would have frozen to death within hours and light-ing a fire would have been fatal. The only sensible thing would have been to take refuge with some decent and brave Russians in a village, but far from being allowed to stop in the villages we were chased through them at the double. What is more, the Russians themselves were fleeing from the villages because, following the example of the Germans, we set fire to every village we had to abandon on our retreat. Unfortunately we weren't caught by the Russians in a tight circle, in which case we would have simply raised our hands above our heads and that would have been that. In this sector the circle was too wide and had been left open in the area of the forest in which we were running. So all we could do was run and try to stay as close together as possible, because we knew that if we were left on our own during the night it would have been the end of us.

Even so, the deeper we penetrated into the forest the fewer of us stayed in one knot. People dispersed, in groups or singly, and were left behind. We could hear the thuds as they fell down and the groans as they struggled to pull themselves up—but by now nobody was helping anybody else, Friedländer. After a few hours in the forest every bit of comradely solidarity, every humane reflex or pose, every shred of shame had evaporated—we left each other in the snow, under the firs, like discarded, empty tin cans. To make matters worse, these unfortunate comrades were carrying very heavy knapsacks full of all kinds of junk that they had bartered with the soldiers and the Russian civilians, as well as the few useful and many superfluous things from the long-awaited Christmas parcels that we were lugging with us out of gratitude and love for our friends and relations at home. The overfilled knapsacks pulled the people backward till they were dancing on the slippery snow. I myself had jettisoned everything, except my bread, my cans and my soap, as soon as we had entered the forest. I could hardly feel the weight of my knapsack, and when I fell I easily managed to pull myself up again. But when the others fell their heavy knapsacks came down on them like rocks and they found it almost impossible to throw them off without help. And if one of them, with a huge effort, finally succeeded in scrambling to his feet—where were the others by then? For a while he could still be heard calling, then he probably set out blindly and ended up who knows where.

By the time dawn broke we had been freezing in the snow-storm without anything to eat for a whole day and night, and we were very tired, very hungry, and desperate for sleep. What little vital energy we had left was running out fast. There were two hundred of us when we started out from Seredina-Buda, and seventy when we got to the Desna several days later.

I also made it to the Desna, Friedländer, not least thanks to having impressed on myself, as a lesson to last for ever, that if your life is in danger and you want to live you mustn't cling to objects but only to life itself. My wife had clung to the nine suitcases in Paris, which is one of the reasons why I found myself in the white hell of Rudna Forest then, and why I find myself here now, my friend. Later I saw the Russian peasants fleeing because, if they had stayed at home, the retreating Hungarians or Germans would have set fire to their houses over their heads. Well, these Russian peasants had also piled all kinds of stuff on their sledges, even mangles and birdcages. Then they got stuck in the congestion and were held up on the road for half a day at a time—until suddenly the planes arrived in a low dive, and that was the end of the mangle, the cage, the bird, and the peasant . . . These Russians, particularly their womenfolk, wouldn't leave their sledges unguarded even when the machine guns were strafing them from twenty-five metres overhead—they would stay on their sledges and die rather than lose anything or have a solitary wrench or jug stolen by a neighbour.

My friend, if I were to escape from here thanks to this typhus scam, I swear I'll never have a home again as long as I live, and I'll only have one suit, which I'll wear till it falls off me in tatters. I tell you, after what has happened to them in this war, people should remain nomads for at least a hundred years, ready to move on at any moment. They shouldn't let their homes and furniture worm their way into their petty-bourgeois sentiments and paralyse them. I'll never have a library again. I had three thousand books, Friedländer, but if I survive, against all the odds, I'll read like the eccentric Professor Friedmann, whom I considered a vandal and a madman because whenever he had read a page in a book he tore it out and threw it on the ground. Nor will I ever again have a suitcase, not one, not nine—I'll put my toothbrush, my toothpaste, my soap and my comb in my pocket and change my underclothes in a department store, simply leaving the dirty ones behind.

Twenty-two

At daybreak there was shooting from both sides, but we saw neither Russians nor Hungarians. By now I was dragging myself along with only two other men—Roder, who had been a barber at home, and Weitzier, a former plumber and burglar. The barber, with a child's face and the bones of a bird, was weak but brave. The burglar was the strongest man in the company, bold, enterprising and resourceful. Decrepit as I was, and sixteen years older, these two had stayed with me because they had become fond of me over the long months and wanted to look after me. The barber was attached to me because at home, while working, he had enjoyed arguing about politics, and he had been my reader and political follower. Since we had become forced labourers he had been coming to my quarters, whenever he could, to pick my brains about intellectual matters, books or the private lives of famous people. The burglar had taken a liking to me because he felt that I had no prejudices against him and treated him without either revulsion or curiosity. He was a generous and chivalrous comrade, and a criminal not only by ingrained habit but also by conviction. I had once offered to find him an employer who would help him resume his honest occupation, if we were ever to return home. 'Look,' he said, 'there's no point in promising to try, because I wouldn't keep my word. It isn't only a question of easy money—you can't imagine how exciting it is to pull the skeleton key out of my pocket in the dark.'

It was with these two that I was painfully dragging myself through the howling storm, being pelted, so it seemed, with splinters of glass in the twilight. They supported me left and right by my arms and they even fed me as we staggered on. The burglar's pockets bulged with packs of sweet coffee he had stolen from a supply wagon, which were soaked by the melting snow and which he stuffed into my mouth. The barber had a hundred German cigarettes that tasted of nothing but bore a sonorous name, which of course I couldn't light but sucked till they crumbled away, sodden with snow. Meanwhile the blizzard had become even more furious and we could see even less than during the night, although it was almost morning. All we could do was to keep tunnelling our way through the white darkness, bumping our foreheads against trees at every other moment. Descending relentlessly at an incredible rate, the curtain of snow with its millions of flakes turned into a solid wall in front of us. I could hardly go on, but these two kept pushing me along.

Finally we could go no further because it became impossible to find our bearings in the blizzard. Thirty steps ahead we saw the outline of what looked like a hut, but when we had managed to crawl to it we discovered that it was a neatly built stack of wood, no doubt cut and assembled by Jewish forced labourers. We decided to wait behind the stack for the blizzard to abate. The rumble of the battle could be heard from both sides of the forest, louder and closer at some times, softer and more distant at others. While the battle itself remained outside, the forest was combed by patrols at irregular intervals and brushed by salvoes from the guns of tanks speeding along the highway. Bullets hissed over our heads and shrapnel kept breaking the branches, but the only thing we were afraid of was that the snow would eventually bury us alive, because it was already waist high even where the stack of wood provided some protection from the wind. To keep my spirits up, the burglar began to sing 'Katyusha' in Russian and the barber accompanied him in his titmouse voice.

Then it was like a film—a sudden revolver shot, followed by a soldier stumbling towards us through the trees. The wind was almost carrying him like a piece of newspaper. He was a Hungarian soldier, with his hat pushed back, his forehead bandaged in a bloody, dirty cloth. His coat was a sheer lump of ice, his beard and moustache a single block of snow. The wind hurled him against the stack of wood. He stopped with a jolt, shook himself, and swore.

'Jesus Christ with his seven bleeding wounds,' he bellowed

and proceeded to list all the saints in the canon. Then he said in a condescending but threatening voice: 'Who are you lot?'

The burglar answered insolently: 'We're Jews.'

'You're skiving, aren't you?' he continued like a disapproving and contemptuous superior. Then he announced boastfully: 'I come from Mikhailovka. I'm a lance-sergeant and I commanded a whole company. But the rank and file have all had it. They're gone for good, the lot of them. I was the company commander as long as there was a company.' And he swore again at great length.

'What happened to the officers, company commander?' the barber asked innocently.

'They scrammed by car, right at the start. But I held the railway crossing with my Mannlicher* for four hours against two hundred sub-machine guns. Even with my temple bleeding and my boot torn open by shrapnel,' he said, contemplating his boots in the snow.

Then he threw his chin up and barked:

'Well, who's going to swap boots with me?'

We stared grimly at him, saying nothing. He raised his revolver.

'Make it snappy, Jews. Hand over those boots! A Hungarian soldier fights, freezes his feet off and croaks, while you're prancing about in fancy boots as if you were promenading on the Danube Embankment.'

In a flash the burglar had thrown himself at him and grabbed the revolver. 'Listen, pal,' he urged quietly, 'stop throwing your weight about, or I'll stick a bullet in you so quick you won't even be able to say good-bye to these saints you keep on about. This caper's finished. One more sound out of you and in five minutes you'll be covered by snow so deep that even the Russki crows won't find you till spring.'

'Now it's us who've got the gun,' the barber, for his part, began to explain in his titmouse voice. 'It's always the man with the gun who gives the orders. You lot have been ordering us about because you've had the guns. Now it's the other way round, and I think from now on it's always going to be the other way round. The Russians have beaten you, pal, and now you'd

* semi-automatic rifle

better get used to not being able to grab whatever you want. And you can't nick the boots off our feet, either, just because we're Jews.'

The company commander plucked up his courage:

'I'm in your hands, Jews, but I'm a Székely,* he declared bombastically. 'I may get out of this forest or I may not. But if I do, you'll all be hanging from a tree, one next to the other.'

The burglar went up close to him and waved the revolver under his nose:

'You know what, pal? We'll make sure that you don't get out of the forest. You're staying here for good. You've tried to rob your comrades.'

'Comrades? Whose comrade are you?' the company commander sneered.

The burglar raised the revolver and I could see that he was about to fire.

'Don't shoot,' I said to him softly.

The burglar stepped back a little. The company commander stared fixedly into the barrel.

'I'm not afraid of you, Jew. I wasn't afraid of the Russki, I'm not afraid of God. And even less of you, you dirty Jews. Shoot if you dare.'

'I'll show you how I dare,' the burglar roared. 'Why shouldn't I dare? You think I'm afraid to waste a bastard like you?' He fired, and would have hit the company commander if the barber hadn't knocked his hand to one side at the last moment. The bullet whizzed past the man's head.

After the shot we stood silently for a moment, gasping for breath. Then the barber said soothingly in his child's voice:

'Look here, pal, don't let's argue. We're never going to get out of this forest in any case. We're going to die here together, and the crows won't give a damn in the spring whether you're a Székely and we're Jews. Or, just as likely, the Russkis will catch up with us. Then we'll tell them that you wanted to nick the boots off our feet and—do you see that tree, pal?—that's where they'll hang you, on that very tree. But I've got a suggestion to

* Member of an ethnic Hungarian group in Transylvania.

make, to show you we're good chaps. You're not getting our boots, but in my knapsack I've got a large piece of sacking the Russians gave me to bandage my foot with in case my boots wore out. I'll give you that, and you can wrap your foot with the bad boot in it. And then all will be sweetness and light.'

After brief reflection, the company commander said:

'All right, let's see that bit of sacking.'

The barber laboriously dug the piece of sacking out of his knapsack. The company commander, leaning against a protruding log, started to swaddle his foot in it, saying:

'But if you think that we're beaten, you'd better think again. Our job here was to trick the Russians. We were supposed to make them think that we had large units here so they wouldn't dare to attack prematurely. We managed to do this, because, as you see, they haven't dared to attack before now. Once they attacked we had no intention of defending this sector because we didn't even have proper arms. If the supreme command had wanted us to hold the front we would have been given proper arms. But everything was set up like this. Now we're retreating from here as far as the Desna, all according to plan. And there we'll get them.'

'Did the officers also scram according to plan?' the barber asked.

'The officers,' the company commander waved his hand dismissively. 'They're school teachers, civil servants, not soldiers. They were drinking, womanising and playing bowls all summer. But what you don't know is that they have no say here. Here the Germans are the only ones in charge. I've spoken to a German who told me: now you must beat it from here, that's the tactic. The Russians are supposed to think that they're strong, so they get complacent. Then the fresh German and Hungarian armies are going to arrive and the Russkis are going to run on to their open knives. That's why we're getting out of here now, understand? And the German also told me what's going to happen in the spring. At Leningrad there are nine million fresh German soldiers and at Kiev four hundred thousand Hungarians—but not rubbish like these here, not old territorial reserves and Romanians, Slovaks, Ruthenians and Jews, but all of them young regular soldiers from the Great Plain and the Székely regions. At Leningrad they'll turn the front upside down and we'll go back in, as far as Stalingrad to start with.'

He went on explaining the new strategy, ever more knowingly and expertly. What do you think of that, Friedländer? He had seen his officers fleeing and his entire company dying, his head was bloody, his foot in his split boot was frozen, he didn't have a crust of bread or a single cigarette because he'd thrown everything away as he was running. But as he ran, desperately, blindly, forlornly through the forest, he still believed that he was actually luring the Russians into a trap. He didn't believe this out of fanaticism, because this brigand, this Székely peasant in a soldier's uniform, wasn't motivated by a cause, say, fascism or nationalism, but merely by a childish belief in the invincibility of the Germans—just as we used to believe in the heroism of the Red Indians—and by the conviction that even in his miserable plight as an individual he had a share in the inevitable final success, the certain victory. That was what gave him superiority, arrogance, even courage, in a quandary he believed to be only temporary. He thought we were stupid, ignorant and traitorous for not believing that the beating we were receiving was only a pretence, a deception, a deliberate stratagem, and the Germans were playing with the Russkis as a father plays with his child. This was the most fantastical thing in this war—that the Hungarian peasant soldier could be made to believe in the invulnerability of the Germans.

In the First World War, when my regiment was smashed on 6 August 1914 at Yanow in Galicia, in the chaos the soldiers climbed on to any kind of vehicle—carriages, carts, trains—and didn't stop till they reached their villages in the Little Plain, where they changed into civilian clothes, because they believed that the war was over. As far as they were concerned, it was finished. But now, Mr Friedländer, we were running as no beaten army had perhaps ever run—I don't believe that the Insurgents* had run more disgracefully than these badly armed, badly trained, mostly older territorial reservists abandoned by their officers at the very first moment, who were only supposed to have been

---

* An army of Hungarian nobles defeated by Napoleon at Győr in 1809.

used for hunting partisans and who had now been stranded in the main front line. And yet, as they were running, throwing away their inadequate weapons, their scarce food, and many even their greatcoats, they believed, my friend, that they were merely obeying orders to imitate a beaten army, craftily luring the Russians to their doom when the Germans . . .

Listen, Friedländer, these people were unable to imagine that they could be beaten in this war, even when they had long since been beaten. Take, for instance, my earlier meeting with János Háry himself.* We were still digging graves at Seredina-Buda, and the day we learnt from leaflets dropped by Russian planes, that the Germans had ordered a period of national mourning because of Stalingrad, we were sitting round the fire in Uncle Kovács' birch chapel, debating the situation. The clear-headed milk-cart driver from Tihany told us that the officers were keeping silent about what had happened at Stalingrad and the rank and file weren't interested, but he and the company clerk, a man from Budapest, had figured out from the first lieutenant's newspaper that there really was trouble at Stalingrad. As we were talking about this, the door of the birch chapel opened and in came another company commander, six and a half feet tall, with a Hitler moustache and small eyes.

'Good day to you, brothers,' he greeted us in a friendly manner. 'I've come from Susemka to collect the post, but they aren't distributing it at the division till one o'clock. May I sit by your fire for a while?'

'You may,' Uncle Kovács said, not very welcomingly. He wasn't pleased to have been found together with us.

The company commander settled down. After introducing himself to everybody and warming up a little, he began:

'Do you know that Stalingrad's finally fallen?' he asked.

Uncle Kovács muttered cautiously: 'How do you know?'

'The officers said so. But I've also heard it on the radio. And do you know how it fell?'

'We don't,' Uncle Kovács mumbled with feigned indifference.

---

* An old soldier telling tall tales about his youthful exploits, hero of the humorous epic *Az obsitos (The Veteran)* (1843) by János Garay (1812–53).

'Well, I'll tell you,' he said. 'The Germans had been held up at the edge of the city for three months, unable to move either back or forward. If they made a little headway in, they were pushed out again, because the terrain is nasty, full of woods and hills. Then, after Hitler met Horthy in Buda, they threw in three Hungarian divisions and these gave the Russkis such a hard time that, one week later, we're already in there. Because in this war, like in the last, it's always us who pull the Germans out of the shit.'

'Maybe it was like that,' Uncle Kovács growled and shrugged once.

'Of course it was like that. I heard it myself on the radio, word for word.'

This was a million times more attractive, Friedländer, than that Székely company commander in the forest. At least this kind of credulous boasting has a tradition in our literature and our upbringing—Botond, Pál Kinizsi, Miklós Toldi* and the others, including Garay's János Háry. In Jókai† too, we've read of a Hungarian hussar putting a Turkish or Austrian regiment to flight single-handed. The whole 1848 cycle of legends is full of miraculous exploits like that. From the First World War, purely out of dislike for the Germans, we ourselves brought back such fairy tales, in which a lost situation was always saved by Hungarian troops. Three Hungarian divisions or, if you like, three Hungarian hussars, capturing Stalingrad—that's all right, that's an old, regular Hungarian legend, the old megalomania, with an anti-German edge at that. But the Székely company commander didn't expect a miracle from Hungarian bravery, he had been bewitched by Goebbels—as had been, after all, the whole country—and even now the whole country still believes that we're allowing the Russians in, as far as Iasi, Kolozsvár and then Nagyvárad,

---

* Botond: legendary Hungarian general, believed to have led a victorious campaign against Byzantium in 958. Pál Kinizsi: fifteenth-century Hungarian general, who liberated part of Hungary from Turkish occupation. Miklós Toldi: legendary fourteenth-century Hungarian hero, celebrated in particular in the epic Toldi trilogy (1847, 1848, 1854) by János Arany (1817–82).
† Mór Jókai (1825–1904): one of Hungary's major novelists, who played an active part in the 1848 Hungarian revolution.

according to plan. These idiots still believe that the whole thing is a crafty trick to catch the Russians somewhere—which is why they dare to do all this to us here in the ghetto.

Well, let me continue. We were lying low for about an hour and a half behind the stack of wood with the company commander, who even explained to us why, once the war was over, it would be necessary to exterminate us Jews to the last man—because we were showing the Russians, and the British too, where their planes should drop their bombs on the German and Hungarian cities, and where the Christian churches and kindergartens were.

'You want to wipe out the Christians,' he went on. 'You might as well admit it, now that we're in the same boat. The officers have told us that there hasn't been one attack on this front without a Jew in a yellow armband sneaking across to the Russkis with the plans the day before.'

'How did the Jew know the plans?' the barber asked, looking curious.

'You lot know everything you want to know. That's exactly what's the trouble with you, you know everything. That's why it's impossible to live with you. A Christian learns and struggles all his life without getting anywhere. You just come along, look around you, and you already have it made.'

The snowfall had abated, the wind decreased and turned direction. Behind us the sun began to shine through the curtain of snow. The roar of guns was also approaching. Now we could make a start.

The company commander, conscious of his rank, sauntered a few steps ahead of us. The burglar said to me under his breath:

'If we let him live now he'll certainly hand us over to a field gendarme. Or he'll shoot us himself. It would still be better to do him in.'

'We can't do him in,' I objected.

The barber shared the burglar's concern, but waited to hear my opinion. For some moments I wavered. I thought of my comrades, of the sixty-year-old freemason lawyer from Eger, whom the Lord Lieutenant had also sent to the Ukraine. They had pulled his grandchildren from his lap and put him in the wagon, and he had died in Sostka, in the hospital hut, because the commander wouldn't allow him to use the insulin his family had sent after him by field mail with special permission of the Ministry. I thought of the young lads with typhus whom company commander Lieutenant Fazekas—in civilian life an environmental engineer—had laid out in the snow with forty-five degrees of fever to make the thermometer go down. I thought of the men of the 'bone brigade', as the company next to us was called, most of whom had been torn to pieces by mines, frozen, starved to death or beaten out of their minds. I thought of the 135 Hungarian dead we had buried in the heroes' cemetery at Seredina-Buda—mainly landless, penniless peasants and small-timers, who had been rounded up and dragged out there by force, and on whose coffins we uncaringly sat and baked potatoes before we buried them.

I also remembered something else. In 1921 I happened to be in Berlin, when I heard that there was going to be a very important socialist congress to decide which Internationale the German Socialist Party should join. In those days I wanted to be present wherever the destiny of the world was decided—I was young, Friedländer, I still thought that some place, some time, the destiny of the world would really be decided. Next morning I took the express train to Bonn. The congress was being held in the municipal theatre. The orchestra pit had been covered by boards and there sat the great figures of German socialism, whose books in their blue covers I had devoured as a child, whom I respected, but I must admit, more and more sceptically since the German revolution of 1918–19. There was Scheidemann with his beard, Otto Braun with his innkeeper's face, Hermann Müller, and majestic, grey-haired and smiling Klara Zetkin. The debate was heated and frantic. At times people almost came to blows and there could almost have been blood on the floor. This contest, which was more exciting than a record-breaking motor-cycle race on a narrow track, had lasted from morning till afternoon, and the energy of the people— none of whom had left the theatre for lunch—had begun to flag, when a thick-set man in a velvet coat, with grey hair combed back, a goatee beard and pince-nez, suddenly stepped out from behind the curtain, and began to speak in German with a typical Russian accent:

'Comrades, I have come through several frontiers with a false passport to warn you before it's too late.'

First, instead of going into theoretical and practical political arguments, he told a story. During the revolution in Leningrad, prey to a humane impulse and, perhaps also to masculine susceptibility, he had saved a general's wife and daughter from the fury of the people. The general was wandering somewhere on the disintegrating front line, the lonely ladies were frightened and attractive, and he, motivated by pity and infatuation, had not only hidden them but even helped them to escape to Finland. Six months later the same general temporarily recaptured from the Red Army the small village where the family of the man with the beard lived, and he learnt that the same general had exterminated his entire family. The thick-set man with the beard raised his arms and begged the meeting:

'Genossen! Nicht gut sein zu der Bourgeoisie!'*

It was only then that he turned to the political arguments. And while he made his points and formulated his attacks in his expertly constructed speech, the fervent warning kept returning at the appropriate points:

'Genossen! Nicht gut sein zu der Bourgeoisie!'

I can still hear his plaintive tones. Having been taught generosity and justice, in other words defencelessness, by the glorious but naive and effeminate French Revolution and the humanitarian–liberal–socialist nineteenth century, we—a whole generation at the mercy of political and social sentimentality—had to be entreated by that Russian speaker, whose identity I've never discovered, to be bad to those who were bad to us. And have we learnt to be really bad since? 'The winner is the man who shoots first,' I was once told by a Mexican revolutionary in Paris, but we can't even shoot *back*! And if we were to survive all this and get hold of the gun, as we got hold of the company commander's revolver in that forest, do you think things would be any different? We would try to intervene, just as horrified, if somebody

* 'Comrades! Don't be good to the bourgeoisie!'

raised a gun against the murderer. We would knock his hand to one side, as the barber did. No, I simply couldn't have countenanced a man being deliberately killed with my agreement and my responsibility. That's why I would never be prepared, in politics either, to accept a role in which I had to make life-or-death decisions, or where maintaining my own power depended on liquidating those who threatened it. I know, the Russian in Bonn was right: '*Nicht gut sein!*'—but in that forest I said to the burglar:

'Don't hurt him. We'll try to stay behind. He's from a different division, we may never see him again . . .'

So we walked on, with the company commander in front and the three of us a few steps behind him. From a distance we must have looked as if we were mechanically, obediently following our master . . .

Twenty-three

We would have loved to stay behind altogether, but the company commander kept looking back, and as soon as there was a fair distance between us he ordered us to hurry up. He was visibly gaining in confidence by the minute. He sensed that having missed the one moment when we could have become murderers out of self-defence, despair and hate, we wouldn't now be able to kill him, although we had the loaded revolver and he was unarmed. Even the burglar, who was only a burglar and no murderer, stopped blustering as he plodded on, sullenly dangling the revolver. He was angry with me for preventing him from doing something that he could have done while the time was right but didn't feel able to do any longer. There were still only the four of us among the snowdrifts in the sunny forest, but the company commander was acting more and more obviously as if he were our leader, and we began to lose more and more of our sense of unrestricted freedom. The reflexes of captivity and discipline had taken hold of us again: I noticed that we had already started adapting to each other's rhythm and walking in step. When the company commander demanded a cigarette over his shoulder, the barber, with his old air of sly, alarmed eagerness, gave him one, and even added: 'Yes, sir.'

That was when I realised that something had to be done, because going on as we were meant certain death. Our 'pal' would indeed have us hanged on the first tree as soon as we got somewhere. I told the others under my breath that we must come up with some bright idea as soon as possible.

After a few more steps the burglar fell flat on his face. He gave an excellent imitation of an epileptic fit, but the company commander, who by now regarded himself as being in charge and therefore automatically responsible for us, kept rubbing snow into his temples and the area around his heart. The burglar jumped up in anger. The ploy had failed. We trudged on, as if hypnotised. Indoctrinated as we were with the idea of discipline and punishment, the company commander could easily have led us to the nearest command post, and that would have been the end of us.

But we were lucky. About a hundred and fifty steps along the trail that led through the forest, a convoy of sledges suddenly appeared. The burglar, who was first to notice, ran towards them, shouting in Russian. The company commander, stopped terrified in his tracks, bawled at him:

'Shut up!'

But the burglar went on shouting. The company commander turned on his heels and ran back into the forest. We hurried towards the Russians.

The convoy consisted of four sledges carrying Russian peasants, old men, women and children. They were from the nearby village of Golukhovka. Having fled from the retreating Hungarians sideways into the forest, they expected the Russians to continue their advance, while they returned to their liberated homes along the forest trails behind the front line. As I told you, Friedländer, the battle was fought mainly on the road. It was primarily a tank battle, and tanks were unable to move in the forest. So if you got off the road and waited in the forest there was a good chance that the battle would pass you by. These Russian peasants had the same idea, and they were convinced that they would be back home in their village by evening.

Of course they knew who we were as soon as they saw our yellow armbands—we were famous on the whole front for being the lowest of the low, the miserable victims of the Hungarians, who specialised in making even their Jewish slaves play at being soldiers. Without further ado, they made us climb on their sledges and warmly invited us to accompany them to their village, where they could always find us some chores to do around the home and some potatoes to eat as long as they themselves had any. Slowly but purposefully the sledges set off towards the interior of the forest—even the horses knew where to go. I had an unimaginable sense of relief—as if nothing untoward could ever again happen to me—partly because the company commander, who would certainly have done for us, had made himself scarce, and partly because perhaps we were at last 'pheasants'. In the evening we would reach the village with the Russians and report to the first Russian officer. I would tell him who I was and ask him, if possible, to send a message to Moscow for Béla Balázs, Andor Gábor and Béla Illés or, maybe, my friend Sándor Gergely, with whom I used to hatch plots in the Abbazia Café in the thirties before he left for the Soviet Union.* I thought these colleagues would arrange for me to be taken somewhere safe, where I could recover physically and even be of some use to them. I would also put in a good word for my splendid comrades, the barber and the burglar . . .

We had travelled for about twenty minutes before the sledges stopped in front of a wooden construction that looked like a corral. The fence concealed a primitive bunker of the kind thrown together by partisans if they camp somewhere for only a few days. The horses and sledges were put out of sight behind the fence and we took shelter in the bunker, where the Russians promptly lit a fire. From the group with whom the barber had travelled an elderly woman came up to me. She addressed me in German. Her black clothes weren't those of a peasant but suggested, rather, a widow living on a small pension. She told me in German, Friedländer, that she was the village teacher. The barber had told her that at home I had been a writer and she cursed the Hungarian fascists for daring to treat a writer thus. To them a writer was like a count or a prince had been under the czar. When she was at university in Moscow under the czar, the Russians had treated writers the way the Hungarian fascists were treating them now. They were sent to jail, starved to death, or allowed to die of tuberculosis. Every writer worth his salt was a revolutionary. She hadn't personally known any writers and was pleased to have met one at last.

We chatted for about an hour and a half in the snow-covered

---

* Béla Balázs (1884–1949), Andor Gábor (1884–1953), Béla Illés (1895–1974), Sándor Gergely (1896–1966), Hungarian communist writers, in exile in Moscow before and during the Second World War.

bunker, with the heat of the fire searing my face but leaving my back and legs cold. She was proud and truly grateful to hear that I knew the names of Russian writers, both old and new, and she was ashamed of knowing only French, German and Scandinavian, but no Hungarian ones. When I told her that I had been to Paris several times I had to tell her everything I knew about Paris. 'I'm at home in the Paris of the Goncourts,' she said excitedly. 'I could find my way round with my eyes closed. For me Turgenev's Paris is as if I'd spent my youth there.' Do you realise, Friedländer, what this new Russian world is like? It's as replete with literature and a belief in some ultimate justice as the Christian world is with God. Most of this new Russia was dreamt up by emigrés in Western literary cafés. I'd never felt anywhere else that literature was such a mass religion, not even in France. Imagine! *L'Education sentimentale* in a kitchen, in the hands of a peasant boy, and the Goncourts in a bunker under the snow in a forest, while German and Russian tanks were wrecking each other on the road and the lice were devouring us both below and above the belt. We would have gone on talking about literature for a long time if the burglar hadn't come up to me, looking frightened.

'Listen,' he said dejectedly, 'I think there's something wrong. I can't hear any shooting. It's dead quiet up there.'

It really was dead quiet. From time to time we heard a bang— it sounded like people shooting rabbits in peacetime, in a reserve, with hunting permits and Lancaster shotguns. Then silence. The snow had stopped falling, the sun had come out, and the cold was even more bitter than it had been during the night, in the middle of the blizzard.

The Russians were also listening with sombre faces. What was going on? Could the attackers have advanced so far that we were no longer able to hear the battle? Or had they been repulsed? In any case why didn't the victors pursue the losers? Why had they stopped? Had something gone awry? Had the company commander been right after all?

After deliberating for a while, two men on a sledge went to investigate. They returned late in the afternoon. It transpired that the Russian troops hadn't been stopped, but had stopped of their own accord. They had taken up positions three villages further back, where the road turned at a right angle, that is, at the most suitable strategic point of the forest and the road network. The battle beyond that line was only a reconnaissance and nuisance raid carried out by an armoured advance guard. The tanks hadn't been followed by the main units and had pulled back by daybreak. The Germans, who had believed that the Russians wouldn't stop till they got to the Desna river, were cautiously advancing again along the section of road that they had recently surrendered. For the time being, Golukhovka, where these Russian villagers lived, was empty: the Russian soldiers had withdrawn and the Germans hadn't yet arrived.

The men would have preferred to make their way through the forest behind the backs of the Germans and join the Russian soldiers, but the women wanted to go home at any price. Now their only concern was their unguarded houses. They were determined to get back as soon as possible to recover the things they had abandoned or hastily buried. The teacher agreed with the men, but of course the women won. The convoy, with the dejected men and the tense, silent women, departed towards the village.

We got there at about ten o'clock in the evening. One row of houses had been burnt down and nothing but an irregular line of black, snow-capped posts stood in the white moonlight to show where they had been. The villagers were trickling back sporadically. Only our quiet, stealthy convoy brought a little more movement into the empty settlement. We took refuge in the teacher's house, which hadn't been damaged. She had no oil, but the moon illuminated the cold kitchen with its stove and the bedroom with a brass bed in one corner, some icons with family photos stuck in the frames above the bed, and a wardrobe, a bookshelf, a table and two chairs made of soft wood. In this sparse interior, reminiscent of a student's digs, the moonlight drained the life out of everything. It painted us, too, the colour of corpses and made words freeze on our lips. The burglar was the first to recover. He asked the teacher where he could find some wood. She directed him to the classroom at the back that had been used as a woodshed since the teaching stopped. The burglar and the barber set to work. Eventually the damp wood started hissing in the stove and even its suffocating reek seemed to warm us. Then the two of them brought some straw into the kitchen and spread it around the stove. The teacher set a pan full of unpeeled potatoes on the stove, and at long last we began to look forward to having something hot to eat and a few hours' rest in a warm place.

Outside, a car spluttered and came to a halt. We watched the window. Presently there was a knock on the pane and somebody shouted in Russian: 'The Germans are here.' We knew very well what happened when German field gendarmes found straggling soldiers in a Russian house, and so did the teacher. The soldiers were shot on the spot and the Russians hanged in front of the house to make others less eager to hide fugitives. I knew that we couldn't stay there. We had to get out at once, not only for our own sake but also for the sake of the teacher. I said to her:

'You'll be in trouble if they find us. Can we get to the fields from the yard?'

The teacher didn't hide her terror, which made it even more astonishing that she was reluctant to let us go.

'You can't go to the fields. Everything's covered in ice and full of bumps and holes. Even a Russian who knows his way couldn't go there now. You've got to hide here somehow till the coast is clear.' She looked round helplessly. 'If only I knew how and where.'

Finally the burglar decided that we should hide in the classroom behind the piles of wood. There wasn't much point in this, because if they were to search the house, the classroom would follow immediately after the living space. But we had to do something, if only to prove to ourselves that we weren't completely passive.

In the windows of the classroom there was no glass left. The wind blew in with equal force from both sides, and through the musty smell of the damp wood the cold felt even more solid than it had done in the forest during the night. We lay down flat behind the piles of wood, pretending rather than seriously trying to hide, because we knew it was madness to hope that the gendarmes wouldn't find us if they came in with their torches.

Soon we heard the slow and steady rhythm of footsteps typical of a patrol hell-bent on doing its worst, followed by the arrogant, merciless knocking on the doors, which reverberates wherever fascism reigns, draining the blood from the faces of any decent people huddled, with their beliefs, desires and fears, behind them. Now they were inside the house. An immeasurably long time passed. Our eardrums stretched to breaking point, we listened without hope: what was going on, what were they saying? A door opened—a German spoke in a rough, insolent, almost jovial voice. Now they were deciding which way to go: back to the street or into the yard—to us? For a few moments they just stood there. Then they left.

After a quarter of an hour—a quarter of an hour as long as this whole miserable life—the teacher's frightened shadow fell across the snow in the yard, and she called softly through the window:

'You can come in.'

We slipped back into the house, bent double to cast as small a shadow as possible. The teacher was paler than the moon. Her flat chest heaved as she told us that the men had been German field gendarmes, looking for fugitives, particularly Germans. It had been lucky that she could speak German. Fed up with having received nothing but a '*ne ponemaiu*'* and a shrug from the many Russians they had tried to interrogate along their route all day, they had been downright grateful for her German words and had immediately become less suspicious. So they had just looked round briefly, warmed themselves by the fire, glanced at the family photos, asked a few mechanical questions, and almost politely taken their leave.

'That was a close shave,' I said, with a deep sigh of relief. 'But now they'll be coming every hour. We can't stay any longer. The woodshed's no good, and you can't hide us anywhere else, can you?'

The teacher insisted. 'You'd better stay till we think of something. At least till morning.'

'In the morning they'll be even more likely to catch us. With

* I don't understand.

159

the moonlight it's already as bright as day, but by morning the road'll be full of Hungarians and Germans into the bargain.'

We stood helpless and silent. It was again the burglar who spoke:

'Wait. I'm going to take a deco out there.'

As he went out his face showed both anxiety and pleasure— the excitement of pulling the skeleton key out in the dark.

A few minutes later he returned to report:

'The village is quite empty. The troops aren't here yet and the gendarmes have gone on to the next village, towards the front line. The coast is clear. If we go right now we'll be able to reach the road without any problems. If we meet someone on the road we aren't fugitives, we've only been left behind . . . Or we tell them some fairy tale about escaping from a prisoner-of-war camp. They can't hurt us if they see us looking for our company.'

For a while we continued to discuss our options, but in the end all we could do was to set out for where we thought the company was. In short, Friedländer, we were going to 'escape back', just as the red-haired Grosz escaped back here to the ghetto yesterday afternoon. I'll never forget the moment we stepped out into the moonlight. We looked around us with our hearts beating, as if we were running away from slavery and afraid of being stopped before we could reach freedom. Only we were escaping back *into* slavery, and what we were afraid of was that we might get caught before we could make our plan to return to slavery seem plausible and our desire to return to slavery look sincere. We hoped that if we met any gendarmes or Hungarian soldiers as we were making our way on the open road towards Novgorod-Seversky, where the troops were being reassembled, they would somehow believe that these Jews hadn't wanted to escape but had been left behind through no fault of their own, like any upright Aryan soldier separated from his scattered unit. They would certainly beat us up, but perhaps they wouldn't kill us, unless they happened to be in the mood for killing. On the other hand, if they had seen us stealing out of the house they would have immediately realised that we had been try-ing to lie low till the Russians arrived, in order to betray the fatherland.

After a brief good-bye we were out in the dead, burnt-out street. As soon as we'd left the black, snow-capped posts and the dead windmill at the edge of the village behind, the cross-wind began to tear at us, as if the steppe had concentrated all its rage on the road. I had never before felt such a razor-sharp wind on my face. I almost expected to see strips of bloody flesh dropping before my feet. I had never felt as cold as I did under that cruel white moon that made the landscape seem like a whole province of China devastated by yellow fever, with not a soul left alive. I couldn't bear it any longer—even a field gendarme would have been better. I wished I had given up the ghost in the teacher's yard. There's nothing heroic about such a longing for death to release one from physical pain. One is seized by a final impatience: I've had enough, and that's that. Enough of the cold, of the unsalted cold potatoes, of the pile of dirt that is now my body, of the latrine freezing to my backside. I'm no longer prepared to let the lice chew my cold body till it's on fire—I can't scratch myself, I can't tear all the junk off me, my sweater, my winter shirt, my summer shirt, my vest. Everything's swarming with lice and the only way to get rid of them would be to burn the whole heap of rags, with me inside. I can't open any buttons with my mittens on, and if I take the mittens off, my frozen fingers, spread out, point towards the sky—ten frozen fingers pointing to the moon! If the nine suitcases hadn't arrived at the Gare Pajol in Paris at the last moment I might now be in Lisbon, bored with my life, with the endless war, with the contradictory reports of the enemy news agencies, with the confinement, with the rotten boarding-house food. I would be dreading the weekend when the rent would be due and I wouldn't have the money. I would be hating Salazar's pious lies and his secret police, the dirty, stupid locals, and the unbearable heat. I would be arguing all night with my wife about whose fault it was that we were at this dead end, stranded in this boarding house. I might be desperately unhappy—after all, I've been unhappy often enough in Paris, Venice, even on the Orient Express, not to mention Budapest. If we had made it to America I might hate myself—and the whole world—for begging cents from acquaintances in cafés, for not working, or for doing some work that was beneath me. But—I—wouldn't—be—itching—like—this—without—being—able—to—scratch—myself!

'I'm not going one step further,' I yelled. 'Leave me here,' I bawled at the burglar and the barber. 'Leave me here, damn it! Go on!'

'What's the matter?'

'I can't bear this itching! I can't bear it! I can't bear it!'

'All right,' the burglar said. 'We'll scratch you. Where does it itch worst?'

'Everywhere. On my back, on my stomach. In my shoes.'

Yes, the most hellish thing was that the lice had installed themselves in my ragged woollen toe-rag and my tattered socks, and I couldn't even push my finger in because I hadn't taken my shoes off for days and the leather had frozen to my skin. The barber and the burglar, pretending to scratch me by rubbing and kneading me with their gloved hands, kept pushing me along the road. And I sobbed like a child.

Then a truck approached. The imminent danger distracted me from my obsession with the lice.

We always used to scuttle off the road when we heard a car from afar—these people drove out here as if they didn't give a hoot for the life of a pedestrian, or even their own. We would have done the same now, but the road was bounded by a deep ditch full of snow. So we stood on the edge of the ditch, facing the road, as if we were prepared for anything. On the distant truck a red cross glinted in the sunshine, but this didn't put our minds at rest—we had seen more than enough of the cruelty of doctors. About a hundred steps away the truck braked and skidded to a halt in front of us. The driver called down imperiously:

'Get in. Come on.'

We would rather have continued on foot, but in response to the brusque command we climbed into the tarpaulin-covered truck.

We had no idea what they might do to us—help three comrades stumbling on the road, or deliver three Jewish stragglers to the gendarmes? Inside the truck two pince-nez flashed from a pair of grey, fur-collared German car-coats. One of the soldiers was fair, plump and youthful: he couldn't have been more than twenty-five or thirty. The other was older and more sallow-faced. They wore red-cross armbands and red-cross badges in their buttonholes. We didn't expect anything good from them—our experience of doctors had been about as bad as our experience of priests. We sat down at the end of the bench as far away from them as possible and, huddled together in silence, waited to see what they might decide to do. From our yellow armbands they could of course tell immediately that we were Jews. Perhaps they'd taken pity on us because they hadn't noticed them from the speeding truck. But now that they had discovered them they might do anything if they got angry, even push us off the truck at full speed. Such things had happened before.

'Do any of you speak German?' the older man asked.

'I do,' I said.

'Where have you come from?'

'From Seredina-Buda. We got left behind.'

There was a short pause.

'You're cold, aren't you?'

'Very,' the burglar said.

'Do you want some rum?' The older man offered me the flask.

I drank and passed the flask to the others.

'Where's your company?' he asked.

'We don't know. We were scattered near Chernovskoye. We came through the forest.'

Again the German was silent. He took a mouthful from the flask. Then the younger one spoke.

'Are you workers back home?'

'Yes, he's a barber and the other's a plumber.'

'But you're an old guy. How old are you?'

'Forty-five.'

'Did you serve in the first war?'

'I did.'

'What rank were you?'

'A lieutenant.'

That surprised him.

'And what do you do at home?' he asked more curiously.

At first I was going to say that I was also a worker, but every time I found myself facing intellectuals in a similar situation I was tempted to try and make them feel the shame that I would have felt if things had been the other way round, with me in a superior position meeting a fellow-intellectual who had been outrageously humiliated and thrown into the most beastly slavery. This had often been a mistake, particularly with Hungarian intellectuals, who weren't at all ashamed but delighted in my appalling plight, more than any resentful proletarian, any envious pauper, could have done at the sight of a VIP's distress. On one occasion, for example, a hospital consultant, shaking with laughter, took a picture of me as I was digging a grave, and by way of farewell shouted down at me from above: 'Well, Mr Editor, this picture's going to appear in *Tolnai*.* People will love it in Budapest.' In Krasicka, where we met a battalion from Budapest, the young officers from the capital ordered the sergeant to pull me out of the company. They stood around me as Lance-Corporal Bota, like a horse trainer in a circus, made me run in circles as fast as I could, while he hit my head with his rifle butt. They wouldn't even let me go to one side to relieve myself. They were all young graduates but they had no sense of shame or solidarity, and when they left towards evening, having become bored with the performance, even the brutal guard felt moved to spit after them at they went. And yet, in spite of all my experiences with such intellectuals, I let slip:

'I'm a writer and journalist.'

They stopped talking and abruptly turned away from me. Then, in an embarrassed and extremely friendly manner, they began to question the barber and the burglar about their lives at home. Using a familiar mode of address, they asked them about all kinds of trivialities, just for the sake of talking and not having to talk to me. Eventually the older man once more offered me the flask, asking in a formal style whether I would like another drink. I thanked him and drank. From then on they always spoke to me in the same formal style, and although they kept up their harsh and soldierly Prussian tone they did so mainly in order to hide their embarrassment and perhaps their sense of shame.

Eventually the younger man got to the point. He asked what

* Popular Hungarian magazine of the period.

kinds of things I'd written. Yes, novels too. And had anything I'd written been published in German? Yes, some time ago, by Erich Reiss publishers. The conversation developed in short bursts. In between, they talked to each other, but they kept coming back to me with questions. The younger one in particular couldn't stop. 'Literature is stagnating everywhere, isn't it? It's stagnating in our country,' he said, 'but in an experimental age like the present that's understandable.'

What could I answer? That in England, America, and wherever else humanity still remembered itself, it wasn't stagnating? I tried to give a cautious reply.

'The older generation is still holding on,' I said.

'Is there any literature in America?'

'Yes, there is,' I replied quietly. 'There is some.'

Then the older man said unexpectedly: 'And there must even be science.'

We continued our journey in silence for about a quarter of an hour. Then the younger man spoke again:

'Tell me, is Remarque* in America?'

'I'm not sure,' I answered. 'I haven't kept up with him. I must admit I don't think he's a significant writer.'

'But', the younger man insisted, 'the way he describes war is astoundingly true. I only realise now, after fourteen months out here, how true every word of it is. At home the book isn't available. I got hold of it by chance before the war. Do you know, I didn't believe that such things could be true.'

I didn't say anything. Were they trying to trap me after all? On the other hand, could they be bothered to trap and hand over a Hungarian Jew? They wouldn't even get a commendation for that. All the same, I didn't dare to make any remarks or express an opinion on the war itself. And the young German was once more silent, as if he sensed that it would be tactless of him to extract an admission from me that would place me at their mercy.

The older man offered us some biscuits, and they chatted again

* Erich Maria Remarque (1898–1970), German writer, most famous for his novel *All Quiet on the Western Front* (1929).

to the barber and the burglar. At midday we reached the bridge over the Desna, opposite Novgorod–Seversky.

On the hill stood a cathedral with a dome, like that of Esztergom back home, surrounded by palaces that looked like monasteries. But what interested us more was a chain of German and Hungarian gendarmes in front of the ramp leading to the wooden bridge. Here was the net, or rather the noose, because all those who had been scattered during the retreat had to cross the one bridge that led from this sector of the front line to the other river bank. The river had been frozen since November and it would have been possible to steal across the ice, but on the near bank there was a guard at every twenty steps, and on the far bank there were men with machine guns watching. You can imagine, Friedländer, how a Jewish straggler felt when he reached the Desna bridge, with German and Hungarian gendarmes awaiting him. Other stragglers were also questioned, and if they were unable to prove where they had spent the time since they were separated from their units, they were handed over to court-martial. But at least they weren't immediately beaten up. We would first be kicked till we were half dead, and only then would the official part begin.

Twenty-four

The German truck stopped at the bridgehead. For some tense minutes we wondered whether or not they would hand us over to the gendarmes. They didn't. The gendarmes couldn't be bothered to take a closer look at a medical truck, and within a few seconds we were on the other bank. We could have got off as soon as we were there, because people would have thought that any soldiers moving about freely on this bank would already have been been checked and allowed through by the gendarmes. I was about to thank the German doctors for bringing us this far, so that we could go and look as quickly as possible for our company, where we would now really have been safest. But I didn't say anything because I had vowed a hundred times since I arrived in the Ukraine that I'd never interfere with the chances that shaped my fate and never 'take up position', as they say in the army. So we travelled on with the doctors across the whole town, till the truck stopped in front of a two-storey building.

'Well, this is it,' the younger German said. 'If you like, you can stay here for the night and have a rest. Then you can look for your unit tomorrow.'

The big building was a German military hospital. Before the war it had been a school. The warm corridors, smelling of hospital and food, were teeming with soldiers, wounded men hobbling on crutches and blonde German nurses flitting to and fro. Nobody took any notice of us as we walked up to the second floor behind the two doctors. They led us to the end of the corridor, where there was an empty room with one window. The centrally heated room was warm and the floor was covered with fresh straw. Along the corridor we had been joined by an elderly German soldier. He turned on the light, as it was becoming dark.

'Delouse these men and give them a bath and clean under-wear. They're staying till tomorrow morning and then they'll be moving on. *Die Leute sind meine Freunde*.'*

The medical orderly stood to attention, but gave us a sly wink. Then the two doctors left. We didn't feel comfortable, Friedländer. This was too good to be true. We were afraid that things going suddenly so well for us could only mean that they would end badly. Of course it would be nice to have a bath and get rid of the lice. But what then? What if a German beast, an SS man or field gendarme, came through the door and found us? And what was going to happen in the morning? How could we get out of the building without a *Schein*?† We knew that the Germans were demanding *Scheine* everywhere.

The old man returned.

'Get undressed, quick, there in the corner. I'll take your clothes to be boiled and then we're off to the baths, at the double.'

We undressed in the corner in silence. At last I could kick the toe-rags and socks off my feet and tear off the mass of junk that was setting my whole body on fire. We looked diabolical, Friedländer. Our bodies were one single louse bite.

Even the old German was surprised. Snapping his fingers, he said: 'You really are full of lice. I've never seen anything like it.'

Then we set off along the corridor to the baths. Round the corner a door led into the 'Douchebad'.‡ As he opened it the old German whispered into my ear:

'Cover yourselves in the showers as well as you can. There's no need for the attendant to know what you are.'

The attendant was also an old, fat German medical orderly. He was sorting out towels in the semi-darkness. Our man engaged him in coversation to divert his attention from us. I don't need to tell you how wonderful the hot shower felt. Then we went back to our room naked. The old man brought us some clean underwear, a brick-shaped German loaf of bread and jam. Then he left us and locked the door from outside.

The burglar suddenly became very cheerful. He shouted with

* These people are my friends.
† pass
‡ showers

168

joy, and I tried to silence him. To make me feel less nervous, the barber forced himself to join him in the high spirits. I alone kept asking myself: what if they come through the door, what if they demand to see our papers? What are we going to tell them about how we got here? We don't even know the doctors' names. And tomorrow morning? How do we go on without any documents?

'Don't worry,' the burglar shouted cheerfully. 'The main thing is we're alive. It's all gone like a dream. We've eaten, we've had a bath, and now we're going to have a kip. Then something else will turn up, like it has up to now.'

We lay down on the straw.

The key rattled in the lock, and the old orderly came in with our disinfected clothes. Then he locked the door from inside.

'You poor devils,' he said, 'don't get up. Where are you from?'

'From Budapest.'

'I'm from Karlsbad,' he said. 'Do you know where Karlsbad is?'

'We do.'

'It used to be called Karlovy Vary. I mean in the days when we had it so bad'—and he winked with a bitter smile.

'This gentleman has been to Karlsbad,' the burglar lied, pointing to me.

'Really? Where did you stay?'

I'd never been to Karlsbad but I didn't want to give the burglar's lie away. I mentioned the name of the best-known hotel:

'At the Pupp.'

'Then you must be all right. Perhaps you've even been in my shop. The first barber's shop, at the corner to the left of the Pupp, that's mine. The smartest barber's shop in town.'

'I think I've had a shave in your shop,' I said. 'But perhaps you'll be interested to know that my comrade here's also a barber.' I pointed to little Roder.

'You're also a barber?' the old man said happily. 'Why didn't you tell me straight away? Where are you from?'

'From Budapest.'

'Have you got your own shop?'

'Yes.'

'Men and women?'

'Yes.'

'Well, I'm really glad to hear it. I'm sorry I didn't know sooner, my friend. I would have brought you some more decent nosh. I can imagine you're hungry, you poor devils. Here in the hospital there's always something to eat—but back home! It's better not to read what they're writing. Tell me, how much longer is this bloody war going to last?'

'It could last a lot longer.'

'I tell you, we in Karlsbad needed it like a hole in the head. When this thing started I immediately told people: you'll be sorry you didn't keep quiet. A world-famous spa needs peace and quiet, otherwise there won't be any guests from America, Argentina and Sweden . . . Before the war the express train ran as far as Karlsbad. People were coming from everywhere. From your part of the world, too, masses from Budapest, and Jews from Poland in silk caftans. They had sidelocks, but who cared? They paid. They brought most of the money, because many of them had stomach trouble, and the chiropody alone paid for the rent of the shop, because their feet were full of corns and bunions. Then this bust-up happened. All right, in thirty-nine we had guests from the Reich, but they're best forgotten. Our classy Karlsbad was like a Bavarian village. In my main shop there were hardly any customers all day. Only the little shop survived more or less, thanks to the Karlsbad locals. Then war broke out and I was drafted on the very first day. As a medical orderly I'm not having too bad a time. I'm always at the hospital and when people go on leave I can even give them some food to take to my people back home. But at home they're literally starving. My wife hasn't written to me how things really are at home, because she doesn't want to upset me. But I've been on leave twice, last time a year ago, and I could already see what was going on. There's no bread, no jam, no lard. All the lovely luxury hotels are military hospitals, and the boarding houses are closed. The whole of Karlsbad is bankrupt. I didn't like the Czechs either, but at least they lived and let live. They didn't do anybody any harm, and you could say what you liked. The taxes were high and they pestered you with one thing or another, but business was booming and you didn't starve to death. Now of course the women are whining the loudest, as if they hadn't been the ones that got most excited when our brothers arrived. They are our brothers and I feel German, just like you feel Jewish. There's nothing wrong with that. But under the Czechs I could also be German and my children didn't even speak Czech. And neither did I. These doctors who brought you here are also pretty sorry now. They don't say so openly, but I can feel they're sorry. The older one was a spa consultant, and was better off than anybody. He specialised in the intestines and he was the first to have a machine that washed your guts out like pants in the laundry. His surgery was full of Americans and rich Polish Jews, but he too turned wild when this business started. At least at first, when there was no controlling him. The younger one is the late spa doctor's son. His mother, if it's true, was a Jewish woman from Vienna, or at least a half-Jew. He'd gone to school in Vienna, and when the Czechs were driven out he was over the moon. Of course he couldn't know then that his practice would go to the dogs and he'd end up fighting for three years in Russia. But neither of them is really a bad guy. They treated you decently, didn't they? They told me to look after you and not let anybody in during the night.'

'Yes, they treated us very decently, really. You too. We'll never forget it. But tell us, Uncle Rauscher, how are we going to get out of here in the morning?'

'You'll be given a slip saying that you've been patients here. The doctors will see to that in the office. Write your names and unit on this piece of paper. With this you'll be able to leave the hospital and it'll also do as an ID on the road.'

I stretched out on the straw with relief. The Sudeten German barber continued:

'But the things they're doing to you!' He shook his head. 'A man like you, who has stayed at the Pupp in Karlsbad. And decent tradesmen. I've always said, Fair enough, I can understand that they're suppressing the Bolsheviks and driving out the Czechs if Germans are going to live in Karlsbad. But what does the Führer want from the Jews? I never understood what kind of problem he has with you. If he wants to make Germany great, fine. The Germans really are a great nation. They deserve to lead

Europe. But is that a reason to do these things to the Jews? Because the Jews wanted to make money? Who doesn't want to make money? I've also wanted to make money all my life. The factories were taken away from the Czechs so that the Germans made money and not the Czechs. Let everybody make money if the country profits from what they're doing. If everybody was killed for wanting to make money nobody would be left alive. Perhaps not even the Führer. He doesn't live on air either. To persecute, never mind kill, somebody for that! . . . You see that office building out there,' he pointed out of the window into the darkness with his index finger. 'There are a hundred and seventeen Jews in there. They were rounded up only three days ago. Apparently they're all that's left in the whole of Russia. They were left alive in forty-one because the patriotic Ukrainians who worked with us asked us to spare them when the Jews who'd collaborated with the Red Russians were done in. There are a lot of businessmen among them, hauliers, and a famous eye doctor—the patriarch himself had asked the general to allow the doctor to go on healing, because the people loved him and there was a lot of trachoma around here. There's no eye doctor like him in Prague or Berlin. They're all a better class of people and they were left alive because they liked the White Ukrainians and the Germans. But now, with the Russians approaching, they've also been pulled in, and I'm told by the SS that tomorrow or the day after at daybreak they'll be taken to the minefield at Pirohovka, to make sure that not one Jew's left alive by the time the Russians get here. But they were decent Jews, who liked the Germans. They've been helping us, and now they're going to be killed. If they'd spared all those clever Jews who know about business and haulage, who can rustle up merchandise even when the borders are closed and we're told in the shops and markets that everything has run out and there's not an ounce of anything left—I'm sure there would have been a lot more to eat at home and here too. And more of the raw materials, too, they're always talking about. The worst thing that would have happened would have been that the Jews made some money. Am I right?'

'Yes, you're right,' the barber agreed.

'Of course we ordinary people don't understand these things,' he continued. 'At least that's what the big shots in Berlin say. But when it's all gone wrong we'll be proved right again. A barber is told to shave and be quiet, and not to talk politics, because he'll cut the customer. But all the barber's shops in the world haven't drawn as much blood as you can see in this hospital in one hour. I wouldn't dare tell anybody else what I think. Now lie down and don't worry. I'll lock your door in case some wild boar tries to get in.'

Twenty-five

Yes, Friedländer. In the morning we walked out of the hospital gate, puffed up with pride, because we had papers, real *Scheine*, which enabled us to walk about the town legally. But if you have a regular ID, of course nobody wants to see it—they only think of questioning you if you're cheating or doing something forbidden. Every minute we met gendarmes, SS men and Hungarian officers, who didn't take the slightest notice of us. We saluted formally and courteously, and they seemed to return our salutes benevolently, as if they knew that these Jews were all right. Novgorod-Seversky is a pretty town, I'd enjoy spending a holiday there one summer. Believe it or not, it's rather like Nagyvárad—the Desna reminds me of the Kőrös river, and the long High Street, with its yellow bungalows, old trees and small front gardens, looks like Lukács György Street. Of course it was winter, the trees were bare, and the flower beds in the gardens could only be seen in outline. I also saw rose beds covered in straw—a rarity since the occupation—and at the bottom of almost every yard beehives painted red. The burglar knocked at each house in the street, begging for bread. The people were generally friendly, only in a few places were the doors slammed in his face by nationalist Ukrainians who were packing because they were sure that the Russians were on their way back and they intended to scram together with the Germans. The priests, who had been most in cahoots with the Germans, were also nervous. The Germans themselves didn't expect to hold the town and were obviously going through the routines of withdrawal— for instance, they had set fire to the haystacks at the edge of the town and these had been glowing for three days. The smell of burning in the misty air reminded me of sweet caramel in a confectioner's kitchen. It filled my nose and turned my stomach.

In any case I was feeling queasy, probably because I'd too greedily devoured the canned beef the barber of Karlsbad had given us for breakfast. The amount of meat he had given each of us would have been the ration for ten men in the company, not to mention the pumpkin jam and three mess tins full of cocoa boiled in water each of us had drunk. I immediately knew that I had upset my stomach, although the barber and the burglar, who had stuffed themselves no less thoroughly, didn't turn a hair. We also had ample provisions for the journey: three whole loaves of bread, a large can of meat and two cans of fish—all by courtesy of the medical orderly—but the burglar went on begging in every house and collecting anything edible. There was such a lot that we didn't know where to put it, and our knapsacks were getting heavier and heavier. By now the burglar was begging out of habit—in this war armed soldiers looted, while we forced labourers begged, most of the time from people who had already been looted by the soldiers.

We called at various offices to enquire about our company. The German field gendarmes knew nothing. At the Hungarian town command we were told that the company had probably been taken back to the other bank of the river because—as a sergeant with a terrifying moustache told us with fervent optimism—we were advancing again till we were blue in the face. But we couldn't get any accurate directions here either, and when we asked where we should go the sergeant told us to look for the collection point for Jews in the town, where we would receive further orders. We didn't like this idea and kept on wandering through the town with our German *Scheine* in our pockets. Late in the afternoon we bumped into a corporal who had been working as a postman at the divisional command in Seredina-Buda, and he told us that the company might be somewhere in the region of Orlovka, seventy-five kilometres west of the town. Seventy-five kilometres is a three-day walk. Evening was falling, and we didn't feel like starting. So we had to look for some accommodation for yet another night. We wished we were still in the German hospital.

At the outskirts of the town the peasants' houses were scattered, with great distances between them, as if they had been in

175

the country. Most were uninhabited. We asked to be put up in two of them, but the doors were shut in our faces by old, suspicious, lonely women, and we were followed for a long time by dogs baring their teeth. It had become completely dark. All we could do was hide in a half-burnt-down barn. I can't recall exactly how we got to the barn because I was shaking with cold and my stomach ached dreadfully. I do know that I had a hellish night, and the barber and burglar lay on top of me to keep me warm with their bodies. And I also remember lying in the morning on a stack of wood in a windmill with one sail missing. There was a lot of slush everywhere because, just as the snow and frost had arrived within minutes on 12 November, during that night it had suddenly started thawing. So I was lying on a stack of wood in a windmill, and as I was lying there I could see the road with the snow water running along it.

Then I saw some trucks with the mud squirting high up in the air behind them, and a convoy of sledges floundering in the mud where the snow had melted underneath them. Right in front of the windmill somebody shot a horse that had broken its leg. By the way, Friedländer, I've never told you how much horse blood we had waded through. Then a long procession of people arrived, covered in mud up to their ears, Germans on motor-bikes, followed by men, women and children with white bundles on their backs. Such processions were an everyday sight. That was how captive Russian civilians travelled when they were taken with their families to wherever there was suddenly some work to do, and that was in fact how almost everybody travelled along the roads. Transports were the normal human condition— every move, for better or worse, took place in transports.

Anybody on his own was suspect and defenceless. This transport that I saw through my fever shuffled along in the mud, unsuspecting and carefree. The people were chatting, adjusting each other's bundles if they had slipped, smoking pipes or cigarettes rolled in newspaper, and some were swinging bags made of oilcloth, like those carried by doctors. Yes, it was those bags that reminded me through my fever that one of the people transported here was the famous eye specialist the Germans had allowed to live at the request of the White Ukrainians, even though he was a Jew—the eye specialist who had been unsurpassed either in Prague or in Berlin.

The rear of the procession was brought up by more muddy Germans on motor-bikes. Then came muddy German and Hungarian soldiers. Then, herded along by Jewish labour servicemen, came countless unruly, kicking horses with scabies. Their hairless skins and revolting sores made me feel sick. I vomited up everything I had eaten, and fainted.

From then on I only regained consciousness from time to time. My companions later told me that about nine o'clock they had heard a series of mines exploding. Perhaps the barber of Karlsbad had told the truth and the hundred and seventeen Jews who had sided with the Germans and Ukrainians had been taken to the minefield. But mines could in any case be heard exploding here at any moment. Of course, we never managed to find out what had happened to them, Friedländer. But my companions had heard the explosions from the direction of Pirohovka, the village where the medical orderly had said the Germans were going to kill the Jews who were still alive after two years in occupied Russia.

I only know from hearsay what happened after this. In the German hospital the typhus had already been inside me and in the barn it had broken loose with full force. In the windmill I had been delirious. It was a special miracle, Friedländer, that I didn't give up the ghost on that road.

Twenty-six

Later, when we had rejoined the company, the barber told me what had happened. First I lay in that windmill for two days. The barber and the burglar, stopping every vehicle on the road, asked the drivers to give me a lift so that I could continue my journey, or at least be taken back to the town. But neither the Hungarians nor the Germans were prepared to help me—they either wanted this Jew to die or were afraid of the typhus. The kind chaps were trying desperately, while racking their brains what to do. Eventually the burglar decided to go back to the town to ask the medical orderly from Karlsbad for help. On the third morning he left and I remained behind with the barber. The poor bloke hadn't slept for two nights and at daybreak he was overcome by tiredness. When he awoke with a start half an hour later he discovered to his horror that I had gone. He rushed out of the windmill, but couldn't see me anywhere. Eventually he found me lying on the road with my face in the mud. That's a typical symptom of typhus, Friedländer, the 'getaway', the break-out into the open: the unconscious patient is suddenly mobilised and thrown out of his bed by his fever as if he had been hit by the shock wave of an exploding bomb. When the barber found me I was almost entirely covered by the melting snow and must have regained some consciousness thanks to the icy water, because I said to him:

'Listen, Tibi. Listen to all these beetles buzzing. Big green beetles humming "*ne boisa*".'

'*Ne boisa*' is Russian for 'don't be afraid'. I don't remember knowing that before I had this fever. Perhaps somebody walking past had addressed me in Russian and it had stuck in my ear. I wasn't afraid. I had never been so brave. I felt very much at home in the mud. I protested when the barber pulled and pushed me, so that I would at least be lying with my face up. The poor little man couldn't lift me. He just squatted next to me, sunk in the mud up to his knees. Eventually, with a huge effort, he managed to turn me. He placed a large rock under my head and begged me to try to get to my feet. But I neither could nor wanted to get to my feet. Finally, in his helplessness and misery, he burst into tears.

By now it was evening, and this time there were some clouds. We had every chance of being squashed by a truck, as there was no moonlight. But since dusk no vehicles had come that way because soldiers driving on their own were afraid of the partisans. After a very long time a sledge drawn by three horses approached, faintly lit by an oil lamp hanging on the shaft. The melted snow and mud had hardened somewhat because the frost had returned, although it was less bitter than before. The barber stood in the middle of the road, shouting and waving his arms, and the troika stopped.

The driver was a Ukrainian *politsai.*[*] Behind him sat an elderly gentleman in an astrakhan fur hat and black winter coat, and next to the gentleman a lady with fair hair, aged between forty and fifty, in a fur coat and woollen headscarf. She was dressed like a landowner's wife back home in Hungary might be when she was being driven from her estate to the nearby railway station in winter. The barber, moaning in broken Russian, told them what the matter was with me. The gentleman in the astrakhan fur can't have been bad because he was inclined to pick me up from the mud. The militiaman dismounted to give a hand with lifting me. But the woman objected irritably:

'I won't have it. We'll all be full of lice. I'm not taking lice to the new house. You lot, what are you?'

'Hungarians.'

'Ah, Hungarians. Thieves. They steal all they can. The German commander turned you out of Grinevo because you were stealing bicycles.'

The barber tried to appeal to the Ukrainian woman's sympathy by telling her that we were Jews:

[*] Local militiaman collaborating with the Nazis.

'We're forced labourers, Jews, not Hungarians.'

'Jews too, that's all we need,' the woman screeched, and the barber saw the humanity also rapidly draining out of the man in the astrakhan fur.

'Well, if you're Jews you can just as well stay here,' he said.

The militiaman tried to put in a good word for us.

'Sir,' he said, 'let's at least take them as far as the village.'

'The devil take them,' the woman shouted, and both she and her husband urged the driver to get the horses going.

They were probably middle-class Ukrainian traitors. But the behaviour of the militiaman, who had addressed the gentleman in the astrakhan fur with the title of 'civil engineer' and who had also defected to the Germans, was very typical. You never knew whose side these characters were on, Friedländer. There was a humorous saying: by day *politsai*, by night partisan. Perhaps this coachman, who must have been a schoolboy after the revolution, suddenly remembered learning that a man should help if he sees another man dying alone on the road. All right, thousands and thousands of people were seen dying in this war: let the medical unit or the army doctors take care of them. But all the same, if you see a single individual stretched out in the mud on a road at ten o'clock on a winter's night, it's shameful and barbaric not to help him. Such thoughts may have crossed the mind of the *politsai*, because he was very reluctant to start the horses. He drove off slowly, looking back several times and shouting something. But then he loosened the reins and the tiny light of the oil lamp disappeared in the dark.

For the next hour and a half nobody came. It got colder. The barber put his coat on top of mine to prevent me freezing. Meanwhile I, of course, remained unconscious. The barber tried again to drag me to the edge of the road, but was soon exhausted. So I stayed there on the frozen mud.

Later still a peasant sledge approached. It was driven by a boy aged twelve, and an old Russian couple were dangling their feet from the sides. As soon as the barber told them about me the boy jumped down, while the old couple continued to stare into the distance indifferently, without giving me a glance or budging. The barber begged them to allow me on to the sledge. The boy, crouching down close, took a look at me and felt my head. Then he rejoined the old people, and at once a heated argument started between them. The old peasant said:

'These are deserters. If we meet any Germans they'll finish us too.'

'We aren't deserters,' the barber assured them. 'Here are our IDs.' He showed them our crumpled *Scheine*. 'We're Jewish forced labourers.'

'There are Germans in the village,' the old woman lamented. 'They've got a hospital for German horses with scabies there. If they find us they'll kill you anyway like all the Jews.'

'Don't worry about that,' the child shouted at her. 'Can't you see this man's freezing to death. He's old, too, like the pair of you.'

The old woman went on:

'Where are you going to put him? There isn't any room on the sledge. Do you want us to walk?'

'I'm going to walk,' the child answered. 'You don't think I'll leave him here on the road, do you? Grab his feet,' he said to the barber and took hold of my shoulders.

I was as heavy as a sack of salt or a dead body, and the boy of twelve didn't have the strength to lift me. So they dragged me on to the front part of the sledge. The barber and the kid followed the sledge on foot. The old couple grumbled for a while, then calmed down and nodded off. We travelled like that for three hours till daybreak, when we reached the village and a new complication arose. The old couple wouldn't let us into their house. They argued, with the old man roaring and the old woman screaming at the boy, till they agreed to compromise, allowing the boy to put me in the stable. In the stable there was a cow and the horse that had pulled us this far. I was laid on the straw and dung under the manger and the barber snuggled up to me because he was also terribly cold. He later told me that I'd opened my eyes and asked him:

'Are they home yet?'

'Who?'

'The women.'

'Where from?'

'The Terrace Restaurant.'

'What Terrace Restaurant?'

I closed my eyes without giving an answer. Later I figured out that this question must have belonged to one of two serial dreams I had had while I was suffering from typhus—or, rather, one of two daydreams. The first dream was confused and corrupt. It was probably based on the fact that I still couldn't believe that what was being done to me in the Ukraine could really be done to a man who was used to civilisation, a well-known journalist who, despite his oppositional behaviour, had maintained tacitly chivalrous relations with the authorities, and even with his opponents, which ensured a somewhat exceptional status for his occupation and his social standing. I was in the Ukraine, digging graves by day, but dining with my wife, another lady and the company commander himself at the Terrace Restaurant in the evenings. Do you know what this Terrace Restaurant might have been, Friedländer? Probably that big, brightly lit inn at Tátrafüred where the Poprád road crosses the tram lines. That was where we used to go late at night when all the other restaurants had closed. It seemed to me that I was meeting my wife here in the evenings after work. The company commander was only pretending to make me dig graves during the day because he had to, but in the evenings we were again gentlemen, wining and dining together. During the day we were merciless adversaries, but at night both of us hated this disgraceful predicament equally. The woman with fair hair might have been the company commander's wife and my wife's friend. The two women had been asked by some young men to dance, while we husbands continued our conversation, and they were having a good time. I didn't want to disturb them and left early, because I knew that I had to get up at four o'clock, in time for the roll-call at half past four and the start of the gravedigging soon after. But before I took French leave the head waiter prepared the bill and, of course, I also paid for the lady with fair hair and the company commander. Then, back at the hotel, I had woken up with a start because my wife and our female companion, 'the women', were still dancing and hadn't got back yet. Obviously this was the source of the question I asked the barber in the stable.

It was a stupid dream, but a Hungarian dream. Apparently I couldn't believe for a long time that Hungarians ever did anything that didn't involve nepotism and string pulling—that an oppositional journalist, who was called 'buddy' by József Vass,* who was invited to the soirée of the chairman of the bank together with the chief of the general staff, who was after all on first name terms with everybody in parliament, should be unable to contrive a way out of having to play this terrible game in earnest, to pick up the phone and fix things somewhere in the Ministry, so that he didn't have to stay any longer with these small-timers, these 'readers' who didn't know anybody. Even as a forced labourer I couldn't imagine not staying in a hotel while digging graves.

Do you understand, Friedländer? For us somehow things had never been as black as they now looked. That was where that stupid dream came from. It still seemed improbable that things were not only as black as they looked, but even blacker. Of course they did in fact allow some rich and well-connected people to stay at home or to go gravedigging from a hotel. But to us intellectuals they showed no mercy. They hated us even more than the rich. This is what I still don't understand—how relatively tolerantly and gently they treated those who really sponged off them and who patronised them, till the Germans arrived. But us intellectuals, who only wanted to teach them that it's possible to think and live differently, they immediately decided to send to kingdom come, so that we could no longer disturb their stupid intellectual laziness by forcing them to adopt a point of view that extended beyond their own back yard. 'I want to see people with doctorates attending to the horses,' Major Körösztös brayed when we arrived in Kiev. Not bankers, manufacturers, or even currency dealers, Friedländer, but people with doctorates. It isn't so much the Jews these people want to kill, Friedländer, but civilisation itself.

If I weren't a confirmed rationalist I'd think that my second serial dream gave me a foresight of our own situation tonight. In that dream, like now, I was lying at the end of a long row

* József Vass (1877–1930), professor of theology and Conservative Minister for Education and Culture in Budapest.

on some kind of plank bed in a hut or cave. I was dressed in white, in the *kittel*, the Jewish burial attire, but on my head I wore an Arab burnous, attached to my forehead by some kind of clip. The scenery was from the era of the great migrations, and I was in a tribal lodging, waiting in the empty room for the tribe to return. After a while the room was filled with people dressed like me. I don't know where they had come from or what they were doing. First they stood around my bed, but I don't know what they said or what they wanted from me. Then they lay down on the plank beds that were set out in a regular line, and it got dark. Sometimes I was the oldest member of the tribe, a kind of chieftain, and their respectful behaviour seemed to be addressed to my age and rank; at other times I was the youngest, and they seemed to cosset me because of my youth. In the morning we stood in line and I was always at the end. With martial steps we set out in the bleak, rocky, yellowish biblical landscape and marched faster and faster, as if we were taking our rhythm from drums or were being harried from behind. At last we reached a river. The water was hidden by the blue mist of the dawn. Without thinking, the tribe ran into the mist and disappeared without a sound. I lost my courage and stopped short on the bank, not daring to enter the mist. I turned round and hurried back home. In the empty hut or cave I lay down again on my plank bed and waited all day for the return of the people who'd disappeared in the mist . . .

I dreamt all this under the manger. The boy had covered me with a clammy horse blanket. He milked the cow and tried to pour some milk into my mouth, but I clenched my teeth in refusal and constantly asked for water. The boy gave me some water, till he noticed that it made my diarrhoea worse. The barber tried to persuade the boy to fetch some medicines by repeating 'Aspirin' and 'Ultraseptyl', till the boy ran to the horse hospital, where his sister, Marusia, worked for the Germans as a cleaner. He said that he needed the medicine for himself and was given some paste that was supposed to be good for diarrhoea. I was in a bad way, Friedländer. According to the barber I was shaking so hard that even the horse and the cow were continually listening to the chatter of my teeth.

In the morning the old woman came out to the stable several times. At first she still nagged the boy and the boy answered back. They argued about me for hours. But towards midday, still cursing under her breath, she poured a cup of *chai** into me. I was much worse again. The barber could hardly feel my pulse, and my lips had turned blue. They thought I would be finished within minutes. Now the old woman told them to take me to the kitchen. They put me down on the straw in the corner. Of course I don't remember any details. The only thing I remember is the pink nose and moist, round eyes of a small calf. The calf lived in the kitchen, because in the stable it would have frozen to death. The Russian peasants' stables were built of wood, not bricks or adobe, and only the hardened adult animals could survive the forty degrees of frost in them. The calf must have been tethered to something in the kitchen, because it kept coming towards me before it suddenly stopped, unable to reach me. As it approached, its nostrils grew huge and it stuck its bluish tongue out to within a few centimetres of my face. I wouldn't have minded if it had licked me and I even offered my face to be kissed—perhaps because I hoped that it would cool my hot skin or because I longed for some tenderness.

By the afternoon the barber saw that the boy, who was called Kolya, and the old woman were presenting a united front on my behalf against the old man, and even more against their daughter Marusia. The old man only grumbled, but Marusia raged and uttered threats. Working as a cleaner for the German soldiers who looked after the horses with scabies, she regularly brought home their laundry for the old woman to wash and iron in exchange for bread, margarine and soap. As a result Germans often came to the house, which aroused great disapproval among the Russians in the village. Four days earlier, when it had looked as if the Russian troops were about to cross the frozen Desna, the horse hospital had also received its marching orders. At that time the family had been wondering whether or not to go with the Germans. Of course the boy hadn't wanted to go, but Marusia had almost persuaded the old couple to pack.

* Russian tea

185

Now it was also the girl who tried to terrorise them into kicking us out of the kitchen. But even the old man was no longer very firmly on her side. After lunch she went off to work in the horse hospital, slamming the door behind her, muttering more threats. When the *starosta** took the boy away to clear snow for two hours, the barber was left on his own with the old couple and me. He finally managed to placate the old man by trimming his greying red beard. The old woman, for her part, had gone to the other extreme by the late afternoon: she was constantly fussing over me, applying compresses and cleaning me up.

About dinner time Kolya came back. He'd managed to get hold of some medicine that contained salicyl, and he and the barber made me take it. Then the girl arrived with a huge, dim-looking German groom. He'd come for the laundry that the old woman had been ironing all afternoon while nursing me. The girl had probably done her best to inflame him, because he let fly at the barber as soon as he set foot in the house:

'You filthy skiving Jews! I'll teach you to make yourselves at home in the house of these honest people. Get out at once!'

The barber, frightened out of his wits, begged him:

'My mate has a very bad fever, sir. Please allow him to stay at least till morning. Here are our *Scheine*, sir, we aren't desert-ers.'

'Fever or no fever. Get out at once or I'll throw you out into the street.'

The barber backed towards me as if he were trying to hide and protect me with his small, scraggy body.

'At the double,' the soldier chivvied him.

Now Kolya, the boy aged twelve, stepped between them.

'Leave him in peace, comrade. *Kaputt*. He's finished anyway.'

'If he's finished, so much the better,' the German said. 'Then let him croak out there in the ditch.'

The old woman wailed: 'Leave him alone, *pan ofiser*. He won't hurt anybody.'

'He will. He will, as long as he lives. It's because of them we're

* village chief

here. It's because of them there's a war. It's them you can thank for this war.'

The old woman continued to reason with him: 'You're even putting horses with scabies in hospital, you can't let a man die just like that.'

'They're worse than a horse with scabies. Everything's their fault. It's because of them that my home town, Barmen, has been bombed to pieces—the engine shop where I worked, the silk factory where my wife worked. If he dies there'll be one devil less in the world. Out, double quick!'

Now the old man stepped in front of him:

'Listen, *pan ofiser*. I beg your pardon, but this is my kitchen. Please, don't throw this sick man out of my kitchen. He isn't a deserter, and you can see he's on his last legs. I'm a good Christian and so is my wife. I've nothing to do with these Jews, but I don't want to be in trouble with God.'

The German soldier gave a coarse laugh and spread out his arms: 'All right, if that's how you feel. He can snuff it here in the kitchen for all I care. Marusia's asked me to throw him out. But if you don't want to, if you'd rather wait for the gendarmes . . . Well, Marusia, what do you say?'

The girl's eyes flashed. 'When you're in trouble you'll be begging these Germans to help you.'

The boy clenched his fists and seemed about to charge her. In his high-pitched voice he cursed her at such a rate that the German scarcely understood a word.

'You won't be in trouble,' he said. 'The whole village knows that you dance with them. You clean for them, at night too. And you'll be leaving with the horse hospital. But you'll . . .' he choked.

Marusia set upon the child. He head-butted her in the stomach. They tussled till the old woman, crying and clawing, separated them.

The German, with a quieter and somewhat embarrassed laugh, backed towards the door:

'All right, all right, don't squabble. A brother and sister tearing each other apart for a Jew! I'd love to squash him,' he said, lifting his foot. 'Now, old woman, give me the washing. And you, brat,

I'm not going to hurt your Jews. The devil hurt them. But if the gendarmes find them, don't come running to me. Well, Marusia, are you coming? It's nearly time for supper. They're giving us jam pie.'

The girl straightened her dishevelled hair in front of the mirror. Then she picked up the ironed laundry from the table and, walking towards the door with the soldier, continued to curse the boy in screeching staccato outbursts. Kolya sat in front of the stove on a block of wood, ready to pounce, staring at her full of hatred. The old woman stood behind the table, dabbing her eyes with the corner of her apron. The old man leaned against the window sill with his hands folded behind his back, blinking rapidly and rubbing his freshly trimmed beard.

The barber later told me that the girl hadn't come home all night. The boy and the old woman took turns sitting by me till morning. Of course the old man continued to grouse, but more faintly. Clearly he was only trying to stick to his original attitude in order to preserve his authority. At the same time he kept offering the barber *makhorkas*,* boiled potatoes and vodka. When it once more looked as if I was about to pop off he stepped closer and watched me with spontaneous compassion and frightened interest. These three were no longer just sorry for me but also prepared to face whatever the consequences of my being there might be. Luckily, the gendarmes didn't come.

Towards daybreak the remnants of a labour-service unit from Miskolc limped into the village. Their unit had been building a bridge over the upper Desna, and the sappers hadn't allowed them to pull back even when the Russians were already firing at the wooden frame of the half-finished structure. Dozens of Jews had fallen from a height of eight metres on to the frozen river and those who hadn't immediately died had frozen to the ice with fractured skulls, legs and spines. Then the sappers had scrammed and the thirty-one surviving Jews from Miskolc had dragged themselves to Novgorod-Seversky. There they were put in the charge of a lieutenant, a fifty-year-old, humane but help-

* hand-rolled cigarettes

less teacher from Abaúj county, who had lost his own company. Now they had stopped in this village for a two-hour rest during their retreat. When the barber told them that there was a sick journalist from Budapest in the peasants' house they immediately asked the lieutenant for permission to put me on one of their sledges. One of them was a former secretary of the Social Democratic Party who had once met me when I was giving a talk in Miskolc. This young man, according to the barber, carried a great deal of weight with the company commander, and from then on it was he who looked after me. Before they put me on the sledge the old woman draped me with a quilted Russian peasant's coat, which I actually brought back to Budapest. I then had to surrender it at the reception counter in the Margit Boulevard prison and I don't know what happened to it, except that I didn't get it back when I was released. The old man, still with a grim face, gave the barber two *makhorkas* as a parting gift and forced him to accept a gnarled stick to make walking easier. But at the gate he said:

'Well, I'm glad you're leaving at last.'

So we left with the sledges of the men from Miskolc. Behind the sledge that carried me the barber walked like a relative following a hearse. Kolya accompanied us as far as the end of the village. The two of them kissed as they said farewell. Kolya gave the barber his address and asked him to write after the war. The men from Miskolc didn't expect me to arrive in Orlovka alive. But when we arrived in the evening I was still breathing. Our own company was in Orlovka and the company commander was going to tie us up as a punishment for falling behind, but when he saw me in the *kolkhoz** stable where I'd been deposited, and was warned that I had typhus, he didn't dare come too close to me. Instead he gave orders for me to be taken to the medical unit's hospital.

There I was examined by an overbearing, thick-set, rude doctor with greying temples, who held the rank of an ensign. When he heard my name, he cursed violently, threw his coat down and roared for the the nurse to bring the hypodermic syringe and

* Soviet collective farm

ampoules. Then he stuck the needle into me so roughly, Friedländer, that you would have thought he was trying to kill me—but he didn't move from my side till morning. The ward of the medical unit was a large windowless hall, which could once have been the common room of the *kolkhoz* of Orlovka. The patients were lying on palliasses spread all over the floor. There was only one iron bed, with a sick sergeant on it. The barber, who had accompanied me to the hospital, told me later how the rude doctor had snapped at the sergeant:

'Climb down on one of those palliasses, sergeant. I need the bed for this man. I have to give him injections and I'm not going to keep bending down for him.'

So he gave me the only bed there was, Friedländer. At the same time he went on effing and blinding. He cursed everything, including the Jews. The sick soldiers on the palliasses couldn't understand why he stayed with me all night and, at the same time continually bared his teeth, as though he wanted to bite through my throat. Normally after seven o'clock in the evening just the nurse remained behind in the ward and the doctor only appeared if somebody was about to kick the bucket. But now he stayed with me till morning. It was already light when he left and by eleven in the morning he was back again. His name was Dr László Kovács and all I know is that in civilian life he had been a doctor in Sopron. Here the whole medical unit was scared stiff of him, and the soldiers thought that he was yelling at me because I was a Jew. Gradually they began to feel sorry for the unconscious, gravely ill patient he was treating so brutally. Even later on, when I had regained consciousness, he never had a kind word for me. When he stopped at my bed during his rounds he would always make some rude or sarcastic remark, for instance:

'Well, you pathetic cemetery case, all skin and bones! Why don't you stuff your face? Write down first-class diet for him.'

The sick soldiers didn't suspect anything. They were merely surprised to hear him constantly yell at me and then order me a first-class diet—chocolate, rice pudding and chicken— in much the same tone as the officers ordered handcuffs or chains to be put on prisoners about to be interrogated. The people down at the supplies office were also shaking their heads because the army command had expressly forbidden such things to be given to Jews in the hospitals. But I sensed, of course, that this man would do anything for me that a doctor and civilised human being could do. I guessed that there must be some earlier connection between us. He knew at once who I was and what I had been trying to achieve with all the futile and hopeless scribblings I had published for decades in newspapers and books. I was sure he also knew that I had never felt any malice towards the Hungarians when I had preached to them about freedom and culture. As he hurled his insults at me almost twice a day, the sick soldiers tried to comfort me and called him a wild boar. Even the arrogant NCOs, who applauded Hitler and explained to the men in the ward why the Jews had to be exterminated, shook their heads. They didn't approve of a hospital doctor indulging in such behaviour.

One evening three weeks later, by which time my weight had shrunk to forty-seven kilos but I had managed somehow to scramble to my feet, I staggered to the WC at the end of the corridor. As I was dragging myself back along the wall the doctor came towards me with quick, angry steps. There were only the two of us in the corridor, with the oil lamp glimmering faintly in the distance. He suddenly stopped in front of me, grabbed my hand and said with quiet fury:

'To hell with this bloody world! I'm so sorry for you. I'd love to send you home and I'm going to try, but I don't think these bastards will let me.'

He left me standing and walked on with even more ferocious steps and an even more livid face. In the ward he was roaring again: he had caught the sick sergeant and the nurse playing pontoon. And the next day he was also roaring at me, as always. But he had saved my life, Friedländer. He was a doctor from Sopron, a gentile, Dr Kovács. If I were to get out of here alive I would tell everybody that such things also happened. The milk-float driver from Tihany, that intelligent, smart, warm-hearted peasant, was also called Kovács. I was lucky with the Kovácses, Friedländer. That's why I say that things could change for the better, that someone or something could turn up by some chance, at any moment. Believe me, Friedländer, I can even imagine surviving this hell . . .

Twenty-seven

Day began to break. The clock of the Capuchins struck half past four. Friedländer rose from my mattress.

'Miracles can doubtless happen,' he said. 'But they've rarely happened since biblical times. In fact, I don't trust in miracles and I trust in this doctor even less. If they really take this first transport away today, they'll take us too. That's a fact. In any case, if we can go out to dig graves my son will come with me . . . Perhaps it'll work . . .'

Now the friendly gendarme who had slept with the girl with the long legs and the squint stomped into the room.

'Wake up, folks!'

Everybody started and those who could move sat up, blinking and confused.

The gendarme announced:

'If those people in the first transport have hidden anything with you—watches, jewellery, money, foreign currency, documents, stuff like that—put it down next to you. You'll be searched in a moment and if anything's found on you you'll go straight to the wagons.'

Perhaps somebody at the command post thought that the people who knew that they were going to be taken away on the following morning had smuggled their valuables into the hospital during the night. They had been searched a dozen times and their quarters in the ghetto had also been turned over, but they were still supposed to have hidden something. These gendarmes were really convinced that Jews had money, even under their skin.

The friendly gendarme stomped out. The ward was frightened into activity, and all those who were able jumped up from their mattresses and began to fumble and rummage as if they thought that during the night, without their noticing it, somebody had hidden something in their pillowcases or mattresses. They all but searched themselves. A young woman tore a medallion from her neck in horror—a little angel leaning with his elbows on a heart, hanging from a thin gold chain. She might have got it for her tenth birthday and worn it ever since, as naturally as her hair or nails. Now that this little light blue angel had become concealed Jewish jewellery, she tore it from her neck so convulsively that she choked. Then she threw it far away into the corner where the brooms were kept, leaning against the wall. Others searched their pockets in case some 'national property' had been left there, frantically tearing up letters, slips of paper and even used tram tickets. When they had finished searching themselves they searched the mattresses of their neighbours and of the patients who lay helpless and dying. In the corner taken up by the people from the poorhouse one mattress was occupied by the head waiter of a night club, an incredibly thin, unpleasant and cantankerous fellow with a loud mouth. He had actually hidden three hundred-pengő notes on his person. After fiddling with them uncertainly for a while, he suddenly sneaked up to the mattress of Uncle Krausz, the paint merchant who had died during the night, and slipped them into the pocket of the dead man's nightshirt. A lawyer, whose mattress was close by, noticed this and called out:

'Attention, everybody, a corpse has been desecrated. Head waiter Jenő has hidden some money in Uncle Krausz's pocket.'

'So what?' the head waiter defended himself. 'They won't hurt a dead man if they find it on him. But they'll beat me to death.'

'This dead man was honest all his life,' the lawyer, who had once held some public position in the town, retorted. 'He never did anything illegal. And you . . .'

The ward split into two factions. One faction fell for the rhetoric of the lawyer and abused the head waiter for cheating even here. The other faction tried to silence the lawyer, arguing that people had the right to use any possible trick to defend themselves against these gendarmes. The discussion was about to degenerate into a theoretical argument but came to a sudden halt, when the door was thrown wide open and three detectives in civilian clothes—who had been torturing the healthy inmates for hidden valuables to the sound of the gramophone in the empty brewery—strode in. With them came Dr Németi, as pale as death.

'Now, folks,' the tallest of the detectives shouted. 'Out of bed! Sit down in a row, there in the corner. The whole gang of malingerers!'

Those who could padded to the corner on their bare feet, pushing and shoving in their eagerness to obey.

'Hey, why don't those over there get a move on?'

'They can't move, sir,' Dr Németi said. 'They're dying. Some are dead.'

'Dead! I don't believe you Jews, alive or dead.'

But they didn't go to check the dead. They turned to the living, the group of men, women and children in their scanty underwear gathered against the wall, dirty with neglect, revoltingly ugly with sleeplessness and disfiguring fear, and yet infernally comic—puffed-up and flabby old women, old men with hernias and paunches, cruelly illuminated by the glare of the rising sun. I would never have believed that the philistines of George Grosz,* whom I had loathed with such heartfelt laughter, would reduce me to fits of crying if I met them face to face. I stuffed my fist into my mouth to stop myself howling. And, shaken by sobs, I stood among them, hating myself more than the gendarmes—because I was such an abject coward who didn't even shout at or spit into the faces of these impudent torturers when they said things like:

'Listen, Grandma. Nobody's interested in your thing. Cover yourself. Are you trying to seduce me even here?'

And so on. For minutes they lashed the women with their brutal and filthy jokes in order to squeeze the last drop of enjoyment out of their obscenity before the search began. Then we men were ordered to turn towards the wall. The women, old and young, were herded into the smaller room next door to the ward, where the wonder-rabbi from Wisznice once used to don his robe in order to conduct the divine service. There the naked

* German satirical cartoonist (1893–1959).

bodies of the women were searched by an expert midwife brought in from Budapest. Cries and wails of shame and revulsion broke against the door. Then women of seventy, ashen-faced and looking a thousand years old, dragged themselves out, and young girls with blood-red faces and black circles round their bewildered eyes came running as if they were trying to run out of the world. We men just stared at the wall of the wonder-rabbi's synagogue, and I went on chewing my fists so that nobody could hear me sob—while the others didn't even clench their fists but dangled their hands with trembling fingers.

With us they finished quickly. They made us pull our pants down, laughed coarsely and spat at our feet. Then it was the turn of the mattresses. They poked around with knives tied to sticks, and if they became suspicious they slashed a pillowcase or a mattress cover open. They pulled the blankets off the dying and, with expressions of disgust, prodded them with their sticks like piles of dirt. They kicked the dead half-heartedly with their lace-up boots, and when none woke up they walked on. Finally they found something: near the Ark of the Covenant one of them picked up a discarded wedding ring.

'Who does this ring belong to?' he roared. 'The owner must answer at once.'

Nobody answered.

'If the owner doesn't answer, the whole lot of you will be going to the wagons in five minutes.'

'Please, Mr Secretary, it may not belong to any of the patients,' Dr Németi stammered. 'There have also been visitors here. I guarantee that none of the patients was wearing a wedding ring.'

'Don't you guarantee anything,' the detective blustered. 'You've never drawn an honest breath in your life, even if you are a doctor.'

'Believe me, Mr Secretary . . .'

Of course they didn't take us to the wagons, because the transport wouldn't have been reorganised for the sake of 'Mr Secretary'. These gendarmerie detectives liked high-flown titles. In Soroksár, for instance, they had to be called 'Chief'. Here the gendarmerie NCOs in civilian clothes had opted for the rank of 'Secretary', although their whole exterior made it glaringly obvious that they were upstart peasant lads, gone mad with the intoxication of unlimited power and unlimited opportunities for robbery, trying to seem like gentlemen. They all had unwholesome-looking faces, not necessarily from birth, but probably because they hadn't got to bed before morning ever since the start of this carnival of cannibals. They were drinking themselves to death with booze obtained for nothing or paid for with unrecorded money stolen from the 'national property'. They certainly also womanised for all they were worth, and may in addition have been worn out by the pleasure of the cruelties they committed in the torture rooms. There was no spark of humanity left in their eyes, but they had sideburns like the bailiff or sheriff back home in the villages of their childhood, and moustaches that were not like Hitler's but dense and silky like those of the hero in trashy Hungarian films. One could tell that their looted civilian clothes hadn't been tailored for them; their ties were garish, they had thick stolen rings on their fingers and plundered watches on their wrists, and some wore white gloves. They synchronised their bestial behaviour and their crude rural dialect with gestures that they imagined to be those of an army officer or civil servant, but they copied these classy movements so clumsily that, far from being elegant, they recalled the repulsive mincing of homosexuals.

It took the 'secretaries' three-quarters of an hour to search the mattresses. They did their work thoroughly, and even found the little angel that had been thrown among the brooms. Triumphantly, they waved the angel wriggling on its chain while, salivating with conviction, they expatiated on the baseness of the Jews, who tried to rob the fatherland even here, even in hospital, even when they were dead. Then they departed with their booty, and the men, women and children lay back down on their mattresses as if they wanted to die on the spot. A few minutes later Dr Németi returned. Nine people had died during the night, and he had them taken to the morgue. When the old paint merchant was lifted onto the stretcher the head waiter sneaked up to him as swiftly as an arrow and stole the three hundred pengős back from the pocket of his nightshirt. The lawyer once more accused him of desecrating the dead, but nobody was listening. Somebody stuck his head round the door and announced in a sonorous voice that yesterday's gravediggers were to line up in front of the morgue. Thank God, Friedländer would now be able to go out with his son . . .

It was a quarter past six in the morning.

Twenty-eight

Like an orchestra testing its instruments before a performance, the railwaymen made the thirty cattle wagons wail a few times after the night's silence. The engine gave the thirty wagons a shove and under the unoiled wartime wheels the worn-out, rusty rails resounded like vibrating strings. This sound effect was as characteristic of the whole event as the shrieks of vultures are of a battlefield or the howls of jackals are of the desert. Now the train was pushed a few metres further—possibly this wasn't even necessary and the railwaymen had only done it out of professional self-importance and the urge to show off and draw more attention to their contribution. The men in uniform were constantly competing with each other, and although here, as everywhere, soldiers and gendarmes took precedence over railwaymen, the railwaymen wanted to show that they too were on hand and needed for this patriotic deed. So they whistled, waved their flags and shunted. And finally the wagons were almost exactly where they had been before.

I watched it all from a small chamber smelling of onions in the synagogue of the wonder-rabbi of Wisznice. In the wall of the chamber there was a window like an embrasure, where Dr Németi, with his teeth chattering, made me join him—in my nightwear—to watch the first group being deported. From the window we could see and hear everything clearly. I felt like an outside observer, indifferent and almost without emotion. This state of mind—in which one is, as it were, merely a spectator, or voyeur, not only of unimaginable horrors unfolding in front of one's eyes, but even of improbable events and sufferings undergone by oneself—had become familiar to me in the Ukraine. It is no brutish apathy or callousness, but rather an inability to believe that what is happening is really happening. If one encounters varieties and degrees of horror that go beyond any possible horrors known or imagined so far, one can only suffer but not really experience them. For instance if, having believed in monsters with seven heads in one's childhood, one meets a monster with seven heads in a cave as an adult, one is meeting an impossible thing that, as a child, one nevertheless expected to exist. But this wasn't happening in fairy tales, nor in the stories of Edgar Allan Poe, E.T.A. Hoffmann or Erckmann-Chatrian, nor in films about Frankenstein, nor in past history. Yet, since it was nevertheless happening, one was inclined to regard oneself as a hallucinating madman rather than believe that there was an actual world in which these hallucinations had become reality.

So I was standing at the window, the embrasure, like a man who doesn't believe any of it—at times I didn't even believe that the wall, rendered with a mixture of plaster and glass splinters, that I was scratching was a real wall and the blood pouring from my finger as a result was my own blood, although my pyjamas were already covered in it. The nail of my index finger had been almost torn off, but I just let the blood pour out, like somebody who hasn't noticed that the cork has fallen out of the bottle, and goes on letting the liquid escape. It didn't hurt at all. And neither did it hurt that a hundred paces from me the gendarmes, jeering and bellowing, were corralling these people—who were carrying white bundles and wearing dark clothes—with rifle butts, bludgeons and boot tips, herding them into a knot and raising the dust like drovers chasing cattle along the road to the market or slaughterhouse in a heatwave. At the same time, these people with their white bundles and dark clothes seemed to have a lot in common with my nightmare of the previous winter: I had either seen them or dreamt of them while I was lying on the frozen brushwood in the windmill, walking past me like this, with white bundles and dark clothes, men, women and children, the last one hundred and seventeen Jews left in Russia under the Germans, who might have been on their way to the mine-field at that very moment. Those Russian Jews, plodding along the wintry Russian road, had been as apathetic or unaware as the Jews of Nagyvárad, now stumbling towards the thirty wailing wagons with the gendarmes chivvying them from behind. Except that now I suspect it's neither apathy nor unawareness. Again people are not only unable to believe that what is happening is happening to them, but are even unable to believe in their own identity. The disease that splits the personality in two is called schizophrenia, and for some minutes I feel, as they probably do, too, that I, watching them, can't be I, and they, shuffling towards the wagons and about to let themselves be crammed into them, are not even the other halves of their own personalities, but third parties, strangers. That's precisely why they don't comprehend any of it and don't even feel hurt or frightened. Dimly, they just observe these strangers disguised as themselves and suffering this impossibility. 'He's the one walking next to me with my wife and child, between the rails, with his bundle on his back,' the fruit importer registers with a vacant gape when he notices his family shuffling along beside him. And when he looks into the vacant eyes of his wife and child, he doesn't believe that they are real—yes, they too are masks, their own third persons . . . because their real ones must be at home . . . the wife in the kitchen giving instructions to the maid . . . the child gone to the English lesson because it's Thursday . . . That's how it has always been—even though the fruit importer had been taken to the Ukraine in 1942 for forced labour. Yet even then his wife and child weren't harassed by anybody, anybody in office. A nice artillery officer was billeted in their apartment, and he liked the child. How can it be that now, in a place at the edge of the town where his wife and child have probably never been before, they are trudging towards the wagons with their bundles on their backs?

Is it possible that the mayor, the police captain and that nice polite stationmaster know and approve of all this? In the years before the war the stationmaster would always ring up oblig- ingly when merchandise came from Turkey or Italy: 'Mr Kürsch- ner, the wagon has arrived. With perishable goods we don't stand on formalities. You can unload at once.' Of course, the station- master was given oranges and lemons and, each time during the few months when bananas were also allowed into the country, a bunch of bananas for his children. And, of course, at New Year the stationmaster also got some money, five hundred pengős. The police captain was a different kettle of fish, an austere man, who wouldn't accept money. But his wife was a customer at the shop. She paid, although only symbolically. 'At cost price,' as they said to each other with a wink. He practically gave it to her as a present, practically free of charge. And now, could this be possible?

True, the monstrous gendarmerie colonel from foreign parts is standing there with his officers. And the small German officer with the monocle has just arrived, looking like a Premonstratensian priest–teacher, except for the continuous twitch in his right cheek. He looks as if he were laughing, but then, when the twitch stops, his face becomes frightening, like the face of a bull mastiff. Now he joins the group. The gentlemen straighten and flush a little: they have great respect for the German and may even be afraid of him. Flushed, excited and smiling, one after the other, they introduce themselves and shake hands with him. Then they start chatting—certainly not about what is happening and what is about to happen here—cheerfully getting to know each other while having a male gossip, like gentlemen meeting for the first time before a hunt. They chat, first perhaps about the previous night's entertainment, then perhaps about women, and later perhaps about the improving military situation or the V1, which will be followed by other miracle weapons. They rock briskly on their feet, ingratiating themselves with each other. The stationmaster is particularly lively, gesturing like a staff officer and talking a lot. He comes from a Swabian region and his German is good, while that of the others is rudimentary. They stand there, with their backs turned on the Jews, the wagons and the whole affair, like those supercilious men in their black ties in the 'stag line' at a ball, who are not dancing and are trying to look as if they despise the merriment. The gendarmes, on the other hand, grow more rabid the more they feel neglected and unappreciated for what they are doing in this godforsaken heat to these godless Jews.

This German officer is an SS officer—yes, we've heard of him, he is the expert. He has 'ghettoised' the whole of Poland and Holland and he has been sending the instructions, the 'recipes', to the Hungarians. This small man with the monocle and the twitching face is the most famous and fastest German 'deporter'. He is always sent to where wagons and time are scarce and Jews copious. Somebody has told me that the Jews of Slovakia were deported to Poland in record time through his system and under his supervision. He is an *Obersturmbannführer*,[*] but must be called *Herr Doktor*, because, like the gendarmerie detectives who are fond of being addressed as 'Mr Secretary', he is fond of a nice civilian title.

The gendarmerie colonel had retired into the shade with his senior and junior officers for a brief conference. Now he rejoined the group and, wiping his forehead with his handkerchief, shouted in bad German:

'*Herr Doktor, wir können anfangen.*'[†]

The monocle in Dr Seidl's eye twinkled with boyish glee. Then, with a sharp military turn, he faced towards the Jews with the bundles and asked:

'Is the rabbi here?'

From the loose ranks, with obliging promptness, a thin, reddish-blond young man of about thirty appeared. He was not the kind of rabbi Dr Seidl had expected. He had counted on finding an older rabbi, who would have been more venerable, but with his sidelocks and caftan a more suitable target for his humour. This rabbi, on the other hand, looked rather like a commercial traveller, a pharmacist's assistant or a student-teacher. At first Dr Seidl seemed nonplussed. He wasn't satisfied with the rabbi and, weighing him up slowly, didn't find him particularly suited to the performance. Still—a rabbi was a rabbi. Now that he was there they might as well start.

'You—have you ever seen a rabbi crawling on his backside?'

'No, I haven't,' the rabbi answered in a sonorous priestly voice, firmly returning the German's stare.

The German turned bright red with angry surprise. The rabbi stood as straight as a soldier. The German was clearly furious because he didn't know how to make this thin young man with

[*] SS equivalent of lieutenant-colonel.
[†] Doctor, we can begin.

the blurred face and magnificently correct posture look ridiculous. I could feel that the rabbi's courage was the studied toughness of a man who—from school books, literature and biblical examples—had already worked out in his mind the role he was going to play in such a situation: the role of a priest who would accept any suffering and humiliation for the sake of his faith. There was a note of fear in the slightly built young man's sonorous voice, but the role supported him like a crutch and saved him from caving in. 'I must show this butcher, and I must also show my congregation,' he might have impressed upon himself. He had only recently become the rabbi of the progressive section of Jews who had abandoned the faith and had no particular respect for priests, whom they regarded as being employed by the parish for the sole purpose of reciting the prayers twice a year, when tradition brought them to the synagogue for the high festivals. So he also wanted to pass a test in front of his parishioners, although he knew that in particular the intellectuals among them were more interested in materialist philosophy, psychoanalysis, politics and literature than in religion.

The German officer naturally believed that he would be able to humiliate the whole Jewish crowd most deeply through the rabbi: if he kicked the rabbi it would hurt everybody as much as it would hurt Catholics if he kicked the bishop. But now, when he had almost raised his foot in its lace-up boot to kick the rabbi, what little sense of proportion he had made him sense at the last moment that he wouldn't create much of an effect if he saw this skinny fellow off with his boot. If he had been old, dignified and paunchy, the gentlemen would have laughed their heads off seeing him crawl in the dust on his backside. But this fellow wasn't wearing the right mask and costume, and his skinny backside didn't present a good target for the point of his boot. Like an actor from the capital making a guest appearance in the provinces when there was no suitable partner in the local ensemble to let him show off the gimmicks that had proved effective in Budapest, he simplified his original plan for the production: instead of kicking the rabbi, he grabbed him by his lapels and shook him, yelling in time:

'*Rabbinerchen*!* You'll be responsible if any one of these people becomes stroppy. Do you understand, *Rabbinerchen*? If anyone disobeys he dies, and you with him.'

He shook him like a dog shakes a rat. The rabbi's pale face moved up and down in time, his hair stood on end and fell back on to his forehead, his tie ripped and his buttons snapped off. And the German still kept shaking him.

The Hungarian gentlemen, standing in a group, watched the spectacle, responding to it in different ways. The gendarmerie officers showed their support and solidarity through hearty laughter. The mayor grinned, but with some embarrassment—only a few weeks ago this young man had been the priest of a religious denomination that was to some extent tolerated, and with whom he, as head of the town, had been obliged to maintain formal, albeit more and more distant, relations. Indeed, two years earlier, on Horthy's birthday, he had had to appear in the synagogue as the town's representative and, with his top hat on his head, listen to that same priest reciting the prayer for the head of state. The police captain watched the scene with the expression of a pedantic official, who is not responsible for the matter in hand, but who doesn't disapprove of what is going on. The stationmaster bore himself like a humorous old gentleman full of sympathy for the young, who, while himself sober, has been caught up at night in tipsy company playing all kinds of 'tricks' and will join in the fun, shaking his head in mock consternation: 'I say, aren't these kids a caution?—All right then, lads, enjoy yourselves, enjoy yourselves.'

When the children of the Jews with the white bundles saw the German shake the rabbi up and down, some started to cry and others to giggle. Why shouldn't the little ones giggle? After all, they had only seen such things in the cinema when slapstick films were shown, or in the circus when the director with the gold buttons taught the clown a lesson. The men and women with the bundles hushed the children, especially the gigglers, whom they squeezed or pinched to make them cry instead. I held my breath and probably they did too, desperately hoping

* Little rabbi

that the little rabbi would see his part through without breaking down or bursting into tears—which he seemed pretty close to doing, to judge from the grimace that was beginning to appear round his mouth. At these final moments all of us who had been submissively lying low in this ghetto from the start expected the rabbi—whom none of us respected very much—to save the whole community's manhood, to win this duel, as if his winning it would make a difference.

It made no difference, but the rabbi won. The German, sensing his defeat, suddenly stopped shaking the rabbi and struck him in the chest with his fist, making him stagger back three or four paces. But the rabbi refused to fall and continued to stand his ground.

'Go to hell,' the German panted. 'But remember what I told you! And you lot remember too!' he screamed at the Jews with the bundles.

Two gendarmes, grabbing the rabbi by the arms, frogmarched him away furiously, like a criminal caught in the act. Before shoving him back into his place next to his squealing wife and babbling four-month-old child, they rolled him over several times in the dust. His priestly dark suit turned grey, his neck-high waistcoat fell open and his face was covered in sweat. One of the gendarmes continued to harass him for a while, shoving his wailing wife with the child on her arm out of the way, so that the people standing next to her with their bundles had to stop her falling.

The SS officer, who had been so cheerful on his arrival, had visibly lost his good mood over this fiasco. He felt as uncomfortable about looking his audience in the eye as an actor who feels that everything has gone wrong that day. He had wanted to show these Hungarian gentlemen what stunts he was able to offer, what fun such a patriotic act could become under his magic guidance. In Warsaw, Bratislava, Vienna and Amsterdam it had probably worked, but here and now nothing had gone well. He hadn't been able to use this rabbi to make them laugh as he had used other rabbis, or even to impress his own superiority on the people with the bundles. To hide his embarrassment and anger, he switched from his earlier good-humoured, urbane conversation to the stiff, official tones of a soldier. Now he alone was talking, in a grating voice and short, sharp sentences, while the others stood in front of him rigidly, gravely, occasionally nodding in unison. The *Besprechung*[*] lasted twenty minutes. Then the gendarmerie colonel, stepping out of the group with his officers, summoned the district's staff sergeants and staff sergeant-majors. After receiving the colonel's orders, the staff sergeants with their Hitler moustaches and the staff sergeant-majors with their ceremonial-coach driver's moustaches saluted and spread out at the double in front of the untidy crowd of Jews standing with their bundles. Having marshalled them into a straight line, the sergeants started counting. Each time they had counted seventy-five they separated the 'contingents' by inserting a gap of three paces between them. When they had finished they reported back to the gendarmerie colonel.

The gendarmerie colonel roared:

'All aboard!'

The staff sergeants passed the message on:

'All aboard!'

The lower ranks amplified:

'All aboard, you goddam stinking Jews, haven't you heard?'

Now the chain of gendarmes unfolded, forming a living fence between the Jews and the wooden one of the ghetto, beyond which lay the town.

And just as if the guard had called out 'All aboard' at Nagyvárad station a minute or two before the departure of the Budapest express, these men and women with their bundles charged the wagons, pushing and shoving desperately, as though they were absolutely determined not to be left behind because they had to go on an urgent journey that brooked no delay, or because they didn't care where the train was taking them if only they could escape the plague, or the war, at the last moment. Of course the reason they were pushing and shoving and hating each other was that they wanted to grab the best possible places— near the window, the door, the water or the bucket—or that families, friends or contemporaries wanted to remain together.

[*] consultation

Men were dragging their wives, mothers were fighting, holding their children in front of them, and from the hubbub whole shrieking, screeching, frightened sentences could be heard: 'Jancsika, where are you?' 'Gerber family, over here!' 'Don't leave Grandpa behind!' and so on. The gendarmes, who had been prepared to force the Jews into the wagons, stood behind them with their hands on their hips, watching in motionless amazement as they filled the wagons of their own accord. Only ten or twelve clumsy ones were left behind. They too jostled and struggled to get in, awkwardly and feebly, but the stronger ones pushed them back. Then the gendarmes fell upon them, kicking and punching them in the stomach and beating them about the head with their rifle butts. And when the poor souls had almost managed to scramble up, there were objections from above.

'There's no room left here, sergeant-major, sir,' somebody called down.

'No room?' the gendarme hissed. 'We'll see if there's no room! Move closer together, you swine, or I'll come up and make room!'

Above, the terrified crowd drew closer together, and the flabby mass swallowed the stragglers one by one. Those who had half wriggled in and were still half hanging out of the wagon were squeezed in by the gendarme like raw meat into a grinder. Here and there arms and legs sawed the air as if they didn't belong to any bodies. Then these waving limbs also disappeared. At the same time there was a chaotic din. 'Just like a synagogue,' the gendarmerie colonel sneered, but gradually the people calmed down. All this had taken barely a quarter of an hour. It was thirty-two degrees in the shade, and the sun, instead of standing still or darkening, was calmly climbing and sending out more and more fiery heat. Then the staff sergeants pushed the doors of the wagons shut. For a few minutes there was such silence that everybody in these mobile coffins with the German notices painted on them seemed to have died. But when they realised that the coffin had been closed on them, the two thousand seeming-dead suddenly began to shout in chorus:

'Water! Water!'

They must have shouted many other things—cursed, prayed,

argued, wept—but this 'Water, water!' was the only phrase that could be heard right to the end, clearly and at almost regular intervals. The thirty wagons, as if directed by a conductor, chanted simultaneously, in unison and in time:

'Water! Water!'

Although only a quarter of an hour had passed since the doors were closed on them, those who happened to be near the water canister had probably drunk its contents within minutes. The sun had never shone hotter. The shunting-engine ambled up and down between the station and the ghetto, but the war had already started to cause stoppages on the tracks: any strategically un-important cargo could wait, the proper engines were needed for something else, for the front line. I had already experienced this when we were being taken to Russia for forced labour: in Katowice we had had to wait two days for an engine, and in Bahmach four days. But we had at least been allowed to get out and use the latrines, in groups under guard. In the mornings we had sometimes even been allowed to wash if there happened to be no German or Hungarian soldiers at the water pipes. And, although we had had to be economical with our money, at the larger stations we had sometimes been able to buy water . . .

'Water! Water!'

Oh, this standstill. It was as if they had dragged themselves across a thousand bloody, excrement-laden, epidemic-infested, crumbling, hungry and filthy kilometres of the New Europe before being forgotten on a siding in distant foreign parts—rather than in the town where they had been born and to which they had always returned—until an engine with some time to spare arrived, ready to take them to the gas chamber, or until the planes came to bomb them.

I am standing at the embrasure with the doctor, listening to the chorus:

'Water! Water!'

The gentlemen, led by the SS officer and the gendarmerie colonel, officiously strut past the thirty wagons. The gendarmerie colonel stops at almost every wagon and tugs at the lead seal or padlock, in order to test them personally. I stand at the embra-sure with the doctor, watching these gentlemen check and complete their work with the seriousness and thoroughness of professionals, with satisfaction and with unmistakable pride. We stand there and watch hands reaching out through the barbed wire barring the wagon windows, fingers both old and young, well groomed and rough, jerking and gesticulating senselessly, like the torn-off legs of a spider. It seems as if they are trying to explain something or to clutch at an imaginary straw thrown to them by their homeland, or by Europe, at the last moment— or at a lifebelt thrown to them by Christianity from the tall towers with the gilt crosses and stars that dominate this town. As I stand there watching with the doctor, a gendarme seizes the butt of his rifle in both fists and, at the very moment when the gentlemen are testing the lead seal on the wagon, with all his strength strikes a blow at an old woman's wriggling hand, which suddenly droops, like fruit about to drop from the branch.

At this point the numb, dazed doctor suddenly says in his normal expert's voice:

'He's broken her wrist.'

We stand there, watching and failing to understand. Did they really get aboard? Why, for the love of God, did they get aboard? Why didn't they turn round, why didn't they run away as far as they could, through the wooden fence, into the town beyond, into the forest? Why didn't they kill, or die, first? They got aboard simply because they had been told to. The magnificent Dr Sebestyén and my other friends, the companions of my youth, my sympathetic and unsympathetic acquaintances, the lovers I have deserted and the lovers who have betrayed me—all the earnest, industrious, clever citizens, intellectuals and workers, all the jokers and spivs—are they all in there behind the sealed doors?

And will I get aboard in five days as they did, dragging my wife with me?

'Water! Water!'

No, there's no voice I know in the chorus. I listen, in case I hear a familiar one, but I've never heard such voices in Nagyvárad or anywhere else. Not even in the war. In Paris the lepers' chorus in a mystery play had chanted in similar tones. I think the play was by Claudel. In those days such a highly stylised, inhuman wailing seemed very alien to me.

'Water! Water!'

About midday the proper engine finally arrived, but it too shunted for about half an hour. When the train was coupled to it, the chorus suddenly grew softer. The people had probably begun to feel more optimistic because something was happening and the standstill, the interim, had ended. The engine immediately gathered speed, as if it had a special pleasure in taking this cargo away—or as if it was afraid that at the last moment an order cancelling the whole affair might come. It was therefore just as well to hurry.

In the smoke, dust and sunshine the train disappeared towards the Rhédey Garden. We gazed after it through the embrasure long after we could see nothing but the dust raised alongside the empty rails, where two thousand Jews with white bundles had been herded together in the morning. Then we saw the gentlemen get into their cars and the gendarmes march away towards the brewery, where the gramophone had been playing all the time.

I was startled by Dr Németi grasping my hand: 'But you're covered in blood! Come along, I'll dress your wound. You could catch some infection.'

He took me to the small operating room—where everything was in disarray, derelict and grubby—to take care of my finger, from which the nail had completely broken off. Somewhere he found some used greyish gauze and cotton wool and bandaged my wound.

Twenty-nine

For lunch they brought us grated pumpkin boiled in water. The NCO from the municipal catering department, an old man with a walrus moustache and lupus rash, whose job it was to escort the Jews detailed to carry the heavy metal containers at mealtimes, seemed to have been somewhat shaken by the loading of the wagons. Perhaps that was why he tried to cheer us up and make amends, as he shouted into the ward in an encouraging voice:

'Here's some yummy, delicious pumpkin, folks! An extra large portion! Today everyone gets a ladle and a half!'

No wonder the ration had increased. Today two thousand people fewer were eating lunch in the ghetto. Even before now, people hadn't eaten a lot, or rather, had eaten so mechanically, so absent-mindedly, so casually that I for one still can't remember what, if anything, I ate. But that lunchtime hardly anybody touched the food or even stirred on the mattresses in response to the NCO's invitation. Only a few greedy old people from the poorhouse and the lunatics, who had good appetites and were always hungry, pulled themselves up and fell upon the deserted, unsupervised containers. They devoured the pumpkin with spoons and hands, pushing each other out of the way and arguing. Within minutes, the revolting bitter smell of the pumpkin had drowned all the other bad smells of the ward. The old people and lunatics were soon wading through the vegetable, which had spilled out of the tilted containers and spread between the mattresses. Even their hair was smeared with it, because they stuck their heads into the containers to get the titbits.

Meanwhile we could constantly hear Lili Marlene, Fatia Negra and all the crackling patriotic, sentimental records. The gramophone had continued to play day and night in the brewery, where the 'secretaries' were 'working' incessantly. It had even played during the loading of the wagons, as if a theatre director were trying to intensify his effects by playing music offstage. Now the people due to leave on tomorrow's transport were being questioned, to make sure that none of them were taken away in the wagons without having confessed under torture where they had hidden their money, their wedding rings, their children's bicycles, their fountain pens, their wristwatches, their grandmother's winter coat with the fur collar—in short, the 'national property'.

The euphoria awakened in me earlier in the morning by the gynaecologist's typhus plan had evaporated. This time it was not replaced by the apathetic state in which I had contemplated the events last night, with indifference not only to life but to death as well. My numbing, schizophrenic detachment from myself and from reality had also ended, and now everything had not only become possible but was true. All the people and all the things—including myself—had again become identical with themselves. As I lay breathing together with the heavily breathing ward, in which hardly any raised voices had been heard since the departure of the thirty wagons, I was blaming myself desperately, impatiently, almost angrily for allowing things to come to this pass, for thinking of anybody other than myself. On 19 March, for instance, that Sunday afternoon when I received a phone call warning me that the Germans had arrived and were already in Budapest, I didn't immediately make myself scarce and go underground with forged documents or slip across the Romanian border, which was just round the corner, but hid and lay low in my apartment. Sometimes I slept in the cellar, at other times in the laboratory of the pharmacy. I wouldn't budge an inch and kept telling myself and everybody I spoke to that I wasn't going to leave my family. From the very first moment, these unfortunate people, my wife's parents and even my wife, had been asking, almost begging, me to flee. They kept saying that I was in greater danger than they. After all, who cared about an insignificant Nagyvárad pharmacist, my father-in-law said, spreading his arms. They were ordinary, humdrum middle-class people, their fate would be the same as that of the other Jews.

'But you, so many of them hate you, because you've written

against them . . . They almost did for you at the front. They aren't glad that you came back from Russia alive.'

My mother-in-law also kept telling me to go, and I must admit I would have liked to. On one occasion, when Jews wearing the yellow stars were still allowed to work in their shops, a young lieutenant who had just arrived from Budapest leaned across the counter in the pharmacy and told my father-in-law in a low voice that he had come to fetch me. He had a small card with the password that I had agreed with my friends: 'Ego sum via'.* My father-in-law ran across to the apartment where I was hiding, waving the card and demanding that I let the lieutenant take me to a safe place in the evening. I knew that he wanted to take me to a castle in Transdanubia that seemed relatively safe. My wife had even packed the basic necessities for me—but I wouldn't go. 'No,' I said to the old man. 'Who do you think I am? I'm not going to leave my wife and family *now*.'

Of course there was just as much genuine affection as vain and determined posturing behind this. I loved these good and loyal people, but I must admit that it was ultimately the compulsive pose that stopped me leaving them. The *shohet*† Gottlieb, a friend of the family who had come here as a refugee from Chernovits twenty years ago, had more experience of the end of the world than any of us. Every day since the German invasion he had been giving us his expert opinion that the only way to make a successful escape was on one's own. Whoever wasn't a Jew nowadays was a detective, and people fleeing in groups, with families, were conspicuous and inevitably gave themselves away. The children and mothers forgot themselves—and that was that! Of course, he explained, there must be an agreed safe place where everybody would meet at the end. But I didn't go even the second time round, when my friends in Budapest sent the front-office manager of the Pannonia Hotel—a member of some resistance movement, who was bringing me forged documents in the name of a waiter called Ferenc Pattermann, born in Sarajevo—to fetch me.

* I am the way.
† Kosher ritual butcher

214

'Not unless they send papers for all of us. The whole family,' I said, playing for effect in front of the family, and sent the manager back to Budapest.

They admired my loyalty, and I was inwardly ashamed of being less than sincere. I alone knew, and suffered pangs of conscience because of that knowledge, that my manly behaviour drew its strength at least as much from play-acting, and from the pressure of the moral imperative that was still automatically operating in me, as it did from my love for my wife and my attachment to my family. Not one day passed without my father-in-law trying to persuade me:

'Look,' he explained, 'it'll also be better for us if you leave. If the Gestapo or the political police come and find you here, we ordinary Jews will also become political criminals. And then it'll be even harder.'

I wouldn't go. 'How can I go when my wife is lying here ill, with a fresh wound after her operation?' I protested. And when Dr Gottlieb got hold of documents for us in the name of Samu Hirschler and wife—because I wanted to shed my own notorious name and be an ordinary, humdrum Jew—I embarked on the most banal petty-bourgeois adventure, hiding with my illegal documents in the house of my wife's family and finally in the hospital inside the ghetto.

I still say that I should have gone, even on my own. I ask myself: what good have I done them by staying with them? Now we are all in the ghetto, and the family, in the third section of the ghetto, will be put into the wagons the day after tomorrow, and we in five days' time. What's the point of having been together to the end, and still being together, without being able to help each other? And now I must even be ashamed of being so helpless in front of the family. At the front line my troubles were always made more bearable by the thought that they couldn't see how powerless and helpless I was. I can't help my wife by getting into the wagon together with her. Even if she doesn't die of her open wound within hours, as the doctor promises, can I protect her from being beaten up, never mind from death? I've seen the Germans beating the women in the Ukraine. Yes, we should all have run in every direction as far as we could see. The nine suitcases pushed and pulled us home from Paris because we didn't have enough presence of mind and enough nonchalance to throw away all that junk. Now the family is here. Now the family has dragged us into this ghetto. And it's dragging us in further. Into the wagon. Water! Water!— and then the gas . . . we ought to have broken free and shaken each other off as soon as all the social and moral bonds came undone around us.

And yet. If somebody now came to my bed and told me that he would save me on my own, would I at least have enough courage to stop lying? To admit that I would be prepared to go on my own?

But I am already answering my imaginary rescuer, in a loud voice, with my head held high, like a bad actor in a bad play in which every word is made of paper: 'How, pray, do you think I could leave my sick wife behind? . . . And the old people? . . . And the child? . . .'

Do I love my wife? Of course, I love her very much. During the nineteen months I spent as a forced labourer in Russia she did so much for me that she almost became a byword among the forced labourer's wives. The cattle wagons had hardly left Vác with the Jewish company into which I had been shoved as a punishment, when she took on the whole military and political gang who had, on their own admission, sent me out to Russia with a written order to the effect that it was 'undesirable from a Christian national point of view' that I should ever return home. She didn't give my personal and political friends one moment's peace, pestering them, knocking on their doors at daybreak, phoning them at midnight. With her relentless harassment she managed to keep my fate permanently in the minds of people who had lost interest in me as soon as I was gone from the town where I had had so many followers. In the winter cold she stood in front of the station, stopping every soldier on leave to ask if he had seen me somewhere, spoken to me, or at least heard something about me. She went around with the mistress of the Prime Minister, and she gave her winter coat to the wife of the labour unit's guard, having invited her to dinner. She pushed her way into offices with notices on the door

216

forbidding Jews to enter. By some trick she got as far as the chief of the general staff, and, banging the table, told him to his face that some of his officers were murderers. Finally, her tears, her harassing tactics, her bullying brought me home—I had her to thank for my life, if that was anything to give thanks for.

But if I now ask myself whether it was because I loved her or was grateful to her that I refused to leave her, then I must answer: no, not primarily because of that, but rather because of the moral terror, because a man doesn't, and can't, leave his wife in danger, particularly if she's ill. In earlier days, if I read something like this in a novel, I was bored and threw the book away, or if I heard something of the kind in the Abbazia Café, where the philistine regulars used to deliver themselves of such maxims, I pulled a face of indulgent mockery. A man doesn't leave his wife—what does that mean? Has nobody ever left his wife? Has nobody ever killed his wife? What about those husbands on the *Titanic* who kicked their wives off the ladders hanging from the side of the sinking ocean liner, in order to get into the lifeboats first? Yes, those men hadn't had time to assume the pose, their survival instinct acted instantaneously—they didn't care what their wives, drowning and sinking in the icy water, thought of them, or what society would think of them for the rest of their lives for kicking women into the sea, so that they themselves would live. What if they are blushing with shame? What if they are walking among their fellow-men with their ears burning and their necks drawn in between their shoulders? They are alive!

Fair enough, if there's no time for lying—but a decent man can't deliberately abandon the pose of human dignity and social propriety.

I brushed this painful, embarrassing sincerity aside and, driven by shame and guilt, decided to take some kind of action, to do something. For the moment, the most important thing was to find a way of bringing my wife's parents and her young daughter by her first marriage to the hospital before they were taken away from the third section of the ghetto early on the day after tomorrow, when the third transport was due to leave. If we had to go, we should at least all go in the same wagon. When Dr

Németi looked into the ward for a few moments in the afternoon, I asked him to try and smuggle the family into the hospital. The doctor didn't hold out much hope. He said that it would be difficult, if not impossible. The different sections of the ghetto were now completely isolated. The gendarmes weren't letting anybody out into the streets, and the Jewish doctors were no longer allowed to admit patients to the hospital: only the army medical officer was entitled to do so, in serious or infectious cases, in other words, if there was hope of the patient dying. But he would try, Dr Németi promised. One of his patients was a gendarme who had caught gonorrhea in the town and didn't dare to see the medical officer, because people with venereal diseases were punished. Dr Németi was treating him in secret. He was a peasant boy, but from the north, where he had gone to a Czechoslovak school, and he was doing his job half-heartedly and nervously, because he didn't like what was going on. Dr Németi would have a word with him, he might have an idea. This pathetic plan was our last resort, but if it worked, the family would at least be together in misfortune. I asked Dr Németi to have a word with my wife upstairs and to cheer her up a bit by telling her that we'd all be together soon.

Till late afternoon nothing happened, apart from an air raid that only lasted ten minutes, although the bombing in the distance could be heard for three-quarters of an hour. My neighbour shared his 'information' with me in a whisper:

'They're certainly bombing the train with our people. It's better for them than dying of thirst. Anything's better than the wagon.'

Towards evening more Jews beaten half to death were brought from the brewery on stretchers. By this time the only way of getting into the hospital was through the brewery, if people had been tortured so badly that the medical officer diagnosed them as being beyond help. Now the town's richest Jew was being taken off the stretcher. He was a lawyer, a banker, a hotelier, a brick manufacturer and the owner of almost every building with more than one storey in Nagyvárad. He was seventy-five and, with his gold pince-nez, looked like a scholar, perhaps an old professor of sociology in the University of Heidelberg who had married a rich banker's daughter in his youth, or a Swiss *Nationalrat** from a small town in which, nonetheless, the whole world gathers, for conferences or for the winter and summer season.

This man was the most merciless money-grubber and usurer, the most notorious villain in the town. Although he belonged to the conservative upper middle class, he hobnobbed with receivers of stolen goods on back staircases. There was hardly any depositor in the town whose money wasn't embezzled by his bank, or any debtor who wasn't threatened by him with having his possessions auctioned, down to the last shirt. And his rapaciousness hadn't simply made him a great fortune, but had also given him a unique prestige in the town. People hated him, but admired and envied his unfailing unscrupulousness, shame-lessness and resourcefulness. A bad man, but what a well-mannered and talented man, they would say, and the millionaire was elected chairman wherever a chairman was needed, from the religious congregation down to the sports club. They admired in him what they themselves would have liked to do but couldn't or didn't dare to do—or if they did do it, far from having similar success, usually burnt their fingers or were completely ruined. This man had been a widower for ten years, and his elder brother, who—as if in a novel by Dickens—was his opposite, a really good man, had committed suicide after losing all his savings in his bank. He had driven his two sons out of his house and had neither spoken to them for years nor given them a penny.

When he heard on the afternoon of 19 March that the Germans were in Budapest, he wrapped up his gold, his currency and his securities, and buried them somewhere, without letting anybody in on the secret. He had an old cook, who had worked for him for thirty years and whom he had trained to be as wicked as himself, but even she didn't know anything. When the 'secretaries' arrived from Budapest to beat the 'national property' out of the Jews of Nagyvárad, he was of course the first to be taken to the brewery. Initially they treated him almost politely, because the fame of his wealth had even spread to the capital, and these

* Member of parliament

men with the sideburns had the same involuntary respect for the master of millions as they had for the Jewish tenant living in the castle in their village. When he refused to say anything they started beating him. They beat him more cruelly than any of the others, gave him electric shocks, parched him with salted herrings, and tied heavy weights to his testicles.

After the beatings in the brewery everybody else, without exception, confessed, or at least admitted to something, but from this man they were unable to extort a penny. He vomited blood and pissed blood, but he didn't say a word. He was a clever man, who understood fascism and knew all about the German camps. He knew that he couldn't survive this, and even if he did by some chance survive it, he wouldn't survive the wagon, and if he survived the wagon, he knew what fate awaited the old people at the wagons' destinations. But they didn't make any headway with him. He knew that the hidden fortune would be of no use to anybody because nobody would find it. It would be of no use to the nation, or even to his own sons. Because this very wicked, very smart man had hidden everything so well that it would remain underground for fifty years, until a labourer found it while digging or blasting a drain. But rather than confessing, he let himself be beaten to shreds inside and out—his fingers broken, his nails burnt off with glowing metal rods—and those who had seen him in the brewery told me that he didn't for one moment let go of the discipline, the subtle arrogance, the good manners and the civility that had characterised his most sordid business negotiations. He derived this unique strength from his belief in the sanctity of private property, as a martyr does from a sacred or noble ideal. As he was lying on the mattress, which turned more red by the minute with the blood pouring from every part of his body, his eyes were open and he kept his bloody, swollen mouth firmly shut even when he was un-conscious, lest he should reveal in his delirium where he had hidden his fortune. And by morning, with his eyes open and his mouth clenched shut, he was dead.

Thirty

About seven o'clock Friedländer returned from the cemetery. Yesterday he had told me how he had buried one of his two sons, now he reported how he had got the other to escape. They were escorted again by the pensive, concerned, grey-haired gendarme from Somogy. From almost imperceptible signs—the looks and reflexes of the passers-by, the listlessness of their revulsion and abuse—Friedländer felt as if the town's hostility had diminished since the previous day. Perhaps the people were shocked to see the sudden reality of what they had vociferously but irresponsibly demanded for years: that the Jews be taken away. Many of them probably hadn't wanted it to happen just like that. Perhaps, at the twelfth hour, they were horrified by the enormity of the deportation which was now staring them in the face so starkly that even they recognised it, or perhaps they were slowly awakening to the danger that things might not turn out exactly as they had calculated. The majority of the town would have liked the present situation to be made permanent: we'll let the Jews stay behind the fence, we'll take everything away from them, we won't let them work, promenade, sit in cafés and interfere with our business—but let's not kill them unnecessarily or take them to some unknown place where they might be lost for ever. Somebody might call us to account one day, and if these Jews were to remain in the ghetto we would always be able to say that it was the only way we could save them from the Germans. These Jews are really soft, forgiving, or indolent. If they regain their freedom they'll be delighted to go back to their empty houses. Perhaps most of them won't even demand anything back, they'll be glad to be alive, and, tough and clever as they are, within six months their houses will again be full of furniture and silver.

This might have been roughly how the philistines of Nagyvárad would have liked to settle the whole business and—like a criminal speculating at the moment of committing the crime how he would defend himself if he were caught—they were pondering what they would say if, in spite of everything, the Germans were beaten, the Russians crossed the Carpathians, the invasion of the British and Americans really materialised, and the western or eastern enemy arrived, grabbed them by the collar, stood them on the doorsteps of the many thousand houses and apartments and asked them: 'Hey, Hungarians, where are the residents? Where did you put the people who should be living here according to the list of tenants or the land register?'

The town was nervous, depressed, downcast, Friedländer told me. But it could have just been the result of some bad news of the war: perhaps Budapest had been bombed more viciously than ever, or in the east another large railway junction had fallen. We in the ghetto hadn't seen a newspaper for days and didn't know anything about the front. The last thing we had heard from the eastern front was that the Russians had reached the Gyimes pass.* In Italy the British and Americans were still south of Rome. And nobody was talking about an invasion any more.

'Invasion!' Friedländer said disparagingly. 'According to the gendarme who doesn't like the Germans, the British radio says it's been cancelled. In the west the British and Americans only want to fight in the air now. It'll take longer, but they aren't in a hurry.'

But at least Friedländer's son got away. The professional gravediggers did not have to be rounded up from the inn, but were already waiting for them in the cemetery, and dug the graves in their place—everything was like yesterday. As soon as they had got there, Friedländer told the gendarme that he wanted his son to escape. The gendarme walked away without answering. A quarter of an hour or so later he returned, called Friedländer to one side and asked him:

'Has he got anywhere to go?'

* In the eastern Carpathians.

Friedländer said that he wanted the lad to escape across the border but was afraid of letting him go on the off-chance. He had some close friends in the town he would like to talk to first. He also knew the Romanian consul well, he explained. It would be necessary to contact his friends.

'If you like you can go into the town,' the gendarme said. 'But people probably know you. You could send one of these gravediggers with a message.'

Friedländer gave Uncle Kukucska, the oldest gravedigger, the addresses of his three close Aryan friends. Uncle Kukucska came back about noon, slightly drunk. At the house of one of the friends he had rung the bell in vain; nobody seemed to be at home. At the second house the people had got very nervous when he told them why he had come, and pretended that they had never heard of Friedländer. The third close friend had bundled him out impatiently, saying that he would come out or send somebody in the afternoon. In the afternoon an errand boy arrived on a bicycle, left a food parcel and something to smoke, and turned back at once.

Meanwhile the gendarme had asked several times: 'Well, is there any news?'

'No, nothing,' Friedländer said miserably.

While the gravedigging continued, the gendarme strolled up and down between the cemetery and the road, as he had done on the previous day. On the road the traffic was also as it had been before: army trucks, peasant carts, a few cars, soldiers on bicycles and bombed-out civilians. About half past three a gypsy caravan, consisting of three carts covered with tarpaulins, approached from the town. The gendarme, positioning himself in the middle of the road, raised his hand imperiously, and the carts stopped close together. Large, shiny, frightened, sly gypsy eyes peered from under the tarpaulins. Friedländer could hear the gendarme snap at them:

'Which of you is the chief?'

An old gypsy, two metres tall, with greasy black hair down to his shoulders, a grey beard and gold earrings, stuck out his head and at once jumped off the cart:

'Sergeant, sir,' the old gypsy said, 'we are tinkers and we've got permits. I was a Honvéd* corporal in the first war. You can search us, we haven't got anything.'

'Follow me, chief,' the gendarme growled at him, starting to walk towards the cemetery gate.

The chief followed him, bowed and pale. He couldn't imagine what this gendarme with the bayonet on his rifle wanted to do with him under the trees of the cemetery. The way things were these days, he might easily make him dig his own grave and bump him off without more ado.

Halfway between the cemetery gate and the new grave the gendarme stopped and started quietly negotiating with the chief. The chief's face showed an embarrassed amazement. He couldn't understand that the gendarme was not only not going to hurt him, but was actually asking him, a gypsy, a favour. Instead of threatening him with the law, the gendarme was trying to persuade him to collude with him in breaking it.

When the negotiation was over, the gendarme called Friedländer.

'If you like,' he said, pointing to the chief, 'this gypsy will take your son. He'll try to take him as far as the border. Or, if possible, across the border.'

'I'll take him, I'll take him,' the chief enthused, almost transfigured by finding himself in cahoots with a gendarme for the first time in his life. 'Yid or gypsy—same kind of animal,' he added.

'Now don't get too familiar, chief,' the gendarme turned on him, feeling offended on Friedländer's behalf. He was an old-fashioned gendarme, grey-templed, rugged and tough, but brought up in the stable period before the wars, and he clearly thought that, no matter what was happening now, a gypsy still couldn't talk about himself in the same breath with middle-class people, educated people, people who were gentlemen yesterday and might again be gentlemen tomorrow, like this decent-looking Jew. But Friedländer didn't feel offended. Breathless with excitement, he called his son. When the boy joined them the chief looked him up and down from top to toe.

---

* Hungarian regular army.

'Well, the young gentleman doesn't look very much like a gypsy in these clothes. But we can hide him in the back. Or we'll say he's a musician from Budapest.'

'Put some rags on him,' the gendarme ordered.

'That's very good,' the chief jumped at the idea, eyeing the boy's steel-blue jacket. 'We'll dress the young gentleman as a gypsy. And we'll think of something to do with his clothes and shoes.'

'You can keep the clothes and shoes,' Friedländer said. 'I'd also give you some money, but I haven't got a penny now.'

'You will have again, sir. It doesn't matter, sir. I know you, sir. You'll help me one day, sir.'

Of course the other Jewish gravediggers watched anxiously. The gendarme, who was a really decent fellow, asked the chief:

'Could you take any more?'

'I could take two more,' the chief said, 'one on each cart.'

'Ask them', the gendarme told Friedländer, 'if there are two more who want to go.'

The Jews surrounded Friedländer excitedly. Yesterday nobody had wanted to flee, but today, under the impact of the deportation, people would rather have climbed into these covered gypsy carts than the wagons. After a short, hectic discussion they agreed that two students should go with the gypsies. One was a medical student, the other a high-school student. Let the young ones go. For them it was worth it. They might even get over this if they lived long enough . . .

They waited for half an hour for the traffic on the road to thin out a little. Then the chief hid the lads on the carts under the tarpaulins. He put Friedländer's son on his own cart. When Friedländer got to this point in his story he was convulsed by sobs. He was probably remembering the details of the farewell, the words, the carts disappearing in the dust. One of his sons was lying in a grave dug yesterday, and he had been tramping over it all day. His other son had gone with the gypsies—it seemed like a cheap novel or an operatic libretto. It was by these wild, lying and deceitful nomads, who live in tents, who are born in ditches, who are rocked on tree branches, who steal horses and who eat carrion, that his son had to be rescued from the jaws of a civilisation created by white men who had been christened and had lived in stone houses for a thousand years. These nomads don't worship our gods, they have no homeland, and they live in incest. Yes, they steal and, if they really have to, if they are very hungry, they may even kill. But only then, like wild animals. They would rather eat pigswill and rotten carcasses thrown on the rubbish heap than lay hands on a live human being. And if they have what they need, they don't kill just because the others have something too, as do Europeans living in towns, who have been organised and assigned to states and parishes. The gypsies are Aryans—they are the real Aryans of the fascists. And yet they put Friedländer's Jewish son and the other two Yids on their carts, and while Friedländer was sobbing I could feel that he was relieved: he feared much less for his son from the gypsy chief than from the Bishop of Nagyvárad, the mayor and the superintendent of schools. By now the real Aryans had perhaps taken Friedländer's son as far as the border, or even finessed him across it.

Meanwhile the Aryans in the brewery, with the gramophone playing, had been interrogating the second section, which was due to be packed into the thirty wagons tomorrow morning. The Aryans on the railways were already busily shunting, whistling, waving flags and lamps, making the wagons squeal, assembling the new train for the morning.

Friedländer asked me: 'Do you still think that it's possible to escape from here?'

'How do I know? And what if it is?' I answered gloomily.

We were silent, looking at the dirty floor.

'You know,' Friedländer broke the silence, 'I'm very angry with your father-in-law. When the Germans invaded Hungary I immediately asked him for some poison. He's a real mad chemist: he told me to get a prescription. A prescription at times like this! If he'd given me some I wouldn't have any problems now. I would have exterminated my whole family.'

'That would have been wrong. At least one of your sons has escaped.'

'I hope so. I've buried one, perhaps the other will survive. The rest doesn't matter any more. Who's leaving tomorrow?'

'The second section. Mainly businessmen and lawyers from Main Street.'

'My sister and her family are in that section,' Friedländer said coldly. 'Did you see any of what happened in the morning?'

'Yes, I did.'

He didn't ask me to tell him what I had seen. He sat doubled up, with his chin in his hand. Then he stood up, stretched himself and croaked with a yawn:

'Well, tomorrow I'm not going to dig graves. I've had enough. I'm stiff all over my arms and legs and I haven't even done any digging today. This hellish heat! Well, I'm off. Tonight I'm going to undress and lie down, perhaps I'll be able to sleep a bit. Good night.'

Stooped, he shuffled towards the door of the operating room. A little before midnight Dr Németi came to see me. He was neither more frightened nor paler than usual. He had found Friedländer in the operating room, hanging from the transom of the window by his braces.

Thirty-one

On the following day the second transport left. This time I didn't watch through the embrasure. I was sitting on my mattress, listening. Everybody else in the ward, who was able to, sat like that, hands clasped round knees, eyes bulging, ears pricked. The noises were the same as the day before. Shunting, wheels squealing, whistling, gendarmes yelling in the ghetto, then the hissing of the starting steam engine, the rattle of the train fading as it disappeared into the distance and, from the town outside, the ringing of trams, the honking of cars, the rumble of carts on the cobbles, and the shouts of market-women. The only difference was that today the bells could be heard more often. It was a religious festival, Corpus Christi or Ascension Day, which falls at the end of May or the beginning of June.

On Corpus Christi there is always a procession. The bishop with his red mitre and claret-coloured robe marches meekly under the canopy, as if butter wouldn't melt in his mouth, as if he weren't the owner of the Nagyvárad paper that teaches its readers how to eat people alive. The four pillars of the canopy are carried by four old, distinguished, pious and hard-drinking craftsmen. Before or behind them the young girls about to be confirmed sprinkle rose petals on the board from their baskets. The more illustrious citizens of the town have erected tents with altars in front of their houses, where the procession stops for a few minutes and the bishop says a prayer.

Five years ago I happened to be visiting my wife's parents at Corpus Christi. Their next-door neighbour was a royal notary, whose wife also used to set up such an altar in front of their house. We were having dinner when the bell rang and the notary's wife entered in her dressing gown.

'My dear,' she said to my mother-in-law, 'could I ask you to lend us those two silver candlesticks for the altar tomorrow?'

Naturally, my mother-in-law lent her the two candlesticks, which my father-in-law had inherited from his father, the chief rabbi of Arad. The chief rabbi had been one of the first Jewish priests to preach in Hungarian, and to proclaim the need to introduce Hungarian as the language of the Jewish liturgy. In short, he had been one of the advance guards of assimilation, with the lifestyle at one and the same time of both a provincial Hungarian gentleman and a fashionable middle-class Westerner. He had been a friend of Jókai and had travelled with him to San Remo every winter. He had even been raised to the Hungarian nobility. My father-in-law treated everything he had inherited from his father like an object of religious devotion. When my mother-in-law lent the silver candlesticks, which they used for the Jewish ceremony on Friday evenings, to the neighbour for the Catholic altar, he was perturbed and belatedly made a weak protest:

'You shouldn't have done that.'

'Look,' I comforted him, 'we've done, in a way, what your father would have wanted us to do. He was the first to try and bring Hungarian Jews and Hungarian non-Jews closer together. So the two candlesticks will stand for something like that.'

Where could the two silver candlesticks be now? Before they brought us to the ghetto we were made to hand them over to the gendarmes, together with our silver dishes, spoons and forks and the sports medals of my wife's daughter. The notary's wife probably doesn't borrow candlesticks now. In one of the Nagyvárad newspapers that somehow found its way into the ghetto I've read that the mayor invited the 'needy' middle-class population of the town to report to the town hall, where the clothes taken away from the Jews were being sold off cheap. The invitation wasn't addressed to the peasants and proletarians—after all, how would the Jews' bourgeois jackets or fancy fur-lined winter coats look on them? But in such a small town a thing like this could still prove funny, because people even know each other's clothes. The needy middle-class people will run into each other in the street, and as they say 'Hello, how are you?' one will recognise Dr Sebestyén's check overcoat on the other, and the other my father-in-law's puce winter coat on the first. His winter coat is the same colour as Sylvestre Bonnard's.* The old man is a bit of an eccentric: he won't allow his wife to speak to his tailor, he insists on choosing the material and the style himself. And because he wears his suits for years, they are bright blue in colour and beginning-of-the-century in style, and his wife has been nagging him about them daily for years . . .

Yes, they must be smuggled in here, into the hospital, by hook or by crook. They should all be here, the old couple and—most painful to speak of—the child. My wife's fourteen-year-old daughter. She is a sweet girl, and I have a great deal of tenderness for her, which I tactfully restrain, so as not to disturb her relationship with her father. The girl is attached to me, but I must be careful not to become her father's rival for her affection and make her life even more unsettled. After lengthy, contentious divorce proceedings and many personal conflicts, her parents finally reached a compromise, agreeing that she should live neither with us nor with her father, but with her grandparents. My wife used to travel to Nagyvárad to see her for a week or two every month, and during the summer holidays she brought her to Budapest to stay with us. Their relationship was rather like that of two sisters or two women friends, and my wife, not living with her daughter permanently, never learnt the role of a mother properly: she admired, cosseted and paraded her, but didn't really understand her. She watched her with open-mouthed pride, as if constantly amazed at having been able to produce this child. It was primarily because of the child that she came back from Paris. In the Rue de Grenelle she had thrown into my face:

'You? You can't understand this. You haven't got a child—just like Hitler. How should you know what it's like to be separated from your child by front lines?'

That was the reason, the main reason, why she came home. And now she's here, and so is the child. She is living with the old people two hundred paces from us in Szavacsay Street in the ghetto—and tomorrow she'll be put in the wagon. We travelled

* Hero of Anatole France's novel *Le crime de Sylvestre Bonnard* (1918).

three thousand kilometres, through fortified and mined mountains, tunnels and bridges, almost touching the front line, in order to be near at hand if the child needed us. And now we are near at hand!

Before we were taken to the ghetto, the child, driven by an animal will to live, rebelled when she heard the pessimistic adults give vent to their dread of the Germans in their lamentations.

'I'm not going to die,' she shrieked arrogantly. 'I'm not afraid. I'm strong and healthy. I'll work as a maid or help with the harvest, but I'll live.'

Two days before the ghetto was set up, my mother-in-law's old dressmaker slipped into the house carrying proletarian children's clothes and offering to take the child with her. My mother-in-law sent the dressmaker away.

By then she was in a very bad nervous state and seemed almost demented as she screamed:

'I'm not handing her over. We're going to die and God knows what will happen to this child. She might even sell her.'

The dressmaker was a widow with a good reputation, who was fond of the family and of the child, and wanted to help. But my mother-in-law kept telling us all day that the child would have ended up on the streets if she had let her go. The Gestapo was ringing the doorbells by the hour and dragging men, women and young girls to the cellars of the town hall, but the old woman clung to her peacetime nightmares to the very end. When the mayor's posters appeared with the announcement that Jews were only allowed to keep one set of underwear, she sent for her washerwoman, who was already forbidden by law to work for Jews. She made her wash in secret everything they had and, as always, insisted on ironing the men's shirts herself. While she was ironing, she periodically screamed dementedly: 'I don't care if they kill me. I just don't want to be tortured. Not tortured.' Hiding in the attic, I could hear her screams every half hour.

When the head porter of the Pannonia Hotel came to take me to Budapest with forged documents, I suggested that if I didn't go we should at least send the child. My wife agreed with me. But my mother-in-law, her contorted face as red as a beetroot, objected:

'I'm not letting her go. In Budapest anything could happen to her. A hotel porter! Who knows, he might even sell her!'

We had lost everything, the gendarmes were already clearing out the apartment, in the pharmacy a stranger was giving the orders. But what weighed most heavily on my mother-in-law was the vision of her granddaughter ending up on the streets. It was the petty-bourgeois dread of moral ruin that made her shudder.

I tried to persuade her that the girl would come to no harm. I had known the head porter for a long time, he was a gentleman, opposed to the Germans, and a decent man. He would immediately take her to some friendly Christian place.

'No, no, no!'

My wife joined in the argument, desperately, aggressively. They almost came to blows.

'How dare you stop her? Will you take the responsibility if the child dies because of your obsession?'

My mother-in-law buckled. Lowering her hoarse voice so that my father-in-law, who was walking up and down in the next room, couldn't hear her, she turned towards me:

'Listen. Every night since the Germans arrived we've wanted to take cyanide. But each time either I or my husband stopped to ask: yes, but then what will happen to this child?'

So if the child had gone, the old people would have taken cyanide. There was no doubt that they would have. It was in their pockets in small medicine bottles. We had also been given one each. But—with a sudden burst of callousness—I asked myself: shouldn't this child be saved, just because they would take cyanide if she were? Let's face it: the old people were most probably condemned to die, as we were also. I suspected that in any case they didn't love life very much, had never really loved it. It hadn't been much use to them, even before this disaster. They were quiet, hard-working, tired, passive, joyless people, whose zest for life had evaporated long since, who knows when and why. They were beasts of burden, slaves of work and duty. But this child, with her small fairy apple face, her eager curiosity, her ambition, her vanity, her starry eyes full of energy—should she stay here with us, and die

232

with us, just because, if she didn't, the old people would take cyanide?

It was up to my wife to make the decision. She adored her father to an almost neurotic degree. And now she had to decide that her child should go to Budapest with the head porter and her father should die as a result. She couldn't do it, she didn't have the nerve to do it. She collapsed in tears. My mother-in-law had won: the child stayed . . .

And now I was trying to arrange for the child at least to be deported in the same wagon as her mother. I waited impatiently for Dr Németi, who didn't turn up till about midday, when the second transport had left.

'Today there weren't any scenes,' Dr Németi reported. 'Today everything was more businesslike and dull.' All the same, had anything special happened? Well, Kádár, the lawyer, had died of a heart attack as he was climbing into the wagon. They threw him out and now he was lying beside the rails. And a farm manager, a Jewish member of the gentry in plus-fours with a quail feather in his hatband, had laid into a Polack for unintentionally bumping into him as they were climbing into the wagon. 'Stop pushing, we're not in Poland!' the farm manager had roared.

This farm manager had been waiting for Horthy to return ever since the Romanians had taken charge in Nagyvárad. He sat in the grand café at the table reserved for the gentry regulars, smoking with a bunch of defiant gentlemen, some from the town, others from the country, who had been stripped of their status and their offices, their estates and their rackets. He hunted and visited brothels with them, and he took his pleasures with them mournfully in the style of the Hungarian gentry, lamenting the lost past and hoping for the future. It was no secret that these Hungarian gentlemen were paying for their mournful pleasures with public money supplied by Hungarians on the other side of the border. They were supposed to use it to promote irredentism, but they squandered it on their revelries or, having learnt to 'work', and gone into 'business' with a few determined Jews, they gambled it away on smuggling and other adventures. When it ran out, they got more from Budapest. From time to time, to fulfil their patriotic duty, they made a gypsy play a banned irredentist tune, when there was no Romanian in sight. And, as they could keep an eye from their table on the whole Main Street promenade, every now and then they sent a message to a Hungarian girl they had seen walking with a Romanian officer, warning her that they had made a note of everything and she would be in trouble when the Hungarians returned. The farm manager of course financed his irredentism with the salary he was paid by the Jewish leaseholder in Bucharest and with what he made on the side. Then Horthy's Hungarians returned, bringing with them the law that forbade Jews to be either leaseholders or farm managers.

'This doesn't apply to me,' the Jewish member of the gentry boasted, but within three weeks he had been fired. He was still sitting all day at the table reserved for the gentry regulars, but nobody else was sitting there, because the other members of the gentry were sitting once more in their seats of power and authority. He was left alone at his post, his forehead leaning on his hand, in defiant solitude, the last of the irredentists. On the rare occasions when some of his former companions happened to drop into the café, they either turned back on the doorstep as soon as they saw him, or reluctantly joined him for a moment, listened with embarrassed nods to his long-winded tirades, promised everything, and promptly escaped. The Jews at the tables nearby guffawed and gloated. Even after the German invasion he continued to come to the café and sit at the gentry's table, although Jews were no longer allowed to be seen in public places.

'This doesn't apply to me,' he said arrogantly. And indeed the chief of police, who had been informed that the Jewish farm manager still frequented the café, gave orders that he shouldn't be disturbed. After all, they had drunk, hunted and womanised together for twenty years—even though he was a Jew now, he had been a patriotic Hungarian then.

As soon as any Germans came into the café, the farm manager, who spoke good German, invited them to his table. '*Kamerad*,' he shouted, pretending to be drunk and spreading his arms, '*zu mir!*'* Until closing time he drank, ordered the gypsy band to

* Come hither, mate.

234

play for him and, embracing the Germans, showed them how a Hungarian enjoys himself. The gentiles, who didn't speak German, became envious and finally lost their patience:

'Well,' they murmured, 'this is really a bit much! Who does this Jew think he is?'

One day they informed a group of Germans who were drinking with him that he was a Jew. They were young Wehrmacht officers, the most senior of them a captain, about twenty-five years old, with a commanding face.

'So what?' retorted the German officer to the waiter who had been sent with the message. *'Er ist ein feiner Kerl!*'* It's none of my business. And nobody else's either.'

When the yellow star was introduced, the farm manager went to the café without it. A detective demanded his papers and tried to arrest him. He didn't budge.

'I'm not going. Tell the chief of police that I have a right to sit here. I spent twenty years earning it.'

The detective didn't dare to arrest him and reported the matter to the chief of police. The chief of police waved his hand: 'Leave the poor devil alone, he was a really good Hungarian. He was my buddy.' All day the farm manager pranced about the town without the star, demonstrating, in particular to the Jews, that he wasn't like the rest, who were only allowed to appear in the streets with the star on their chests, and then only for two hours, if the mayor let them. Then came the ghetto. Unfortunately for the farm manager, the interior minister had sent a security force from elsewhere to round up the Jews of Nagyvárad. When they went to fetch him from his home in the evening, he protested, struggled and argued in vain—he had to go.

'Very well, I'm going,' he said threateningly. 'But first I'll write a few lines to my friend, Knight Jenő Horthy. Do you know who that gentleman is? The younger brother of his Serene Highness the Regent. He's my hunting partner and bosom friend.'

'Write anything you like, but you must come with us.'

He wrote a letter to the younger brother of the regent and

---

* He's a fine fellow.

entered the ghetto, with a mocking, malicious smirk: what a reprimand these gendarmes were going to get when his friend heard what they had dared to do to him! In the ghetto he demonstratively shrank back from the many Jews, but to a few of his more classy and wealthy Jewish acquaintances he graciously promised that he would do something on their behalf outside, because his friend, Knight Jenő Horthy, would have him released within a matter of days. In the ghetto he lived in isolation, like a stranger who has assumed a disguise in order to observe things more closely, or a protector who is prepared to help but first wants to see what is going on. He was constantly expecting to be called: 'The younger brother of His Serene Highness the Regent is looking for the farm manager.'

He even walked towards the wagon like a haughty Hungarian gentleman. And as he was climbing into the wagon he behaved as if his brush with the Polack had been a regular affair of honour. To the very last moment he blustered and swaggered, holding on to all the bad habits he had learnt from the Hungarian gentlemen.

When Dr Németi had finished his story I asked him what was happening about my wife's family.

'I'm afraid the gendarme can't bring them here,' he said irritably. 'But maybe he'll try to move them to the fourth section. That way we would at least gain a day. And tomorrow something else could happen.'

I asked him to go and talk to my wife. 'Tell her that they've been taken to the fourth section. Let's lie to her, poor woman. One day!'

The good Dr Németi went upstairs to my wife and told her that her family had been moved to the fourth section. But the gendarme couldn't move them. On the next morning they were taken away in the third transport. When my wife heard the fading squeals of the departing train, she was lying in her bed apathetically, calmly. She was calm because she believed that there was another day left. Calm because they weren't in the wagon, because they were still here . . .

In the taxi in the Rue de Grenelle she had yelled at me:

'What do I care about your ideas, your politics, your literature?

I'm a middle-class woman from Nagyvárad. I want to go home to my parents and my child!'

In front of the Swiss embassy I had knocked on the driver's window and gone in to get a transit visa.

It was because of them that we had come home.

Thirty-two

The fourth transport has also left, and the hospital—that is us—will be leaving tomorrow. My wife doesn't know that her mother, her father and her child were taken away yesterday. The good Dr Németi still keeps her going by telling her that the gendarme has smuggled them into the hospital and we'll be getting into the wagon together tomorrow. And tomorrow we'll lead her up the garden path by telling her that they couldn't be allocated to our wagon. They are somewhere further back, but when we arrive at our final destination they'll definitely join us.

About the departure of the fourth transport there's nothing special to report. The gendarmes, who had mastered the tricks of the trade over the first two days, were working like old hands, quickly and efficiently. Perhaps the only difference between the first two days and the last two days was that their superiors were finding the mechanical nature of the deportation less and less interesting and were bringing less and less ceremony, energy and good humour to it. By now the job was running smoothly by itself and there was practically no need for the gentlemen to interfere. Everything was taken care of by the reliable NCOs and the excellently trained gendarmes, who had learnt to function like a perfect machine. The SS and gendarmerie officers now watched the loading from a distance, like commanders inspecting a drilling ground, who only occasionally glance at the privates and leave the hackneyed everyday routine of 'right turn, left turn' to the subalterns. Each day fewer civilians had been appearing at the departure, probably with the excuse that the Jews weren't the only people in the world and the town couldn't be left without its leaders. The affair was losing its flavour. But tomorrow, when it was our turn to be taken away, the loading would be a bit more complicated. It was announced that the patients would be put into the wagons on their mattresses. A doctor or medical student, a nurse or two, and a pharmacist would be allocated to each wagon, and a special surgery carriage attached to the train. The Germans think in categories. A patient is a patient, and a patient is entitled to be transported even to the gas and the pyre like a patient.

Today a rumour has spread in the hospital that we aren't going to the same place as the rest, but to Nyíregyháza, where the sick from all the ghettos in Hungary will be collected in one huge hospital barracks. Apparently this concession has been made by the Hungarian government in response to Roosevelt's threat of air raids. Some of the people here even believe it, and the healthy who, like me, have been hidden in the hospital for their own protection are particularly optimistic. But I know that we hospital patients, whether genuinely ill or malingering, will be going to our death by the shortest and straightest route. I well remember reading in the report I received from London via Ankara in 1942 that, whereas from the regular transports only the old people and children are selected and exterminated promptly on arrival, those arriving on a hospital train are sent to the gas at once without exception and without a selection process. I know that our wagons will be marked before our departure in order to avoid unnecessary work for the selectors at the other end, who either finish off the Jews immediately or declare them fit for work so that they take a few months longer to die.

Since I came to the ghetto, my attitude to the question of life and death has varied. When I was first brought in, I had two years' forced labour and military prison behind me, followed by a few short days of freedom before the German occupation. At that point I felt that I'd had enough, that that was it. I wasn't just indifferent to life, but rejected it outright. I've already said that I wouldn't have bothered to walk two steps, let alone take a risk or engage in any adventure, to save my life. I had a superstitious belief that I'd be wasting my time even if I tried. The hackneyed simile of the cat and the mouse was more than a mere simile: it was the odds, the law of averages. Then along came that girl with the long legs and the squint, who told me that the friendly gendarme was prepared to help, and my wife would like to escape if possible. This roused me a bit, but it was above all that gynaecologist with his typhus epidemic who really turned my head.

Have they really called off the deportation in Kolozsvár because of typhus? I'm sure they haven't, and they won't here. Nothing has happened, and nothing more can happen between now and tomorrow morning. Now I no longer care if I'm delivered to the Germans in a hospital train—let's get it over with. I haven't the slightest inclination to repeat the misery I went through in the Ukraine, just to live a few more weeks or months—starting the forced labour again in a quarry, a forest clearing, an underground ammunition factory, or I don't know where; getting up again at four o'clock on a winter morning, to walk kilometre after kilometre to my workplace, not knowing at any one moment whether I'll be kicked or shot from behind; starving, stinking and crawling with lice, and not a cigarette to smoke. Then, sooner or later, the Russians will turn up, and either the Germans will murder us, as they did the Russian prisoners on the front when the enemy was within thirty kilometres, or we'll have to retreat with the Germans for the third time.

Still, there's nothing I can do, they'll be taking us away in the morning. It'll be good-bye to this disgraceful town, this rotten homeland, this crazy age, this life.

Although so many things have happened to me in this evil century in which I find myself by pure chance, I have also had a taste of an earlier, almost nineteenth-century, existence. If I ask myself what was the most extraordinary event in my family's home life between my father's early death in 1902 and the outbreak of the First World War in 1914, I can only report that in the carnival period of 1905 one of our bedroom curtains caught fire. My poor mother was getting ready for some charity ball: in those days the proceeds of balls were used to send clothes to children in Africa or to assist the victims of some distant flood or fire, as if nearer home everything was always well. My mother was standing in front of the mirror and her maid was helping her get dressed. Something about her ball gown didn't quite fit and had to be corrected with pins. In our house pins were kept in the curtains. As the maid was looking for the pin, with her candle held high, the curtain material was set aflame. A conflagration, the greatest and most alluring fear of my childhood, had until then only entered my life in the form of alarm bells and trumpet calls. Now that it had really come to us and was only two metres from my cot, I could no more believe that our house with its tiled roof might burn down than that Szuszu, our dog, might catch rabies. There were rabid dogs in the town, but they always belonged to, and bit, other people, and there were fires too, but they always burnt other people. The blazing curtain was pulled down, stamped on and extinguished with a bowl of water. The family continued to talk about the fire for years, and after I had started school I incessantly lied and boasted about it to the other boys. This was our family sensation until 1914. In that period there were fires and there were rabid dogs, but people with a regular lifestyle only knew about them by hearsay. There was also an earthquake, but it was in Messina, and there were wars, but they were in Manchuria and Cuba. There was even adultery, but it was somewhere in Rouen, in the Bovary family—in Komárom before 1914 no wife had ever cheated on her husband.

There was death, too, but it was an easy, simple affair. One didn't have to walk several thousand kilometres, starve, crawl with lice, labour in all weathers, sit in prison, argue about politics and travel in jam-packed wagons for days, just in order to die. When I felt close to death in the Ukraine I envied not the men sitting in the cafés of Budapest, embracing women, making money and carving out successful careers, but my father, who had died in 1902 in enviable comfort. He developed a small abscess and called the family doctor, who advised him to see a consultant in Budapest. He got on the comfortable fast train to the capital, treated himself to lunch in the dining car, took a rubber-wheeled carriage and pair to the Hungaria Hotel and went to see Lujza Blaha* perform in the theatre in the evening. In the morning he took another carriage and told the coachman to drive him to the address of Professor Herzl, who was the best consultant surgeon at the time. The consultant suggested

* Leading Hungarian actress (1850–1926).

an operation, and my father was admitted to a cosy, almost brand new sanatorium on a tree-lined avenue in the city park. Two weeks later my grandfather suddenly took me to Budapest to visit my father in the sanatorium. His room had cream-coloured walls and he was lying in a white bed, cosseted by a smiling nurse in a white uniform. He was cheerful and seemed to be over the worst. On his bedside table were a bottle of seltzer, half a glass of milk and some fruit. The window was covered by a green curtain, and the whole room was lit up like our pergola at home, where we used to have lunch in summer. Outside the window tall plane trees were swaying in the light breeze. I sat on the edge of my father's bed and he put two shells—the headphones of the Telephone News—over my ears. This miraculous invention had just come into being at that time: through the wires leading into the shells I could hear the music of the military band in Erzsébet Square, even though it was at least a kilometre and a half away. Meanwhile my father was reading the paper and joking with me. At noon I said good-bye to him, and when I stepped out of the door almost the whole family was standing in the corridor, whispering with the doctors. On the same afternoon my father died without having to move his little finger.

Out there at the front I constantly longed for that green light, for the curtain at the sanatorium window with the gently swaying trees behind it, for the alluring atmosphere, the frightened, whispering family and the tiptoeing nurses—and for a tiptoeing, tactful, tender death that does all the work on its own and doesn't work the dying to death. And there was something else. Nobody really likes the idea of being scraped under the earth no matter how and where, or of being dropped and left behind while the others simply walk on, as we used to do to our dead at the front. Everybody has a posthumous entitlement to a proper burial of his own, and everybody sometimes thinks of where he would like to be laid to rest. I myself, from the age of thirty, went to funerals more and more often, as we were burying more and more friends and contemporaries. On such occasions I always took a good look at the soil in which I would probably end up. I was familiarising myself and making friends with the sand of

Rákoskeresztúr.* Nor is the time of one's death irrelevant: I always thought it cruel of a family to leave its dead in the rock-hard, frozen ground in winter. In short, it would have been good to die in comfort and to die in summer. And now God knows how much longer I'll have to struggle, and if they find me fit to work when we arrive at our destination, I may not even kick the bucket before the autumn. In Poland the winter frost comes early, and the cemeteries look panic-stricken, as if their inmates had ended up there by chance as a result of some catastrophe, even in peacetime. I had never seen uglier cemeteries anywhere. On our way to the front, when I was observing the Polish village cemeteries from the wagon, all gave the impression of having been constructed at a moment's notice for soldiers killed in battle, or for victims of earthquakes or pogroms.

The good Dr Németi approached, faster and more excited than usual. When he reached my bed he bent down to me:

'Listen,' he whispered. 'Put on some clothes, but try not to be noticed, do it under your blanket. I don't want your neighbours to get any ideas.'

'What's up?'

'You'll be taken to the isolation hospital.'

'Why? Has it worked? And what's going to happen to the rest of the hospital? Won't the people in the hospital be deported either?'

'The people in the hospital will be deported. The gendarmerie colonel is only allowing the typhus suspects and their relations to stay behind. Not for the sake of the patients, but because he doesn't want the soldiers escorting the rest to catch typhus.'

'How many would be staying behind?'

'Twenty-nine.'

'And I . . . I'm supposed to stay behind when they take the others away?' I protested in a whisper. But I was immediately ashamed because I knew I wasn't being sincere. Dr Németi noticed the histrionics in my voice and almost snarled at me:

'Stop fussing! If anybody gets a chance to stay behind, he should. Nobody's going to think you're a traitor or a coward if

* Hungary's largest Jewish cemetery.

you stay. At least there'll be more air and water for the others in the wagon. The quarantine lasts three weeks. In that time something may happen. Or not. I'm glad you're staying. Perhaps you'll be able to report what was done to them. You'll write about it.'

After a long silence I asked him:

'Is my wife staying with me?'

'Your wife is already getting dressed. Of course she's asking about her family. I lied to her that they'll be meeting up in the isolation hospital. It'll be hard to tell her the truth. Don't put on your shoes—you'll be carried on a stretcher . . . and lean on me, try to totter and stumble. You must now have a high fever.'

'Are you staying with us, doctor?'

'No, I'm staying with the hospital. Or rather, I'm going with the hospital tomorrow.'

'And I'm supposed to say good-bye to you and leave all these people . . . ?'

'Let's talk a little less,' Dr Németi interrupted.

It was agonising, but I stood up and set off.

Clinging to Dr Németi's arm, I staggered out of the front door of the hospital. It was a starlit night. At first I only saw the stretcher I was laid on. Then I became aware of the women and children standing in a group on the left—the typhus patients' relations, who didn't have to play at being ill. Twenty minutes later the procession started. We crossed the ghetto, which was completely empty by now. We passed the brewery, where the gramophone had fallen silent. There was nobody left to be searched and tortured: the 'national property' was now in the hands of the nation. The isolation hospital was at the far end of the ghetto, in a large, forbidding building standing on its own close to the fence. With its large wallpapered rooms and glass veranda, it might once have been a factory office or the home of the factory manager. As soon as we were deposited in the rooms the doctors injected us with abdominal-typhus vaccine— which produces a high fever and typhus symptoms—to make sure that any gendarmes or Germans who might come to inspect us wouldn't discover the deception. Meanwhile my wife, together with the relations of the other 'patients', was left in the cellar

244

which served as an air-raid shelter. It took us till daybreak to settle down. By that time the British commandos and American paratroopers were engaged in an unprecedented battle with the troops of the German Atlantic Wall on the Cotentin Peninsula. It was the dawn of 6 June 1944. The dawn of the invasion. The British and Americans had begun the war on the continent. The Hungarians had finished the deportation from Nagyvárad.

Thirty-three

The invasion had started, but I was shivering with fever and my lips were chapped as a result of the typhus vaccine. By evening these symptoms had abated, but I felt battered as if I had been kicked down a hundred steps to the bottom of a cellar. The artificially induced illness had knocked me out. I had no appetite, felt sick and was kept awake all night by my empty stomach and painful nausea. But we had to put up with the daily renewal of this condition, or else the trick could have been discovered at any moment. What made things slightly better was that the gendarmes, by deporting the hospital in the synagogue of the wonder-rabbi of Wisznice, had completed their task of emptying the ghetto and been taken to other towns to do some more deporting. The isolation hospital with its seven patients, twenty-two relations and two doctors was now guarded by the Nagyvárad police.

The guards' commander was a police superintendent who had for years been in charge of the supervision of cafés, bars and small hotels, and had acquired a nice house of his own in the process. The two doctors were old friends of his and they were also well known to the police guards, who in the old days had saluted them, as they saluted the mayor, when they saw them speeding in their carriages on their way to patients or walking in Main Street with women after surgery hours. The doctors had been entitled to such an official salute from the police because they were employed in the public health service. The main reason why the police were less frightening was that we all knew how corrupt they were at all levels, from top to bottom. The gendarmes, who had been brought to the town from Transdanubia at the beginning of the German occupation, had behaved like gangsters. Even before the orders were issued they started requisitioning and searching, in other words looting, off their own bat. In the early days, when Jews were still allowed to travel by rail, it also happened that gendarmes would herd them into station waiting rooms and simply pocket their cash, their watches and their wedding rings, under the pretext that the Jews had in any case acquired these valuables by wrongful means. In comparison, the police had remained cautious and conservative. Even as they saw that now anything could be done to Jews with impunity, they preferred being bribed rather than going in for robbery. This had been an ingrained professional custom with them for decades. For a drink they closed an eye to a bar overshooting closing time. For a cigar they ignored a case of irregular driving. For a twenty-pengő note they allowed a pair of lovers to leave a sleazy hotel unreported. For a hundred-pengő note they let an embarrassing file vanish. And so on. It was above all their traditional corruption that made them more humane, as they patrolled the area at a distance of ten or twelve metres from the isolation hospital in a relaxed and unpretentious way.

The isolation hospital was only an arm's length from the fence that surrounded the ghetto. Immediately beyond the fence ran one of the streets of the industrial suburb. On the opposite side of the street, interspersed with plots of wasteland, like gappy teeth, were a sickly-smelling molasses warehouse, the rear fire-wall of a decaying cold-storage plant, and a smithy with the anvil outside in the yard, where horseshoes were hammered all day long on to the hooves of long queues of peasants' and soldiers' horses. Unlike the blacksmith and his family, who wore Arrow Cross uniforms, the policemen, standing sloppy and casual guard nearby, almost advertised by their posture that they didn't identify with the task for which they were being used. They had resented the gendarmes from the very first moment, on the one hand because they felt insulted by the authorities who hadn't trusted them and had brought in the 'reliable' gendarmes from Transdanubia, on the other hand because they were obliged to watch, grinding their teeth, how the gendarmes feathered their nests thanks to this 'Jewish business', without a soul calling them to account as they filled their kit-bags or fibre suitcases with

'Jewish loot'. The policemen were indignant because in their view the gendarmes had stolen it all from them.

Now the policemen walked up and down, round the hospital behind the fence and along the street in front of the fence, as languidly as they had done their duty in peacetime. They strolled to the corner, where the fence turned at a right angle into the next street, and disappeared for a quarter of an hour at a time, leaving the area unguarded. When this happened, anybody young and supple enough to throw himself over the two-and-a-half-metre fence could have escaped. Inside the hospital our captivity also felt less tight, less suffocating—a situation that practically invited us to make plans for escaping. Relations between the policemen and the hospital became more friendly every day. The officers were relieved every three hours, and when they went into the town the doctors got them to post telegrams asking for help and to bring back cigarettes, newspapers and fruit from the market. With their help the doctors obtained money from the town, which they gave to the superintendent. The tension also lessened as a result of newspaper stories reporting that the British and Americans, counter to the prophecy of the Bishop of Nagyvárad's paper, hadn't been pushed back into the sea, but had already advanced into the suburbs of Cherbourg.

Shivering with fever, I thought of nothing but the invasion, prompted by an automatic political and professional interest, rather than by any hope of survival. In my condition of artificial typhus I could in no way contemplate escaping: I was hardly able to drag myself to the WC. Besides, as I've already said, I considered any kind of escape hopeless and pointless. And then there was my wife, in an impossible physical and mental state. On the third day in the cellar she discovered that she had been misled, and her parents and her child had been deported. After a hair-raising nervous attack, followed by a six-hour faint, she was overcome by a speechless, melancholy lethargy and went on hunger strike. Then she turned to self-flagellation. For two days she writhed on the bare stone floor of the cellar: her operation wound opened and the doctors had to stitch it up again. It was only with great difficulty that they managed to carry her to one of the empty rooms upstairs. When they left her alone for a few minutes, she tore her artery open at the wrist and in a fit of weeping kept biting her fists till they were bleeding. Meanwhile I lay on my mattress in the sick room, among the other Jews with their typhus vaccine, unable to help her even with words. I listened dully to the doctors telling me what the unfortunate woman had done, and when they had finished I asked them if there was any news from Caen. Eventually she recovered somewhat and frantically demanded to be taken to the gendarmes, put into a wagon and sent after her family. When the doctors tried to calm her down she started to scream: if they didn't let her go to the gendarmes, she would reveal the whole deception and report the doctors and the patients. If her child had been deported, everybody else should be deported. In the hospital windows there was no glass, and in the street outside, less than five metres from her room, every word could be heard by the free Aryans of Nagyvárad as they were passing by. The horrified doctors held her down and gave her an injection to make her sleep. A few days later she had tired herself out and become resigned. She was put into a nurse's coat and given some work to do. From time to time she came into the sick room and sat on the edge of my mattress. With her empty eyes worn out by crying, she stared at me, helplessly or reproachfully, without saying a word, and held the basin when the vaccine made me vomit.

In the sick room there were nine of us—nine typhus patients: seven scrawny, waxen, shaggy Jews from Poland and Bukovina in dirty underwear, whose scruffiness and lice gave the typhus a plausible appearance, and two of us former forced labourers, who had survived the disease in the Ukraine and supplied the contaminated blood for this terrifying game. We fretted about being caught every minute of the day, but the shaggy Jews in particular were shaking even more with panic than with fever. They talked to each other in frightened voices, in a Yiddish that was neither like German nor like the jargon common in Hungary. I didn't understand a word of it, which constantly irritated me, as did also their exclusiveness that wouldn't unbend towards the two of us even in the face of this shared fate. Their families were in the cellar, sad, ignorant and clumsy women, with masses of children who all day long made a racket that couldn't be silenced.

As nobody seemed to bother about the hospital, the children slipped from their apathetic mothers' hands, gradually ventured out of the cellar and dispersed in the weed-infested factory yard. Their innocent, noisy play made us nervous because we were afraid that it might draw the attention of the local population, or the Germans, to us.

The people across the road, in the smithy, were already eyeing us malignantly. Further into the town, hardly anybody apart from the authorities knew that a few Jews had been left behind in the typhus hospital, and the people of Nagyvárad were living in an uneasy rapture at the thought of not one Jew being left in the notoriously Jewish town. Now passers-by stopped outside the fence when they heard the racket of the children and the Yiddish, and made remarks to the blacksmith and his gang, who were working in front of the smithy. Through the open window we heard a coarse female voice say:

'What, this lot is still here? I thought the place had been cleaned up.'

'This lot isn't so easy to get rid of,' the blacksmith echoed.

A quarter of an hour later a high-pitched male voice piped up:

'What's this? A Jewish nursery school? Perhaps they're even giving milk to these little bloodsuckers when there isn't a drop of milk in the whole town.'

'They're still stealing it from our children,' the blacksmith's wife wailed.

Shivering with fever, I turned to my neighbour, the eternally praying and trembling Mr Leimsieder, who had been assistant rabbi in Kolomea* before he took refuge in Nagyvárad, and whose seven children were squealing outside.

'You ask me ten times a day if we're going to be stood up against a wall. It could happen sooner than you think if they don't sort things out down there.'

The assistant rabbi of Kolomea was trembling, but gave me a spiteful look: 'What's your problem, for God's sake? What should be going on down there?'

* Town in Galicia.

'It would be good if the women took the children back to the cellar.'

'What have the children done?' he asked indignantly, defending the children.

'Can't you hear that racket?'

'What racket?' he asked, listening. 'Well, yes. But that isn't a racket. The children are just talking. They're children.'

Poor Leimsieder, he had got so used to the constant din in the one room in which he had lived for years with his wife and his many children that he didn't even notice it any more. And he jumped to the conclusion that I was only making a fuss because I had an aversion to the minuscule sidelock-bearers and was trying to pin some blame on them, the little scapegoats. He had got accustomed to taking everything, even a fair comment, for a groundless accusation. Everything was persecution, Jew-baiting, pretext. He wouldn't allow his children to be hurt, and he was warning me to lay off:

'How can you expect the poor children to turn dumb and sit on one spot in a dark, cold cellar?'

When I told him that at least they shouldn't speak Yiddish, he took offence.

'They can only speak Yiddish. What's wrong with that? It's their mother tongue.' And finally he actually tried to put my mind at rest with his belief in money and bribery. 'I'm scared, I'm always scared, but there won't be any problem with the children. The police superintendent is getting a fair amount of money from us. If he thought that the children were causing trouble he would certainly have sent them back in. Till then, let these poor children stay in the fresh air.'

There were also some decent people walking outside the ghetto fence. One morning somebody threw in a bunch of mouldy red radishes. We went into raptures about the unknown benefactor—possibly a housewife going home from the market—and these radishes became a source of optimism, a symbol, a proof that there were some human beings outside the fence. The patients' relations, who were up and about, also became aware of a young man on a bicycle who turned up six or seven times a day and threw things—cigarettes, bread, onions, newspapers, sometimes even flowers—over the fence every time he zoomed past, without slowing down, so that the policemen wouldn't notice. The policemen actually ignored him, but the blacksmith in his Arrow Cross uniform, assisted by his family and apprentices, kept a beady eye, and passed nasty comments, on everything that happened in the hospital and the street from morning till night. They not only made a fuss when somebody seemed to approach the fence with good intentions, but one or other of the gang started shouting as soon as a passer-by turned into the deserted street:

'It's forbidden to walk on that pavement. Come to this side, double quick.'

Most people crossed over, mechanically obeying the brassy, official-sounding voices. In any case, the majority of the passers-by had no intention of fraternising with us. But, as I say, once in a while there were some who evaded the evil vigilance of the blacksmith's gang and, without turning their heads towards the fence, threw something over, made some encouraging, shamefaced or sympathetic remarks, or simply swore to express their protest. On one occasion I heard a man, whom the blacksmith's gang had told to cross to their side, answer back confidently:

'It's none of your business where I walk. I'll walk where I like.'

'It's orders.'

'Whose orders? I've just seen a policeman and he didn't say anything. He didn't tell me where to walk.'

'It's the rule,' a female voice screeched.

'You should be ashamed of yourselves. Can't you leave these people alone even now? Do you think I'm afraid of your green shirt? I'm as good a Christian as you are.'

A younger male voice from the blacksmith's side chipped in:

'You a Christian? A Christian doesn't talk like that.'

'You should be locked up with them,' the female voice added. 'Their brats are swilling our milk even now.'

The decent voice didn't give in.

'Who authorised you to lay down the law?'

'It said on the posters that passers-by mustn't go within ten paces of the ghetto.'

The decent voice replied: 'Who's asking you, my good wom/
Why are you talking to me? Do I know you?'

'A year or two ago you still called yourself a Romanian, I'm sure,' the female voice accused him.

'I'm a Christian Hungarian craftsman,' the decent voice affirmed.

'You, a craftsman? People like you are kicked out of the crafts-men's guild. I can imagine what kind of craftsman.'

'I'm master shoemaker Ferenczy from Pável Street. What are you jabbering about? Stick to your horseshoes and don't poke your nose into other people's business.'

'The shoemakers are all red,' the younger male voice claimed.

'Not true. Claret,' the shoemaker defended himself.

'Of course the shoemaker's sorry the Jews have been taken away. The Jews paid the black-market price for shoes. The likes of us can't pay that, only the Jews.'

As I lay shivering with fever, I listened to this as if it had been a radio play. A policeman arrived, having heard the row and wishing to make peace. The blacksmith's gang—men and women—made a dash for him. All were shouting at the same time, pouring out their suspicions and accusations:

'He walked quite close to the fence, officer. He was going to throw something in. If we hadn't stopped him he would have done.'

The shoemaker made a confident denial: 'I wasn't going to throw anything. But even if I had, it's none of their business. That's what the police are for.'

'What do you say to that, officer?' the female voice stirred things up.

The policeman didn't speak for a while. Then he said:

'The question is, did he or didn't he throw something?'

'I didn't,' the shoemaker insisted.

'Did you see it or didn't you?'

'He was going to throw something. Just search him, officer.'

'I'd like to see anyone search me. I'm a free Christian Hungarian craftsman!'

'I've no right to search him,' the policeman said after some reflection. 'And you,' he said more sharply to the blacksmith's gang, 'you've no right to harass the passers-by. Are you the authorities, or what? It's our job to keep order.'

'It isn't quite like that,' a male voice from the blacksmith's gang demurred. 'The edict says that everybody's obliged to keep an eye on the Jews. And on the agents of the Jews, who wear red ties, while Budapest is being bombed to pieces. We're only doing what the law says. We're assisting the authorities.'

The policeman became uncertain. 'You've a right to do that. But you've no right to suspect people without reason. If this gentleman had thrown something in . . .'

'He was going to throw something.'

'Going to isn't enough.'

'My son is at the front,' the female voice screeched.

'My son's already fallen,' the shoemaker retorted.

This and similar dialogues took place outside the fence. We could only hear the voices, but the doctors and the relations who were up and about could see the protagonists through the windows. Within a day or two they knew all about the black-smith's gang and the young man on the bicycle—our most hated enemies and our best friend. About the blacksmith's gang they knew that during the deportation the gendarmes had been constantly dropping in on them loaded with parcels. The black-smith either kept the 'Jewish loot' safe for them or, acting as a receiver of stolen goods, sold it on their behalf. Every member of the gang proudly wore the tight Arrow Cross uniform, even while they were forging iron and nailing horseshoes. On one occasion we heard the blacksmith's wife call after her teenage son, who wore the uniform of the party's youth section:

'Brother Jóska, I forgot to ask you to get some spirits.'

The Arrow Cross mother addressed her own son by the party title of 'brother'.

In the evenings men and women in Arrow Cross uniforms gathered in their house. They ate, drank, argued, laughed, and clattered with plates and glasses. When there was an air raid they didn't go down to the shelter—they still believed that the British and Russians were incapable of any serious bombing and were allowed to hang about here by the Germans for tactical reasons, in order to weaken their fronts in the east and west. They had only bombed Nagyvárad once, and even then they had only hit a hospital and a few measly shacks. The blacksmith's gang turned the volume of the radio news up high, so that we could hear it, including the German broadcasts, of which they didn't understand a word and which they probably believed were reporting victories and abusing the Jews all the time. In fact by then nobody apart from us was deriving pleasure, albeit of a wistful kind, from the German Wehrmacht reports. The British and Americans were at Avranches and the first Russian patrol had arrived in Csíkszereda* . . .

The personal circumstances of the young man with the bicycle had also been ascertained in detail in the hospital. He was a tailor's apprentice and the best striker of the Nagyvárad football team. His name was Sanyi Papp, his father was a Hungarian, his mother a Romanian. The hospital had established direct contact with him. Somebody was always waiting for him to approach on his bicycle, and at the last moment threw out a paper pellet. The footballer, like a galloping cowboy, bent down from his saddle at full speed and picked it up. If somebody, in his despair, remembered a last, unlikely address, the footballer forwarded an SOS or at least a farewell message-in-a-bottle from a sinking ship on their behalf.

We were the only ones not to send a note to anybody. I never even thought of it, and my wife was still wandering through the rooms, rigid and soulless like a mechanical wax puppet. But my neighbours were full of excited expectation—their notes had gone out and they were breathlessly waiting for the rescuer. We weren't waiting for anybody.

* In eastern Transylvania.

Thirty-four

At dawn on the eighth day we were once more woken by the screeching of wagon wheels on the industrial siding. The hospital was frightened to death. The doctors discovered that during the night the Jews from the county of Bihar had been brought in. They had been 'ghettoised' here and were awaiting deportation. Some gendarmes, but not our original ones, had come with them. We were still in the hands of the police.

From newspapers and reports that had filtered through from the town, we had understood that the Jews were only being deported from the frontier region and the war zone, while the rest were left in the local ghettos in the interior of the country. Everybody envied the Jews of Püspökladány in their ghetto, a few kilometres from us, for being spared the wagons. Now we realised that those rumours hadn't been true, just as it was probably also untrue that the deportation of the Kolozsvár ghetto had been called off because of typhus. The ghetto had caught up with us again, it had returned together with the gendarmes. When it was first deported—however much we suffered to see our families, our friends, our colleagues being dragged away—we all felt, with a cruel sincerity, as if we had survived an epidemic that had killed our neighbours, or had escaped from a house on fire, in which all the other members of our family had been burnt. Now we had the ghetto round our necks again, and it was certain that we were irretrievably lost: inexorably, the ghetto would suck us in and soak us up.

It had been clear from the outset that the typhus trick could at best give us a respite—certainly no more than the officially prescribed three-week quarantine—and by now the highest praise we dared to give aloud for our 'good fortune' in being left behind was that our journey would be more comfortable with only twenty-nine of us, rather than seventy-five, in a wagon. But deep down—perhaps because nobody had bothered us for a week— we had almost come to believe that we would be completely forgotten and left here till the end of the war.

Every day we had reported a new case of typhus in order to strengthen our position in the eyes of the authorities in the general hospital. Within ten days we had had four 'positives' to prove that the epidemic was spreading at a tremendous rate. Even the doctors had hoped that we could start counting afresh each time, since the quarantine period always began with the date of the most recent case. But now that the ghetto had returned, the hospital, including the doctors, broke down. We expected to be thrown together with the Jews from Bihar within days or hours. And those who had been preparing their escape plans with a certain optimistic deliberation now started to thrash about in a panic.

On hearing the screeching of the wagons, my wife suddenly recovered. Psychologically, the reactions caused by the emotional traumas she had suffered during these weeks were of a peculiar kind. They resembled most of all a physical illness involving a crisis—pneumonia or meningitis. After an acute period of oscil- lation between life and death, a swift process, either towards death or towards life, sets in. During the critical days one either dies of the blows or takes poison, or one unexpectedly finds one's feet and is seized by manic activity. When my wife had learnt that her family had been deported, she very nearly committed suicide. I had dreaded this for days and been prepared for being told at any moment that she was dead. But when she heard the screeching of the wheels—the monstrous music that had been the family's funeral march nine days earlier—she suddenly became herself again, straightened up, and vindictively, recklessly went out into the courtyard to watch out for the cyclist. She threw out a paper pellet with the text of a telegram to Budapest. She wasn't driven by the will to live but by an aggressive grief and the hope of revenge. For revenge one must stay alive, or at least try to. She didn't tell me that she had asked for help. She was afraid that the lad wouldn't post the telegram, and she didn't want to raise my hopes in vain.

257

The escapes from the hospital began that evening. At first the doctors held the patients back, but when it had become dark and the gate could no longer be seen from the smithy, the patients' relatives slipped out one by one. Three bribed policemen had agreed to let Jews out for a thousand pengős per head. The women and children from Galicia and Bukovina had somehow got hold of Romanian and Hungarian peasant clothes. When they stepped out of the ghetto the footballer awaited them at the corner and took them to safe houses, mainly Romanian ones. The footballer didn't accept any money.

Thirty-five

The typhus hospital was housed in the central offices of a decommissioned chemical factory. Over the years the machinery had gradually been dismantled and sold as scrap metal, and many components of the building carried away to other construction sites. The courtyard was overgrown with weeds, which also covered the factory's rusty industrial siding that we hadn't even noticed under the weeds, although it was only forty or fifty paces from our window. By now we had been in the typhus hospital for ten days and we expected to be called out and attached to the new ghetto at any moment. In the morning three drays turned into the yard, loaded high with travel baskets made of straw matting, cabin trunks, valises, portmanteaux, overnight bags, suitcases. They were unloaded in the yard by German soldiers, who then drove away on the drays, dangling their feet. A single guard with a bayonet stayed behind to keep an eye on the luggage. About a quarter of an hour later a number of lorries arrived with similar loads, and then long lines of German and Hungarian soldiers, followed by unshaven, ragged tramps picked up from the streets, came on foot with more luggage, with which they began to build a high wall. About midday the wall had reached the height of several storeys, and they departed. Only the German soldier with the bayonet remained, walking round the wall of luggage and smoking.

From her window, my wife watched the wall being built with the luggage of the Jews of Nagyvárad. Suddenly she turned and came running to me in the ward.

'I say,' she said with great agitation, 'I've just seen the suitcases.'

'Where?'

'They've just put them down in the yard. I'm quite sure they're ours.'

'What have they brought them here for?'

'I don't know.'

She ran back to the window and stared at the mountain of luggage, spellbound. Yes, here were almost all the Jewish suitcases in Nagyvárad in one great pile. Here were the pigskins that had gone on honeymoon to Venice or Paris, and the trunks that had accompanied the adventurous and curious globetrotters of Nagyvárad to the Canary Islands on the ships of the Cosulich Line or to the North Cape with Hapag: there hadn't been one travel group from Budapest or Bucharest without its contingent of Jews from Nagyvárad. Here were the smart suitcases in their green and brown covers, bearing the labels of the grand hotels, and even here they squashed the petty-bourgeois cases made of imitation leather, cardboard or vulcanised fibre which, filled with all the wordly goods of their owners, had already been knocked about by decades of endless journeys in the third class of slow trains. Here were the proletarian travel baskets made of straw, tied with string because their locks were broken. Here were the travelling salesmen's sample cases and the cunning holdalls with the double bottoms, in which contraband and forbidden currency had slipped across borders. And here, too, were our suitcases— at least according to my wife, who swore that she had seen the red labels of the Paris Gare Pajol, with 'Colis exprès' printed on them in black letters.

So, here were the nine suitcases . . .

Then, at noon, panic broke out in the hospital. Two wagons had been shunted on to the rails under the weeds, and everybody thought that they had come for us.

In fact it was the luggage that the Hungarian and German soldiers and the tramps loaded into the wagons, on which they painted in large white letters:

'A GIFT FROM THE HUNGARIAN NATION TO THEIR BOMBED-OUT GERMAN BROTHERS.'

My wife watched the loading, standing on tiptoe. She swore that she had seen our suitcases. But whether she had really seen or only imagined them, it was definitely the nine suitcases that had brought us home when there was no room for them either on the train to Madrid or on the train to Marseille. There had been room only on the Simplon express, which transported us back to Hungary like a gendarme, hurling us relentlessly across hostile foreign borders, and across the even more hostile border of our own country.

I've already mentioned that I had asked my wife in Paris to leave these suitcases behind, to throw these objects to the wind, because we could always replace them with new ones. But she had wanted only these nine suitcases and *these* objects. And *this* town—the greater the upheaval in the world, the more she needed her native soil, where her father was working in his pharmacy, her mother was insisting on her right to iron the men's shirts, and her child was speeding along the avenue on her bicycle. The town where every Tom, Dick and Harry knew her—in short, the most dangerous place in the whole world.

The least unbearable thing in this restless European pandemonium was to be an alien. One was harassed by the authorities, one had to report to police stations, complete endless forms, even have one's fingerprints taken like a criminal, and the population had also become suspicious, distant and nasty, but these inconveniences and insults that one suffered as an alien in a foreign country were directed at a large category, the vagrant, the *méteque*. They were directed at the alien as a political abstraction, not at the alien individual. But here, at home, in one's native town, where every Tom, Dick and Harry knew one, even the political hatred and retaliation were virtually nothing but excuses for personal revenge, for the summary resolution of decades of squabbles between neighbours, unsuccessful competition, secret envy and petty injuries.

'In 1926 they hardly acknowledged my greeting. Now they'd be happy to greet me,' or 'Once I had to jump out of the way, otherwise this Jew would have run me down with his car.' This provided sufficient justification for the master stonemason or the assessor to the orphans' court to call, with great satisfaction, for speedier gassing.

My wife had wanted to come back to her native town, come what may. In Paris she had defiantly described herself as a middle-class woman from Nagyvárad, who was not interested in politics, who was not interested in ideas, who simply wanted to return home, with her nine suitcases, to her parents and her child—and ten days ago the wagons had taken away her family, and this afternoon the wagons had also taken away the suitcases. In tidy, separate consignments—as if they had learnt such distinctions from grammar—they had first taken away the people and had then taken away the objects: everyone we had, then everything we had. All that had so far determined the life of a European had ceased around us. We had no native land, no parents, no children, no homes, no addresses, and no possessions. We were still alive, but we were more dead than the old dead, who at least had a pit and a mound a fathom long for their grave, and a wooden marker with their name burnt into it. We didn't even have a name and were going to die bearing the name of a stranger. And yet perhaps this was not a superfluous precaution— perhaps it was advisable to bear a false name, even when approaching God . . .

Over fourteen days the population of the cellar had decreased. Thanks to the bribed policemen, the women and children had been escaping steadily, almost methodically, after sunset. So far we hadn't heard that any of them had been caught—the football-playing Pimpernel was functioning magnificently. It seemed as if the authorities in the town had actually forgotten the typhus hospital: we saw no sign of them being interested in us. By night, at the other end of the ghetto, on the industrial siding near the synagogue of the wonder-rabbi of Wisznice, the wagons awaiting the Jews from Bihar were once more shunting, but in the hospital—where the policemen had not been replaced by gendarmes and nobody came to look at us—the panic of the first few days had abated and we had got used to the idea that we weren't in immediate danger. It was only yesterday that we had admitted another positive case to the hospital, and we calculated that we would be left here at least till 7 August. People were again beginning to believe that we were a special case and receiving exceptional treatment. Those who had previously been prepared to escape were now more inclined to stay, which they thought was less dangerous than stepping out beyond the fence and running into an acquaintance or a detective, or walking along one of the familiar streets, which were once more teeming with gendarmes. The Bihar ghetto had arrived with a large contingent of gendarmes, who were so experienced that they could recognise Jewish fugitives at first sight. There was also the dread of being discovered in one's hiding place, or being denounced, or caught in a raid. Moreover, the supposed typhus cases had been weakened by constant injections for a fortnight. If you didn't have to go, it was better to lie on your mattress a little longer, better to lie low and wait . . .

At half past nine in the morning I was tossing and turning on my mattress with a high fever, when one of the doctors approached me. In a low voice he told me to hold on to him and let him take me to the doctors' room. Clinging to his neck, reeling and swaying, I made it with great difficulty. The entire furniture of the doctors' room consisted of a kitchen table and a stool. On the stool sat the wife of my friend and fellow-writer, István Szabó. My wife was embracing her in tears. Of all our friends in Budapest, the Szabós were most likely to risk everything to save us. Whenever I thought of our friends and tried to work out who might take the most active, most ingenious and most persistent interest in our fate, they alone came to mind as naturally as one considers only certain actors suitable for certain parts. Now I wasn't even very surprised to see Lili here. I didn't even think it strange that she had managed to get into the ghetto past the fence, the policemen and the gendarmes. Lili was the kind of person who could get in anywhere she wanted to, without using force or guile. She was trusted by everybody at first sight. Her determination was disarming rather than aggressive, and what gave her authority was her modesty and calm. She was the kind of person who would be allowed through the gate by the most suspicious guard, not because he thought her a VIP, but because he couldn't imagine that her errand wasn't legitimate, the kind of person who would make a dog that had slipped its chain stop in its tracks, by just standing there. Her father was one of the leading figures of the Hungarian Social Democratic party, and her mother the most Christian woman I had ever known.

She had come to fetch us from the ghetto, and after the first shock of seeing us here she proceeded to tell us magisterially what to do. She had brought some documents with her—the same that the head porter of the Pannonia Hotel had brought when he tried to help us escape to Budapest before the ghetto. They were 'originals', because it was too risky to use documents forged by a printing press. I was a waiter called Ferenc Pattermann, born in Sarajevo. My mother's name was Ilona Kranc. I had been employed in Nagyszeben at the Római Császár Hotel, in Kolozsvár at the Astoria, and in Budapest at the Debrecen Restaurant, before I finally got my job at the Pannonia. The details of Pattermann's age and person roughly resembled my own. My wife's documents were in the name of Júlia Tóth, a divorced kitchen maid born in Komád, currently employed at the Pannonia Hotel. Lili also gave us two official statements, written on the notepaper of the hotel, to the effect that we were spending four days' paid leave in Nagyvárad with the knowledge and permission of the management: it all looked as if a licentious waiter was taking the kitchen maid to the country for a few days' fun. She had also found a way to 'persuade' the police inspector. She hadn't told him who we were because she was afraid that he might be frightened by my 'famous' name. Instead, she had explained to him that we were related to her and although we were Jews, most of our relations were Christians. And modestly, almost imperceptibly, she had slipped him ten thousand pengős.

We were due to leave the ghetto at nine o'clock in the evening. That was the time when one of the police guards, who had been letting out the people from the cellar for a thousand pengős per head, came on duty. Mrs Szabó would go to the station at half past nine and wait for us on the platform in front of the first-class waiting room. On the platform there were only three blue lights, and the first-class waiting room—as I already knew—was at the darkest part of it. The train wasn't scheduled to leave till half past ten, but it would be shunted to the platform before ten, when we would be able to get on it. It would of course have been better to spend the intervening period in the home of some reliable friends, but we didn't have any. Still, the important thing was to get out of the ghetto. It occurred to my wife to let the footballer in on the act. The doctors knew the lad's

264

address. Mrs Szabó was to call on him at midday and summon him to the street corner on the left-hand side of the ghetto for nine o'clock.

Then she went back to the town.

I slumped on my mattress, exhausted, with the fever reaching its climax about that time, shortly before midday. As far as I was able to concentrate I examined the possibilities and details of the escape in my mind. I thought about the question dispassionately, almost technically, like a soldier who has to carry out a task, whether or not he likes it. Rather than suddenly bursting into enthusiasm for life, I merely pondered the chances of success and the consequences of failure. But my wife began to make her preparations as eagerly as if we were about to leave our apartment or hotel to catch the ten-thirty train that evening. From the way she set about packing, with feminine pedantry and meticulous expertise, one might have thought that she was merely excited by the prospect of going on a journey.

Even before we were brought here, this building had served as an isolation centre for the genuinely contagious patients of the ghetto, people with scarlet fever, diphtheria, typhoid and dysentery. These had been deported together with the main hospital two weeks earlier, just as they were, lying on their mattresses in their underwear. Their outer clothing and other belongings had been left behind, piled up in one of the small rooms facing the yard. Now my wife was in that room, busily collecting things for our journey. There were also some suitcases, and she had already filled two of them to the brim. The nine suitcases had scarcely been taken away when—like a bee that has seen its honeycomb destroyed and can only think of putting its honey into a new comb of the same shape and layout—she began to collect new objects in new suitcases. When I had recovered a little and found her in that room, she abandoned the two suitcases after a heated argument, but continued to insist that we couldn't start such a journey without any luggage. Finally we agreed on a small valise and a battered patent-leather vanity bag that seemed more or less appropriate for a kitchen maid.

From the clothes left behind by the contagious patients we selected costumes that matched our documents. For a waiter on leave from the Pannonia Hotel in Budapest I chose my disguise without much flair, even though I had spent a considerable part of my life in the company of waiters. I dug out a creased brown pair of trousers, a grimy blue shirt, a frayed tie and a jacket with food stains and shiny elbows. I looked like a discarded old waiter from a low tavern in a disreputable outlying district of the city: it didn't occur to me that a waiter on leave from one of the most upmarket hotels in Budapest, on a jaunt to the country with his sweetheart, would try to copy his smart guests in his civilian clothes. My wife's costume was more plausible. She had found a tight, faded blue skirt, a red blouse, a pair of stockings with ladders, and a dusty, scruffy velvet hat. She really looked like a kitchen maid from the country, worn out by all kinds of work and all kinds of love, to whom a few days' honeymoon with a superior waiter enjoying his leave meant happiness and great honour.

Thirty-six

That was the hottest day of the exceptional heat wave. About seven o'clock in the evening the sirens went off and we could see a few planes, but they soon disappeared because a thunderstorm was approaching from Transylvania. In the smithy across the road the company reassembled, and immediately after the all-clear the radio started blaring again. I had been sitting in the doctors' room since donning my disguise. In the afternoon my wife had waylaid the cyclist. He had explained to her in sign language that Mrs Szabó had found him in his lodgings and that he was expecting us at nine o'clock. From the window of the doctors' room we could see the gate and the guard standing in front of it. By half past eight we were beginning to get ready, like athletes warming up before the start of a race. Outside it was hellishly muggy, with black clouds and constant flashes of lightning. Shortly before nine the policeman who was to let us out arrived at the gate. He saluted his colleague and they exchanged a few words. Then the other policeman set off towards the town. From the corner he called back once more and then disappeared in the gathering darkness.

It was time to go. I picked up the vanity bag and started walking towards the gate. My wife followed me. The clouds hung so low that we could hardly see two paces ahead, except when there was a flash of lightning. We reached the gate. The policeman gave a small start, then opened one wing of the gate and murmured:

'Take care you don't come to grief.'

It was as if a stage manager had given the signal: the moment we stepped out of the gate a tremendous downpour began, accompanied by violent thunder and lightning. I had rarely seen such a downpour. It was like a stage cloudburst, not building up by degrees but erupting instantly at full force. It brought to mind the thunderstorm in the fifth act of *Rigoletto*, or a tropical downpour, in which—I had read—the rain descends in a solid sheet.

'Run,' I shouted, grabbing my wife's hand. We ran towards the corner, where we were almost imperceptibly joined by a shadow in a raincoat. It was the footballer, who immediately took the lead and made us follow him at the double across the square and the great marketplace. We ran, flustered and anxious, like hikers surprised by a thunderstorm and desperate to find shelter. Soon we were no different from any ordinary pedestrians who were trying to escape from the thunderstorm, puffing and panting and struggling against the wind and rain. The people running next to us, cursing or shrieking with the sudden cold, never suspected anything, never looked at us, never guessed that we weren't escaping from the thunderstorm, but from the gas. Our soaked clothes and my wife's matted hair legitimised us in the world outside the fence—drenched to the skin we were just like the Aryans. As we ran, the lightning fitfully illuminated the black raincoat that was showing us the way. The far end of the square was bounded by a row of two-storey houses. The black raincoat with the footballer in it headed towards a dimly lit door. He pulled the door open and we stumbled into the inn, where an innkeeper in shirtsleeves stood behind the counter. The only other people in the inn were two old men, looking like beggars and blind drunk, sitting at a table with two long-necked brandy bottles between them. The innkeeper hustled us into a dark private room. We collapsed at a table covered by a red cloth. The innkeeper brought us some brandy. The rainwater was running down my spine. I was cold, but the brandy soon warmed me up. My wife squeezed the water out of her hair.

And now? What next? The innkeeper was the footballer's brother-in-law. He didn't ask any questions but just brought more brandy. The footballer went out to get a hansom-cab. The innkeeper locked the door of our room from the outside. My wife was so exhausted that she immediately fell asleep. I went on drinking the strong spirit and became more and more recklessly confident. The cuckoo clock in the room showed ten minutes to ten. It seemed an eternity till, a few minutes before ten, the footballer returned with a cab driver. He came in and locked the door from the inside. The cab driver sat down in the bar room and drank three decilitres of wine. Then the innkeeper bundled the two old drunks out. A little after ten o'clock we got into the cab and the innkeeper pulled down the blinds. The footballer whispered into my ear that the driver was a friend of his and we needn't be afraid of him, but we didn't say a word during the whole journey. The downpour had abated and seemed to be turning into steady rain. The air had cooled down. I shivered. We crossed the square with the church of St László in the middle—its tower stretching towards the sky, menacingly, like a club drawn back to hit us. In Main Street only the café was lit up. A house on the left, worse luck, was my wife's birthplace— she stuck her head out of the hood of the cab and then dropped back into her corner.

'No crying!' I told her in a low voice, almost rudely. She sat up and once more became the worn-out, soaked kitchen maid. We reached the station. In the semi-dark concourse the peasants were sleeping on their baskets and bags. The platform was almost completely dark—the planes came this way every night if they hadn't got rid of their bombs. A policeman stood under one of the blue lamps.

'Good evening, officer,' I said to him in a friendly voice, feeling that I had become tipsy with the brandy that I had poured down too fast in the inn. 'Tell me, where does the Budapest train come in?'

'It's already here,' the policeman pointed his finger into the darkness. 'The long one over there, on track three.'

The alcohol made me feel very confident. At the same time, with what vigilance I had left, I kept repeating to myself: 'You're Ferenc Pattermann from Sarajevo . . . You're Ferenc Pattermann from Sarajevo.'

'I'd like to get on, if possible,' I said. 'I feel a bit funny.'

'I can see that,' the policeman laughed. 'But you'll sleep it off on the long journey.'

'You make a good wine in these parts,' I said. 'And cheap. Well, good night, officer.'

'Enjoy your journey,' the policeman said.

Nobody had thought of this—being drunk was better than any disguise, any false documents. I felt I had to hold on to my tipsiness, because nowadays even the smartest detective wouldn't sniff out a Jew in a drunk.

As we were walking towards the first-class waiting room, where Mrs Szabó had agreed to wait for us, my wife quietly told me off for overacting my part. But I wasn't really overacting and felt that my slight drunkenness made my behaviour seem more natural and credible. In front of the waiting room Mrs Szabó joined us without a word. In the cool rain, which was falling evenly by now, we crossed the wet rails to track three, where the long, dark Budapest train was standing. The footballer got on to see if he could find us seats in a compartment in which there seemed to be nothing untoward. There was a lot of room and the passengers were snoozing. We climbed up the steps and sat down in a spacious third-class carriage. I sat next to the window. Distrusting my wife's nerves, I told her to sleep, or rather to pretend to be asleep. Mrs Szabó and I chatted in a low voice. My drunkenness made me somewhat voluble, but I managed to speak quietly. Gradually the carriage filled up with tired, sleepy, bad-tempered civilians and dirty, smelly soldiers on leave. A few minutes before departure a gendarme with a soldier's box got on. He was also going on leave.

'Is anyone sitting here?' he asked me.

Opposite us there were two empty seats.

'No,' I said, 'there's nobody sitting there.'

'Well then, I can put my box up there,' he said, throwing it into the luggage rack above me.

Then he sat down.

'Good evening,' he said.

'Good evening,' I replied.

'What time does this train leave?' he asked.

'Ten thirty.'

He looked at his wristwatch, which had a luminous face.

'One minute and a half,' he muttered.

The rain had again become stronger and was lashing the windows. Through the half-open window on the right it even came into the compartment.

'Lovely rain,' the gendarme said. 'You could hardly bear the heat any more.'

'How long hasn't it rained here?' I asked.

'About ten days. In the afternoon there were always clouds, but it only rained a few drops.'

'In Budapest it rained all day last Sunday,' I said.

'In Budapest,' the gendarme said scornfully. 'The asphalt always gets enough, but the fields are ruined by the drought. Somewhere there was even hail.'

'Back in Transylvania,' I said. And then I added, 'It's got very cold.'

'You could close the window, Feri,' Mrs Szabó told me.

I stood up, tottering, and shut the window that had been letting the rain in.

'Well, well,' the gendarme said with a grin. 'Has the wine of Nagyvárad got to you?'

I sat down again. 'A waiter can only drink when he's on leave,' I mumbled. 'Or else he'd drop the plates, wouldn't he?'

Now Mrs Szabó cleverly intervened:

'You also drink on working days, Feri.'

'Do not muzzle the ox while it is treading the grain,' the gendarme quoted a proverb he had learnt in primary school. 'Where do you work?'

'In Budapest.'

'Whereabouts?'

'In the Pannonia. Straight ahead from the Eastern Station.'

'I don't know Budapest very well. I come from Győr county.'

'Are you on leave?' I asked condescendingly.

'Only five days. My father-in-law's just died.'

With a big jolt and a heavy creak, the train started. The gendarme looked at his watch:

'Seven minutes late.'

Thirty-seven

These slow night trains in wartime had their own peculiar voice. While the deportation wagons shrieked like falcons or vultures, this train whined, sometimes almost begged, then ground its teeth in helpless anger, like a beast of burden, or rather like a man carrying an excessive load, who is bent to the ground and whose heartbeat falters, but who is driven on relentlessly whenever he tries to stop. It did stop every five hundred paces, hoping that it would be allowed to stay put on the dark track, but it was given no quarter—it had to get to the Eastern Station in Budapest by noon, come what may. This single, puny engine had to drag the bombed-out people, the soldiers on leave and the black marketeers of half the country to the capital: whoever wanted to travel to Budapest from Zágon, Kolozsvár, Gyula or Szatmár was obliged to clamber into this train, which ran once a day. From time to time the engine seemed to be on its last breath of steam, and at such times its whistle gave the impression of a flute calling for help. But the military trains coming in the opposite direction raced past like fire engines or ambulances on urgent business in a city street.

In fact, this puny engine had almost been polished off by Russian planes on the previous afternoon, if the high-pitched male voice at the other end of the dark carriage was to be believed. This high-pitched voice, which apparently emanated from an expert, also explained that an engine like ours wouldn't have been allowed on a main line in peacetime.

'Its front is full of holes. It's just as well the boiler wasn't hit.'

'Where did that happen?' somebody asked languidly.

'Near Csap.'

As the train continued its struggle, the compartment fell silent. Most of the passengers dozed off, but the gendarme must have been very tired after some great task he had completed, because he was in a deep sleep and his head nodded rhythmically. Without his helmet and the strap under his chin, with his twirled moustache dishevelled and drooping, his soldierly features had loosened and his blank, expressionless face looked like that of a farmhand who has fallen asleep on his oxcart in a country lane, knowing that the oxen will find their way home of their own accord. He sat opposite me with his warm breath hitting me in the face, dreaming and smacking his lips, like a child. The things this man had done before my eyes! Or rather, what had this sleeping peasant with the gentle, stupid face been turned into? With the alcohol still at work in me, I toyed with the idea of waking him and saying to him:

'Listen, fellow-countryman, you're from Győr county and I'm from Komárom county. We're neighbours and almost the same age. We could have gone to school together and swum together in the nude by the landing stage, waiting for the boat from Vienna to arrive. Tell me, fellow-countryman, what have you and your mates done to my poor old mother? Have you gone mad? Didn't I join your ranks, the ranks of the poor, as soon as I was old enough to think? Didn't I say even as a child that the land of the count of Ószőny, the judge of Herkány and the Jew of Bélapuszta should be divided between poor people like you?'

I had almost grabbed the gendarme by his shirt, when Mrs Szabó became suspicious and gave my hand an imperious squeeze.

All right, all right, I thought. I'm not going to wake him. But it hurt indescribably that it was precisely these peasants and other brash small-timers with blood on their hands who had finished us off: people for whom I had fought a thousand times more in the course of my life than for the unfortunate Jews. When the officers tortured me in the Ukraine I hadn't cared. They were my enemies and I was their enemy. Ever since I was first able to think, I had been fighting this stupid, worthless middle class, which was sealed in its ignorance and narrow-mindedness as hermetically as in a tin can, and yet regarded itself as the most intelligent and admirable form of life, even before it had received the gift of racism imported from the Germans. But these small-timers, these proles and peasants—how much had I written on their behalf, although I knew how cold and selfish most of them were in their poverty and lack of education! And whenever a peasant or prole hurt me out there in the Ukraine, I felt as if all my life, all my work, all my beliefs had become ridiculous. In nineteen months in the Ukraine I had met only one man who was grateful to me for defending his interests in my articles. It was the chief cook, who had heard my comrades call me by my name from time to time, as we were chopping wood at the divisional command. Before we turned in he called me to one side:

'Are you the journalist?'

'Yes.'

'You once wrote something good on behalf of waiters. When tips were banned. I read it in Egerszeg, where I was working in the Korona Restaurant.'

'I may have.'

'You wrote something decent. Here,' and he handed me a meatball and a large piece of bread. This waiter—the like of Ferenc Pattermann, whose name I was now usurping—was the only man who ever repaid me for defending the rights of the poor. The rest were just like this gendarme. Yes, this gendarme opposite me embodied the failure of my whole life and career. These were the people for whom I had fought the masters and their power. Where had the Jews been at that time? I am sorry, but out of a disgraceful and false modesty, or an even more disgraceful opportunism, I hadn't so much as written the word Jew, before it became impossible not to write it—before the Jews became the only scapegoats in this country. I had been fighting the injustices and sufferings inflicted on the Hungarian people— and when I demanded land, doctors and schools for the peasants, the masters tried to gag me by saying:

'A Jew mustn't presume to interfere with the internal affairs of Hungarian society. The Hungarian upper class will settle its own business with the Hungarian people.'

But I had still interfered, acting as a self-appointed champion of the people, although deep down I had known that I wasn't wanted even by those I was trying to help. In the Ukraine it had been some penniless peasants who beat me half dead, and another who ruined my left eye. In Komárom it had been the same poor people, in civvies or uniforms, who deported my mother, my brothers and sisters, and my younger sister's four-year-old son. Now I was travelling to Budapest on this train with complete failure in my heart. And I still had no other goal than trying to fight underground for this homeland, in which neither the masters nor the poor people wanted me. Fighting against whom? Against my homeland—for my homeland. Not only against the stupid and venal generals, the rabid bureaucrats and the bloodthirsty tradesmen, but even against these poor people, who had been turned into wild animals and who even now, at the eleventh hour, were fighting only against me. If I woke this gendarme and told him who I was he would immediately grab me by the throat. Would there be anybody for me to join? Was there any resistance, were there any partisans?

Our train was shedding sweat and tears of steel under its tremendous weight. But just occasionally it gathered momentum when the driver was clearly expecting no surprises along the track. We had been crawling for two hours—had we been somewhere between Bobruisk and Minsk in Byelorussia, the partisans would have blown us up long since. Here too I could see acacia forests, corn fields, steppes—but where were the old peasant with the face of an orthodox priest, the toothless grandmother and the high-spirited kid, at whom the German guard would throw contemptuous jibes as he was passing, unaware that a few kilometres ahead the dynamite planted by these dim peasants had already blown up a train? Where was the peasant now? He was sitting opposite me and if I had woken him, and if he had seen me wearing one star more on my collar than he did, he would have killed his own mother if I had ordered him to do so.

But so far he had only killed my mother.

The train slowed and then, after a lot of jerking, stopped for what promised to be a long time. The puffing of the engine gradually died down, as if it had let out all its steam. From below, the steps and voices of railwaymen could be heard. I pressed my nose against the window and saw guards' lamps, painted blue, fluttering in the dark. Our carriage was at the end of the train and the blacked-out station was out of sight.

Now that the train had stopped, the passengers awoke one by one.

'Where are we?' a nasal voice asked sleepily.

'I think in Újfalu,' a Székely accent answered.

'Is that all?' a young female voice complained.

For a while nobody spoke. Then somebody stood up and walked through the compartment towards the door. A deep, elderly female voice asked:

'Does anybody know where the toilet is?'

'At the front,' said the high-pitched voice of the engine expert.

The door at the other end of the compartment was opened and slammed shut. A little later the man who had made this racket returned, bringing news:

'The rain's stopped. We're not at Újfalu but Báránd. We've got to wait an hour and a half, because there are military trains on both tracks. And there's an air raid in Ladány and Debrecen.'

'We'll run into the raid,' an urban voice called out with a start.

'The engine's already been hit once,' the expert repeated his information.

People dozed off again, settling down for the hour and a half's halt. The gendarme, who hadn't even woken, began to snore.

'Who's snoring?' an authoritative male voice snapped.

Nobody answered.

'If you click he'll stop,' somebody recommended, probably a soldier on leave.

Some people clicked their tongues. The gendarme snored more softly for a few moments and then started again. Somebody laughed.

Then the siren went off.

'Well, here it comes.'

'And the moon has come out too.'

'We ought to get off,' the urban voice said nervously.

But nobody moved, because that would have meant having to fight again for seats. Since the start of this war nobody had respected anybody else's seat on a train.

The young woman thought she could hear the murmur of plane engines, but she was shouted down. Half an hour passed.

People drooped again, overcome by the stuffiness of the carriage. They didn't wake again till the all-clear sounded and a few minutes later the military trains rushed past us. Both trains consisted of open carriages, one carrying German anti-aircraft artillery and Goering guns, the other Hungarian sappers. In the moonlight we could see the soldiers' greenish-grey faces. Then, with a din as if a large house were collapsing, our train started again.

My wife had at first only pretended to be asleep, but eventually she really dropped off with weakness and exhaustion. Mrs Szabó sat next to me with her eyes open, watching me. We didn't talk because we had agreed not to exchange one unnecessary word on the journey. The train seemed to be running more easily: now its music resembled that of a gutter in the autumn rain, or a bowling alley in a village on a Sunday afternoon, when the balls roll along the lanes. My lids became heavy and I may actually have fallen asleep in ten-minute snatches, but I kept rousing myself in order to practise: 'If somebody wakes you and asks your name, who are you?' 'I'm Ferenc Pattermann and I was born in Sarajevo.' One of the soldiers had mentioned that on the journey down people had been made to show their identity papers, and I had to prepare myself for detectives searching the train for Jews and leftists. But finally I could no longer resist my tiredness and the soporific gutter music. I didn't wake up till after Karcag. Dawn was breaking.

As the morning light filtered in, the people in the compartment slowly awoke. Stretching, blinking and rubbing their eyes, they asked each other where we were. Then they laboriously lifted their baskets or suitcases out of the luggage racks and took out their food. Everybody ate, the peasants roast chicken and sausage, the townspeople cheese and hard-boiled eggs. The soldiers had canned rations, probably drawn at the regimental depot, and the sergeant now issued the two privates theirs. A thin gentleman with sideburns, pince-nez and a clipped moustache offered a bottle to his neighbours:

'Juniper,' he said. 'Distilled it myself.'

Everybody around him took a swig, even the women.

'Good stuff,' a soldier said. 'Where do you come from?'

'From Gyimes,' the gentleman with the juniper brandy

explained. 'I am a bombed-out notary. All I have left is in my suitcase.'

'Just as well the juniper brandy was left,' the sergeant joked.

'They'll be in Gyimes soon, the Romanians or Russkis, if things go well for them,' a man looking like a horse dealer remarked, leafing through yesterday's paper.

'They're already there, damn their souls,' the notary answered.

'They're coming like the flood,' one of the women wailed.

'Now, now,' an older man in a hunting outfit on the other side of the carriage objected. 'They're coming, but how far? The Germans got as far as Stalingrad, but they've turned back. This lot has got as far as the Carpathians, but they'll also turn back. Am I right, sergeant?'

The sergeant was about to wipe his mouth. Like a cautious expert, he answered sagely:

'Anything's possible in war. They can still be nabbed.'

'Of course they can,' the notary with the pince-nez affirmed. 'It isn't over yet. Only the Jews think it's over.'

This was the first time anybody uttered the word Jew.

'The Jews?' The man with the high-pitched voice gave a coarse laugh. In daylight he had turned out to be a railway brakeman. 'The Jews don't think anything now. They're all finished.'

'To hell with them,' a peasant woman piped up. 'But we haven't been able to sell anything on the market since.'

'That's no argument, my good woman,' the man in the hunting outfit turned on her. 'Just because you did deals with the Jews on the black market . . .'

'Who did deals on the black market?' the peasant woman shouted back. 'But a body doesn't want to work all year to have it requisitioned or sell it for a song.'

'Will it be better if the Russians take it all away? Like we did out there? And if they take you and your son to Siberia? Is that why you're defending the Jews?'

'The devil defends them,' the woman protested. 'All I'm saying is that a body should be paid the proper market price for what she's been working for.'

'Rest assured, you will be paid,' the man in the hunting outfit lectured her. 'Your spinach will also be bought by Christian society. And your goose liver. Christian society will become stronger now. But you mustn't talk like that when you've just heard from the notary that the Russians are in Gyimes.'

The man in the hunting outfit had flushed crimson. His protesting and lecturing had brought him out in a sweat.

For a while the passengers no longer felt like talking. Although the man in the hunting outfit had said nothing directed against them, they wondered whether he might be some kind of official, a detective or an army officer in civilian clothes. With such people around it was better to be silent. It took several minutes before the man with the high-pitched voice started again:

'When they took the Jews away from our village, from Magyarcséke, do you know what they found in the synagogue?'

'What?' one of the women asked.

'A radio transmitter.'

'They found radio transmitters in every synagogue,' the infantry sergeant declared. 'In Poland. And in Russia too. These Jews didn't even have the sense to destroy them before the gendarmes arrived.'

Now the gendarme opposite me awoke and, hearing the word gendarme, enquired sleepily: 'Destroyed what?'

'I was saying the Jews didn't even have enough sense to get rid of their radio transmitters when the gendarmes came. Isn't that true, sergeant?'

The gendarme replied in the condescending and slightly scornful voice of a man in the know:

'You don't know what you're talking about. It wasn't radios they found, but gold and silver. All their secret books were wrapped in it.'

'The Talmud,' the man in the hunting outfit said triumphantly.

'Yes, where it says how they have to finish off the Hungarians,' the railwayman with the high-pitched voice said. 'We've been told at a meeting what kind of tortures for the Hungarians were described there.'

My wife had woken up and was trembling all over as she listened to the conversation. For a moment she opened her eyes. I looked at her steadily till she closed them again.

'I don't know what was in them,' the gendarme continued

even more haughtily. 'All I know is that here in Nagyvárad they didn't have any radios. But it's possible that they had some in other places.' He stood up, lifted his box from the luggage rack and took out his food.

Mrs Szabó took her bag down, and we also started eating.

'Have you slept it off, brother?' the gendarme asked me.

'Yes.'

He looked at his watch:

'Half past four. How far could we be from Szolnok?'

From the other side a man looking like a tradesman answered:

'It could be an hour and a half. If we don't stop too long before the bridge.'

We ate.

'When do you start work again, then?' the gendarme asked me.

'At lunchtime, damn it,' I said. 'I hope we aren't late, because I'd lose a whole working day. And they'd tell me off, on top of it.'

'Is it hard work?'

'It only looks easy. You have to walk a lot. Your back and thighs ache. And the guests are nasty.'

'What kind of place is that Pannonia?'

'Very smart. The guests are aristocrats, lord-lieutenants, sheriffs. And people who own blocks of flats.'

'Any Jews?'

'Not many Jews, even before the war.'

'Does anybody who isn't a Jew own blocks of flats in Budapest?'

'Yes, but not many,' I said impeccably.

'About ten,' the railwayman added.

'No, more than that,' the man in the hunting outfit said. 'I own a quarter of a block myself.'

'In which district?' I asked without looking up from my food.

'In Szent Imre Herceg Road.'

'A nice area. Being developed.'

'It'll be good after the war. The city will be spreading that way.'

He gave me a friendly look. Having heard that I was a waiter in the Pannonia, which was frequented by counts and men of property, he said, in an attempt to increase his prestige in the compartment:

'I remember you. I used to go to the Pannonia too. Last year and the year before.'

'You also look familiar to me, sir. From the bar room. But from the dining room too.'

So now I even had a witness. The man in the hunting outfit had legitimised me in front of the compartment.

When the eating was finished, the green bottle with the juniper brandy somehow also found its way to us. The gendarme drank first, then he gave the bottle to me.

'Wouldn't you like some, madam?' I asked Mrs Szabó, because I felt it was time to draw her into the game a little.

'Not me, Feri,' she refused with a smile. 'You would turn me into an alcoholic if you could.'

'You're in the right line of work, at any rate,' I said.

'What do you do, madam?' the gendarme enquired.

'The lady mends the hotel linen,' I improvised. 'She's a seamstress.'

Thirty-eight

The compartment relapsed into lassitude. Nobody was talking, except the gendarme and me.

He offered me a Levente cigarette. Then, after pondering for a while, he said:

'As a waiter in Budapest you meet a lot of big shots. You know what's what, don't you?'

'A bit. A man sees a few things in my job.'

'Well, look at this problem with my inheritance. I've taken five days' leave to sort it out. My father-in-law was seventy-five, as fit as a fiddle. Then in the matter of a moment he dropped off his chair and was dead.'

'At that age it can happen.'

'Sure, it can happen. But listen, my father-in-law kicked his wife out of his house when he was sixty-two, in the winter of 1934. She'd gone mad in her old age, started drinking and got involved with poachers. She was going around with young crooks and keeping them in booze. My father-in-law didn't drink. When the old man kicked his wife out, my wife took her father's side, and Veronika, my sister-in-law, her mother's. My sister-in-law even moved to Győrzámoly, where the old woman was working for the priests. Then the old woman suddenly died, and my sister-in-law Veronika of course begged her father to take her back.'

'Did he?' I asked.

'He was a weak, gormless type. He did. That was about the time I married my wife. The old man didn't want to be left alone. As soon as my sister-in-law had moved back she married a railwayman, a certain Szulacsik, and he also went to live there. He was a guard. By that time the war had broken out. Me and the wife were living in Szabadhegy, which was where I'd been posted. My third child was born this spring—two are boys, this

282

is the only girl—I only need to breathe at my wife and she's pregnant. My sister-in-law hasn't any. She's sterile. Then the railwayman died. I'll tell you later how. So my sister-in-law was left alone with my father-in-law. I'm being dragged here and there all over the country, first on border duty, now because of these Jews. And my wife back in Győrszabadhegy can only get away from the children and the home once or twice a year. It made no difference that she'd been good to her father her whole life. Now my sister-in-law was with him all the time; she could twist him round her little finger.'

'Did he leave a will?' I asked.

'No, that's the trouble, he didn't. And now my sister-in-law says the old man promised her all four acres. She's also produced two witnesses who say that she's entitled to the whole land because my wife already got her share in the form of her dowry.'

'It's no good producing witnesses,' I explained, with the legal expertise befitting a waiter. 'What is due is due. The children of the deceased are entitled to their share even where there isn't a will. If they've beaten up their father or mother every day of their lives, the children still have an entitlement, unless they've been formally disinherited,' I expounded with voluble pedantry. 'Are there no other siblings?'

'None.'

'Then it's half to each.'

The conversation had been carried on quietly and confidentially. The gendarme was bothered by the issue. He offered me another Levente.

'Look,' he began, 'I know that much myself. A gendarme has to learn some law. But there's something else. The point is that the way I see it they aren't entitled to anything. Everything's due to us.'

'Why?'

'My mother-in-law the old man threw out of his house was a notoriously dirty bitch. Their house stank—and she even beat the old man. She was a big, bony woman and she used to shout so the whole village could hear: "I'll kill you, you bastard! . . ."'

I waved my hand.

'That doesn't mean anything,' I said sceptically. 'If a man and woman quarrel they say things like that.'

'That's true,' the gendarme nodded. 'Everybody says things like that. I've also said things to my wife that I've regretted. I wouldn't have any suspicions, especially as the old woman died six years ago. But my sister-in-law Veronika had lived with her . . . I mean in her house. She might have learnt something from the witch . . .'

'What?'

'Her husband, the railwayman, had nothing wrong with him. He was thirty-one and he didn't even drink. He had an easy life, sitting in the guard's van. Then one day in the early autumn he left his post in Dombóvár and came home. The neighbours say they were beating each other up all night, till the priest, who lives in the third house opposite, came to knock on their door. The next day the railwayman was still walking about, but in the evening he lay down and never got up again. Six weeks later he was dead. And now the same thing with my father-in-law. Nothing wrong with him, and he just falls off his chair. There's only his daughter with him—the old man's like a man of fifty and—suddenly that's it.'

'It's certainly strange,' I murmured. 'But why do you think she learnt it from her mother? She might have discovered it for herself,' I said for argument's sake. 'But if you're suspicious, it's easy for a gendarme. You can have the railwayman exhumed, and the old man too. Then, if the doctors find some poison in their guts . . .'

'I know, I know,' the gendarme shook his head. 'But I don't want to bring the family into disrepute. And it could do me some harm too. It doesn't help the prospects of a gendarme if there's a criminal in his family.'

'That isn't the gendarme's fault.'

'That's how it's judged above. I don't want her to be locked up. But what does she need four acres for if she hasn't got any children? She wouldn't have any children even if she went to bed with half the country, because she's sterile. And I've two sons and a daughter.'

'That's true.'

'A single woman like her should go to the city and be a maid. If she works in the city she'll earn her keep. But how do I know what's going to happen to us after this war? If we beat them maybe we'll be taken to Russia or France to tidy things up. But if they beat us? Then perhaps there won't even be a gendarmerie, never mind ministers and regents. No railways, no houses . . . Look out there.'

I looked out of the window. I saw the fresh ruins of a railway building and, further along, a broken power cable in a tangle. The water from yesterday's downpour, caught in the bomb craters in the fields, sparkled in the light of the rising sun.

'The devil knows what's going to happen,' I growled.

'God Himself doesn't know. Perhaps there won't even be a country. But there'll always be land. And I've three children. Whatever happens the state won't be able to keep all three when they grow up. Who does that sterile woman have to take care of? Who's going to be left when the house collapses on her?'

'That's right,' I nodded.

'You know your way around. What would you do to . . . ?'

'Well . . . it's difficult to talk about such things if they aren't your own business,' I said evasively. 'But wouldn't it be possible to talk to her sensibly?'

'Her? She's like a lynx. Like a cat with kittens. But I can frighten her . . . I can tell her that I'll have her father and the railwayman exhumed. If she has done anything she'll be scared and sign whatever I like. But listen, brother. I've just had an idea.'

'What?'

'Couldn't you get a job for her at the hotel? Apart from that, she's a decent, hard-working woman, not like her mother. And she's a good cook too.'

'She might put something in the food,' I said with a laugh.

'No, she's not really like that. She wouldn't hurt strangers. With strangers she's polite. She was once a cook in Kaposvár, in a Jewish home. They were full of her praises. But listen, brother, you'd really do me a great favour if you got her a job in the restaurant. If I could go back right now and tell her that I've found a job for her in Budapest it would be much easier to persuade her.'

285

'Well,' I said somewhat uncomfortably, 'perhaps we could try. When are you coming back?'

'On Sunday.'

'Okay,' I said reluctantly, 'call in at the Pannonia on Sunday evening. Look for me in the kitchen. Ask for Ferenc. I'll have a word with the boss before then.'

'Couldn't it be today? I've got three hours between trains. Maybe more if there's an air raid.'

'Today's no good,' Mrs Szabó came to my aid, having listened to the conversation without saying a word. 'Today's the boss's day off.'

'But you can take it as fixed,' I reassured him, with my superiority restored.

'They do need female staff,' Mrs Szabó said. 'The girls from the country are frightened by the bombing. Most of them are going home. There will be a job. Just come along on Sunday.'

'Can I bring her with me?' the gendarme asked.

What could I say?

'Yes, bring her.'

'Just let me make a note of your name and address,' he said. Pulling out his official diary, he entered my name and the address of the Pannonia with a pencil. Then, like a man who has carried out a task to his satisfaction, he stretched himself and became more cheerful. Looking round the compartment, he discovered my sleeping wife.

'Is this girl with you?'

'Of course,' I said suggestively. 'This is Róza. She works at the Pannonia too, in the kitchen.'

'She's been asleep ever since we left.'

'She's got something to sleep off,' I hinted.

He leant very close to me and asked in an undertone:

'Is she your woman?'

'A colleague,' I said with a leer.

'You picked a right young one. It looks like you waiters have a lot of choice. But she's very thin.'

'She's from Budapest,' I shrugged.

Thirty-nine

The train stopped at Újszász. Two peasants got on, a neatly dressed old man with a bent back and a young woman in mourning. In front of the train, between the tracks, men were helplessly running to and fro, as if in doubt whether or not our journey would continue. An air-raid siren went off, but it sounded very faint in the distance: perhaps these wartime shortages made it necessary to economise even with noise, so that there was enough left for places in immediate danger. The gendarme stood up, let the window down and called out:

'What's going on?'

'Some paratroopers have been seen near Szolnok,' a voice called back in passing.

The gendarme sat down again.

'Paratroopers,' he waved his hand dismissively. 'Everybody sees them, except a gendarme.'

'On Sunday three were beaten to death. They were all British,' somebody said with a knowing air.

'They weren't British,' the old peasant who had just got on disagreed gently. 'They were local Jews. Deserters.'

'So much the better,' the notary said enthusiastically. 'They must be eliminated. In Gyimes we saw the Jews leading the Russians across the mountains.'

'Then who's leading the British and the Americans in France?' the old peasant asked. 'Because they're in France too now.'

'The Jews again, of course,' the railwayman with the high-pitched voice chipped in.

'Naturally, the Jews,' the notary added officiously.

Unexpectedly, the old peasant said in a decided tone:

'Leave the Jews alone. There aren't as many Jews as there are troubles.'

'Are you trying to say that the Jews are decent people, granddad?' the man in the hunting outfit asked sharply.

'I've never had any problems with them,' the old peasant said with innocent sincerity. 'In the village we only had three: a doctor, a poultry buyer and a cobbler. The gendarmes took them away at Whitsun, but I wouldn't have minded if they'd stayed. It's a pity about the doctor. He'd lived in the village for thirty-seven years. He was a good doctor and he was poor all his life. He asked for hardly any money. He just took what people gave him.'

'And he pulled out people's teeth for free,' the young peasant woman in mourning said.

'For free,' the man in the hunting outfit sneered. 'He earned a hundred times more in other places. I bet he was a usurer and kept his money in town. He probably charged hundreds of pengős for an abortion. These Jews were destroying the children of the Hungarian race even before they were born.'

'I'm sure he didn't kill anybody,' the woman in mourning protested.

'Perhaps you're defending him because he helped you out,' a woman who looked like a market-stall holder intervened.

The old peasant shook his head gently and sadly:

'Don't talk like that, don't talk like that,' he lamented quietly. 'My granddaughter here lost her husband three years ago. He froze to death in the Ukraine. Her only child, a little girl, died a fortnight ago in Szolnok when a bomb hit the school. We're on our way to the funeral. There was nothing left of all seventy children. We can only bury the wooden boxes. Aren't you ashamed of speaking ill of the Jews when you're just as bad? Are you Christians?'

The carriage fell silent. Only the notary opened his mouth:

'Are you saying we aren't?'

'Listen,' the old peasant went on, 'I became a Baptist in the first war because people are so wicked. They don't understand the Word. They upset a poor widow who's just lost her child. That's why we have it coming to us. You know very well what's coming. But we deserve it because the Evil One is among us.'

'You're quite right, granddad, people have become morally

depraved,' the man in the hunting outfit said. 'It's not surprising that these American gangsters are bombing defenceless towns, women and children and old men. But that doesn't alter the fact that the worst criminals, who were trying to annihilate us, were the Jews. The bombs were sent to us by the British Jews. That's why they had to be finished.'

'Of course they had to be finished,' the notary duplicated. 'In Transylvania I saw how they . . .'

Now my gendarme suddenly said:

'The old man's right. Leave the bloody Jews alone. Why do you keep going on about them? We've finished them, full stop. It's boring.'

But the notary didn't give in. 'This question can never be boring, sergeant.'

'There's no question left,' the gendarme explained. 'Now they're taking the Jews of Budapest, too. They're moving them to the houses with the stars. And then the wagons will come and we'll be among our own. That's what we wanted, and we've done it.'

'And we also have to win this war,' a soldier threw in. 'That's still left to be done.'

'Don't you worry, we'll win it,' the notary boasted.

The debate suddenly stopped when a squadron of white American planes appeared low in the blue sky and came straight towards the railway line. Everybody pressed towards the window and watched their flight, awestruck and silent. The notary sat fixed to his seat, white as chalk, crossing and re-crossing his legs. As soon as it had become light and I was able to take a close look at the people in the carriage, this notary had begun to look suspicious to me. His movements, his restless, feverish stare behind his brand new glasses, which didn't fit his eyes and which I could immediately see were being worn by a man who didn't normally wear glasses, his freshly trimmed moustache, and above all the ferociousness with which he kept reigniting the vilification of the Jews—I could read such small signals in such situations with the accuracy of a seismograph. The others also vilified the Jews, but only when the question somehow arose of its own accord. This notary kept almost forcing the conversation back to the

Jews, so that he could abuse them. With those particular signals in mind, I watched him going over the top, and I became more and more certain that with his intensity, his excessive intransigence, his verbosity, he was doing all he could to cover up his panic. I saw with growing concern that if he went on in this amateurish way he would get himself into trouble. He had already made the deporting gendarme himself stop the invectives against the Jews, and everybody in the compartment, apart from him, was getting bored with the topic. I had to find some way of warning him. Especially if—as was rumoured—after Szolnok the detectives were coming to demand identity papers and to search for Jews. If anybody denounced the Jews so massively, an experienced detective would take him to the lavatory and tell him to unbutton his flies . . .

I should tell him to stop it. He should be asleep, like my wife, if he can't play his part. He speaks terribly humbly to these NCOs and peasants: a real notary would behave much more arrogantly. Sooner or later even the least perceptive observer will notice that he's laying it on too thick, and see through his disguise. Only Jews don't know that even the most rabid anti-Semite doesn't think about Jews day and night, or when he is roused from his sleep. Even today non-Jews from time to time take an interest, at least for a little while, in other things in life, for instance in eating when they're eating, in the weather when it's raining, and in enjoying themselves when they're making love. Only Jews think day and night about being Jews. If this clumsy fake notary goes on ramming the topic of Jews down their throats, even when they have lost their appetite for it, he'll awaken their wily peasant suspicions.

But how can I tell him? He's still shooting his mouth off, trembling and white as chalk, even though the bombing has already begun and the whole compartment is listening spellbound to the droning of the planes and to the explosions. He's still blathering and reciting the Arrow Cross mantra he has learnt from the newspapers: the Jews are showing them the targets. The poor bastard thinks that this is what a good Hungarian and a good Christian has to say at such a time, and it's just as well that nobody except me has noticed that the text is not in sync with his gestures. Just as well that nobody's listening to him. They're listening to the bombing, which doesn't end but only grows a little fainter in the distance.

'It was either the bridge', somebody says in a subdued voice, 'or the new refinery on the left.'

'If it was the bridge, we won't be able to get across,' laments the woman who looks like a market-stall holder.

Bang, bang. The windows rattle, and from somewhere we hear the sound of breaking glass. The planes are back again, right above our heads. They roar past very low, almost ruffling our hair. The passengers have hunched up their shoulders. The notary has hidden under his seat and peeps out from his cover long after the planes have moved on. Now all the passengers regain their colour, straighten up and behave as if each has individually passed a test, individually overcome some danger. When they see the notary with his green face crawling out from under the seat, they burst into laughter and mockery in their relief. They all want to prove at the notary's expense that they're not only not afraid of death, but are indeed on friendly terms with it.

Forty

'Well, mister notary,' one of the soldiers on leave jeered. 'No wonder the Russians got into your village first. If a man's as yellow as you he can't defend his village.'

The notary stammered: 'It's not my job to defend . . .'

'But you still don't need to get such cold feet,' the railway-man with the high-pitched voice sneered. 'What do you think you'll do in Budapest?'

'I'm not afraid,' the notary pleaded, 'but can't I protect my head from splinters?'

The man in the hunting outfit had probably also been terri-fied, but he intervened in the didactic tone of a superior arbi-trator:

'That's a question of nerves. Take me, for example. I can stand any danger, but not quite as easily if it comes from above. When I was on the Italian front in the first war I could stand the cannons and the machine guns, but when the planes came . . .'

'If anybody says he likes it he's a liar,' the gendarme remarked, turning to me, 'but you didn't look too worried, brother.'

'Well, you know,' I shrugged, 'I've got used to the bombing in Budapest. At first I had the jitters. But now I serve during the bombing and I don't even rattle the dishes . . . I was born in Bosnia. In the Black Mountains people aren't afraid.'

'Are you a Bosnian?' the man in the hunting outfit asked with interest and got up to sit closer to me.

'I was only born there, in Sarajevo. But I soon moved to Szeben.'

The man in the hunting outfit sat down on the empty seat next to the gendarme. Perhaps, terrified by the bombing, he wanted to draw some courage from a man with better nerves.

'Memphis or Symphonia?' he asked, offering us his silver

cigarette case and lighting one himself. 'I was in Zilah,' he started telling us, as if we had asked him. 'I'm taking home a rabbit and some sausages and butter. At home there's either nothing left or it's prohibitively expensive. How does the Pannonia manage the cooking?'

'With difficulty.'

'You can only bring something from the countryside now,' the man in the hunting outfit lamented. Then he said confidentially: 'Do you happen to know anything about the inspections by the excise at the Eastern Station?'

'It varies.'

'I wonder how I'll get into the city with this little bit of food,' he pondered. 'The family's on the brink of starving. What if they confiscate it? I should get off earlier. Perhaps at Kőbánya.'

'Kőbánya's no good. There are lots of excise men,' I said expertly.

He moved closer to the gendarme and asked him in an ingratiating manner: 'Perhaps the sergeant would be so kind and take it off me at the exit . . .'

'What have you got in there?' the gendarme asked benignly.

'As I said, a rabbit and some pork and lard.'

'Nothing else?'

'Nothing.'

'All right,' the gendarme said condescendingly. 'Give it to me when we arrive at the Eastern Station. Is it a large suitcase?'

'No, not at all,' the man in the hunting outfit answered eagerly. 'It's quite small. The brown one up there,' he said, pointing to the luggage rack.

The train started.

Forty-one

The man in the hunting outfit is nervous about smuggling a rabbit through the excise. I have to smuggle my own skin and my wife's life through the nets of the murderers, and yet I'm not nearly as nervous as he is. I feel like an apathetic tightrope walker performing his balancing act mechanically, no longer really dreading the abyss that yawns beneath him. My instinct for survival is functioning, but my passion for life hasn't been kindled by this unexpected, adventurous escape.

After all that I've been through I no longer believe that life is worth living, and I don't even know whether I'll be able to live. Meanwhile the train is mechanically carrying me towards Budapest, and when I get there I'll do just as mechanically what the situation demands and allows. The events of my life up to now leave me no other way, and no doubt I'll do all I can to make contact with the underground resistance movement or the clandestine press. If I'm given a role I'll accept it, though not because I still believe in the Hungarians, the Jews, the left, or humanity itself. What can I believe in, travelling through this country, in which nothing seems to have changed in spite of what I've seen with my own eyes and felt with my own skin? It's still the same country, with the same moderate climate and the same flora and fauna. It isn't a jungle with pumas and boa constrictors, or a primeval world of ice with palaeolithic monsters, or a desert through which the simoom blows. The same acacia trees drip with rain and the same dogs lie on their stomachs in front of the sentry boxes, chasing the flies away with their tails—the same Hungary! The people haven't grown fangs, and their eyes are where they used to be, as are probably their brains and hearts also. What can I still believe in, in this country whose law demands that every town, village, farmhouse and bush be combed, in case there is a baby or an old woman left behind who was registered as a Jew and has not yet been burned? Whenever the train passes a whitewashed church, I see a church square, where small shopkeepers, publicans, doctors, pharmacists and rag-and-bone men are rounded up with their dishevelled families and driven to the wagons, past rows of peasants passively gaping or venting their half-baked envy and gleeful malice. And once they have been deported, the village goes on living in the same old way, as if nothing had happened. The people go out to the fields, on Sunday the bells ring and the priests preach, and a few days later, having squabbled over and shared out the Jews' belongings, they no longer even talk about them and have forgotten everything. In our carriage too they would hardly talk about them, if the fake notary, cantankerous with fear, didn't keep bringing the topic up again and again.

The unchanging state of the scenery and the world, and the lack of emotion with which people responded to this horror— a horror unprecedented in a thousand years—have confirmed my feeling that there's no point in struggling to keep alive. If nature and eternity are so indifferent to human concerns, all our efforts are in vain: everything will remain the same. But I still wouldn't like to be caught by the detectives on the train and handed over to the gendarmes at a station. I'm afraid of being beaten, and if my wife fell into their hands she'd die straight away . . .

But I feel that I'm playing my role well. Perhaps too well. A bit like a star, like a soloist. I suspect that I've developed and inflated the waiter character to such an extent that even Mrs Szabó finds it difficult to join in. Not to mention my wife who, now that I've upstaged everybody, can do nothing but continue to sleep. Mrs Szabó likewise feels that in my thespian over-enthusiasm I've gradually acted her out of the play, and so she too is, or pretends to be, sleeping.

For kilometres the train has been limping along as if there were nothing but one long, wounded bridge beneath it. In the quiet compartment the passengers crane their necks towards the windows, looking for fresh traces of the bombing. More military trains zoom past us. On the concrete road, covered carts roll east, towards the front, driven by Hungarian soldiers with grey moustaches. At a small station a long line of burnt-out carriages still stands on the rails, but the engine has been overturned. They were probably hit by an incendiary bomb. The stationmaster's arm is in a sling. A gypsy musician with a goitre enters the compartment and starts eerily playing martial hits from the radio's request programme. He's quickly given some money to stop playing. We crawl on. The notary gets up and leaves the compartment. One of the soldiers calls after him: 'Are you going to clean yourself up?'

But the compartment is in no mood for mockery. We stop again. The engine gives a series of long whistles, as if it expected a reply from an accomplice. We're close to the Szolnok bridges. For minutes the steam of the engine hisses earsplittingly, as though it were plucking up not strength but courage: in God's name, perhaps it'll work, let's go for it, let's be devils. Now we're actually crawling across a bridge, with bomb craters around us on both sides of the embankment, and on the left a fresh break in the railing. Sweat is pouring from under the steel helmets of lethargic German soldiers with bayonets. Near the water is a freshly wrecked plane.

We're still suspended on the bridge, above the water. Then, with sudden urgency, we sprint across to the other bank at the greatest possible speed.

'Thank God, we've made it,' the man in the hunting outfit sighs, wiping his sweaty forehead, with the blood rapidly returning to his blanched face.

At Szolnok only half the station is left. Further down the tracks the wrecks of twenty trains are piled one on top of the other, pointing towards the sky or dug deep into the earth. The gendarme stands up and, stepping to the window, promptly discovers that the station bar is unscathed and working. Our carriage has stopped a long way from the station, opposite the bombed water tower. I gaze at the ruins, bemused but with an expert eye—they're genuine battlefield ruins, just like the ruins in the Ukraine. Such ruins haven't been seen in the hinterland until now. What did a talkative Hungarian soldier explain to me in Seredina-Buda?

'Look, pal, I'd rather fight two thousand kilometres from my own doorstep than back in the home country.'

Now the battleground has caught up with him at his own doorstep. I gaze at the ruins, the knot of molten engines and carriages, the tangled pipes, rails and cables, and although I shudder I must admit I also feel a certain satisfaction. After many long years, here is the proof of what they refused to believe, however often we told them: that the country would be destroyed by what its rulers were doing to it, or rather by what its rulers were making its people do.

But the gendarme has no dark thoughts. The gendarme is thirsty and says:

'Well, brother, now we get off. We're going to have a beer in the station bar.'

If a waiter is invited for a drink he can't refuse. I pull myself to my feet, even though I know the risk. This is the first time I have left my seat since we got on the train. It's the first time I've stood up in broad daylight, presenting a 'full target', as they used to say in the army. Here in the carriage nobody knows me. Nor would anybody recognise me from the illustrated magazines that used to print my photo occasionally in earlier times. These people leafed past me even then. But if I now get out of the carriage I'll have to file along the train, with passengers from half of Hungary leaning out on their elbows as if on a grandstand, watching everything that happens on the platform. Even if nobody recognises me with this moustache and the clothes I'm wearing, I could be recognised by my walk, by my movements, by some tic of which I'm not even aware. But I still have to go, because anybody can refuse a glass of beer in a station bar, except a waiter on his day off.

I see Mrs Szabó's nervous gaze following me, and my wife also opens a pair of eyes glassy with terror. But I set off at a nice steady pace, the gendarme and I are chatting like old friends and with the brittle jolliness of two men who haven't lost their mental balance in spite of a bombing raid. If anybody should see me being so friendly with a gendarme he wouldn't seriously suspect me, even if he were to recognise a familiar feature about me and start wondering where he had seen that face before. No, even somebody who thought that I looked like me wouldn't expect a Jew—never mind such a notorious Jew—to be hobnobbing with a gendarme, of all people.

Still, when I stepped down from the train, with a jolt, I felt as if I had stepped on ice. For a moment I was dizzy, but then I pulled myself together and accompanied the gendarme's stride, which managed to seem both martial and boorish, with my own slovenly waiter's shuffle. Walking round the fresh craters gouged out between the tracks, probably less than half an hour ago, by bomb fragments which must have weighed half a ton, we appraised the damage with forced brightness. On the black and white tiled platform a worn-out, bleary-eyed crowd was milling in all directions. Everybody seemed to be looking for a train somewhere else, although there was only ours standing at the station. The platform was slippery with oily water, tinged here and there with streaks of blood. At the door of the third-class waiting room a news vendor stood with the fresh papers from the capital, but he seemed to have lost his voice and, instead of crying his wares, was staring pensively into space. I automatically reached for some money in my pocket to buy a paper. Then, like an overanxious theatre director, I realised that a waiter wouldn't be in such a hurry to read a paper, particularly if he hadn't had anything to drink all night. So, together with the gendarme, I joined the mêlée at the entrance to the bar, which was blocked by soldiers in Hungarian and German uniforms and agitated civilians.

Angry and desperate to get hold of some food for their hungry families in the carriages, unshaven men without hats and collars, and dishevelled, skinny women with rheumy eyes and pointed noses, fought mercilessly with both arms, the men clumsy and awkward, the women ruthless and vicious. Using his authority and his expertise in keeping order, the gendarme cleared a way through, and soon we stood in front of a counter covered by a patched metal sheet, on which some greasy plates smeared with congealed fat indicated that everything edible—the mutton sausages, the cold horsemeat, the smelly cheese, all the wartime rubbish—had already been devoured. The plates were teeming with flies, both ordinary house flies and green dungflies that had

298

flown in from the ruins to make a guest appearance. There was no wine, because the station cellars had received a direct hit. Only a few dozen sticky, dark brown beer bottles stood in a row on a shelf, with the sun furiously beating down on them. At the thought of having to drink out of these bottles, my stomach turned over. I'd never drunk beer—I had an almost abnormal aversion to it—and I could never understand why this bitter drink with the sickly smell was supposed to be so good. But the gendarme had already called out to the grey-haired barman in shirtsleeves and a dirty apron:

'Give us a bottle.'

The barman promptly poured some beer into two unwashed glasses. I knew that there was no retreat—a real waiter will drink anything, given the chance. Not just beer but even petrol and perfume. So I raised my glass full of foamless, viscous liquid and clinked the gendarme's glass with it.

'Your good health, brother,' the gendarme said. 'Cheers.'

'Cheers,' I said and slowly shook hands with him. Then I drained the warm phlegm in one go, the way I used to drain the castor oil in my childhood. It made me reel, and when I opened my eyes I couldn't help exclaiming:

'I say, that was bloody revolting.'

'It isn't the best,' the gendarme said, but much less indignantly than me. He wiped his moustache with a dark brown handker-chief.

On our way back we made a detour. The gendarme took me by the arm and guided me to the concrete huts attached to the station building, in which the Germans had been staying and which had been smashed by the American bombs this very morning. The pile of ruins seemed still to be smoking, but it was the dust rising from the concrete rubble, which had been blasted down to the size of pebbles. The gendarme kicked the rubble with the tip of his boot, and here and there a dented steel helmet, a battered mess tin and once even the skeleton of a charred Leica camera came to light. Finally he found a copper cylinder, about three-quarters of a metre in length, which could have been a shell case. He picked it up and examined it, then put it under his arm, before grasping it firmly in his right fist and brandishing it like a cane or truncheon as he walked on. At the same time he kept chewing over the business of the inheritance and returning to his sister-in-law, whom he was now praising to high heaven—not only her domestic virtues and her diligence, but also her physical charms. Perhaps he wanted me to take a fancy to her buxom figure, so that I made sure she got the job in the hotel kitchen.

Later he unearthed a notebook from the ruins. It was a German NCO's diary, full of official and private notes. I would have given a lot for it, but when, thumbing through it without understanding a word, he asked me if I knew any German, I was alert enough to answer that I only knew a little. A waiter has every right to speak foreign languages, but a man who speaks German could, however paradoxical that may sound, always be suspected of being a Jew . . . In any case the gendarme, with an official air, pocketed the diary. He had probably decided to hand it over to some German authority. Then we went back to the tracks, looking for our carriage opposite the bombed-out water tower. Between the rails the people were still milling up and down.

We were approaching our carriage when the gendarme suddenly stopped, put his hand on my shoulder and said:

'Just a moment, brother. I've seen a mate of mine over there at the pump. I'll be back in a tick.'

He left me standing. I quickly climbed up the steps to the compartment. As I got there, the notary with the glasses was peeping out of the WC. If he hadn't been sure that I had noticed him he would probably have locked himself in again. He had been hiding there since we stopped, thinking that at a station nobody would bother him in a place people were only allowed to use when the train was moving. But now that he had caught my eye he couldn't retreat. He stepped out of the cubicle and asked me with great agitation:

'Sir, did you hear how long we're stopping here?'

The poor, gauche fool. He was kowtowing even to me, a waiter. I decided not to speak to him in the dialect-tinged tones of my adopted part, but in my own voice:

'It's impossible to tell how long we'll be stopping,' I said. 'On the platform people are saying that there are still air-raid warnings everywhere ahead of us.'

The fake notary with the cold feet wasn't too fond of air raids. He turned pale again and gulped. But the air raids weren't what really frightened him, and he couldn't stop himself asking me more questions:

'Tell me, sir, this station is run by the Germans, isn't it?'

'I think jointly with the Hungarians.'

'This is the German fallback line. The Tisza Line. I guess there are also German military gendarmes.'

'Probably.'

'Are they searching the train?'

'Not that I've heard. But I don't think they'd search it here. Most of the passengers are on the platform. They can't be examined on a train standing at a station.'

'They say there'll definitely be an inspection after Szolnok,' he said in a trembling voice. 'Germans and Hungarians . . .'

'I've heard that the train is searched by gendarmes and detectives from time to time.'

'You mustn't think that I've got anything to worry about,' he pleaded clumsily. 'They're quite right to search, there must be a lot of fugitives. But you know I had to flee from Gyimes in such a hurry I could only just scrape my papers together. They aren't even complete. Some are missing. And now I'm afraid I won't get any proper food coupons with them in Budapest.'

I gave him a sharp but benevolent look. He cast his eyes down. After a short pause I said:

'Listen to me. My advice to you is that you go back to the compartment and try to sleep till we get to Budapest.'

'Why?' the notary stammered.

'Look,' I said kindly, 'you've been talking too much. Far too much. The soldiers have already noticed you. They're making jokes about you and pulling your leg. On a trip like this the best thing is not to say one unnecessary word in the compartment. Especially if you can't control yourself. Don't you think so?'

'Do you mean . . . ?'

'I mean that . . . you should go to sleep. You've said enough

301

. . . about the Jews. It would be dangerous to say any more. Do we understand each other?'

He stared at me horrified.

'The others were beginning to get bored,' I said. 'I'd like you to be careful. All right?'

'And if they . . . come and demand identity papers?'

'Then too. Try to sleep. A man who sleeps has a clear conscience.'

He nodded without saying a word. Then, with an ashen face, he sidled into the compartment. He collapsed on his seat next to the window, leaned his head back, and was asleep.

Forty-two

I sat down next to Mrs Szabó again and complained expertly about the sour, smelly, warm beer. I think my wife had really gone back to sleep since the train stopped. The compartment was almost empty. Most of the passengers were wandering up and down the tracks. The few who remained behind were eating, and the compartment reeked of food. At least an hour and a half passed before the guards blew their whistles, and the passengers hastily scrambled back into the carriage, afraid of being left behind. But still we hung around, and the more restless passengers got out again. Then, after about half an hour with a lot of banging and creaking, the train began to move, and the gendarme, out of breath, tumbled in through the door.

'Sorry. I'd seen a mate of mine,' he panted. 'We were in the same training regiment in 'forty-one. He's from Jászkisér. He's come down from Budapest for two days' leave.'

'What's the news from Budapest?' I asked sleepily.

'They've started moving the Jews together today. But the gendarmerie hasn't got anything to do yet. This job's done by the fuzz.' He laughed at his own slang. 'You know, brother, these coppers are the greatest chickens. Do you know what a police sergeant told me in Nagyvárad?'

'What?'

'The first day we started piling the Jews in, the coppers were just watching. In the evening I was having a drink with a police sergeant in a little joint next to the town hall. I'd known him for donkey's years, he'd been a lance-sergeant, loaded with decorations. He said to me: "Listen mate, I tell you, one day all my family will be done in because of these Jews you've put in the wagons today." ' He grinned thoughtfully. 'The devil they will. People will have other worries when all this is finished. Then again, perhaps they will be done in. Who cares? That's what I was saying to my mate just now. A gendarme's a soldier. A soldier can't muck about with orders. Can he?'

'He can't,' I mumbled.

'A policeman's just a skivvy. He doesn't understand this. If I'm given an order by my superior, he may be a Turk or a Tartar or even a Jew—I'll do anything, kill anybody. That's what I'm here for.'

'Well, yes.'

'If they tell you to do this or that in the hotel, and you don't want to do it, you can give in your notice. But I can't give in my notice. I've taken the oath. If we lose the war, the most that can happen is that I'm discharged. I don't give the orders, I only carry them out. That's why I need that land, brother, in case I'm in trouble . . .'

He looked out of the window and cried out as if he had caught somebody red-handed:

'The Germans are stealing the hay.' He pointed with the long copper cylinder, as the train was gathering speed. I saw burnt-out farms and ruins, but his peasant eye had picked out what interested him most. Then he planted the copper cylinder between his feet and leaned on it with his elbows, like a shepherd on his staff. At the same time he went on offering me his sister-in-law, the poisoner, in a low voice so that Mrs Szabó, who was snoozing, wouldn't hear. No matter what the conversation was about, he came back constantly to his sister-in-law and the acres. Every quarter of an hour he made me promise to get her the job in the kitchen, even though I kept assuring him that I would do so. At last he wilted and closed his eyes.

At the other end of the compartment, the fake notary from Gyimes was asleep. The soldiers on leave were also drooping. Their eyes, swollen with sleeplessness, were open, but they were knocking against each other like milk cans. The Baptist with his granddaughter, the railwayman with the high-pitched voice and some others had got off at Szolnok. There were a few new faces in the carriage, including an elderly woman, who looked like a civil servant's widow, and a provincial dame of about thirty. The man in the hunting outfit had been squinting at her ever since he had woken from a short sleep. He could have been about sixty, but he seemed to be a ladies' man and not averse to an adventure on a train. He might have gained some extra courage for socialising when somebody told him in Szolnok that the Americans always returned to their bases at lunchtime, like workers knocking off when their shift ends. This only left the British to be feared, and they didn't come every day. With the air raids temporarily behind him, and the arrangements for his food to be smuggled past the excise in place, he drew himself up and addressed the younger woman:

'Where do you come from, young lady?'

'From Jászberény.'

'What's new there?'

'We've been sprayed a bit,' she giggled. 'The house has had it, and so has the salon. I'm going home to Budapest, thank God. Except I don't know what's going on in Budapest.'

'What were you doing in Jászberény, my dear?'

'I was a manicurist at Zimmer's. The hairdresser's. But the salon's all gone.'

'Manicurist,' the man in the hunting outfit said in a surprised tone. 'Who needs a manicure in Jászberény?'

'Don't you insult Jászberény. There's an intelligentsia, and there are officers and officers' wives.'

'Well, some like the officers, others like the officers' wives. To each his own taste,' the man in the hunting outfit said, pleased with his wit.

'Officers,' she sniffed. 'The farmers are a lot better than the officers.'

'They paid you in kind, did they?'

'Not at all,' the manicurist said indignantly. 'I worked very hard to get some food for my mother back home.'

'Good for you. What have you got?'

'This and that.'

A cloud passed over the face of the man in the hunting outfit. He remembered the excise men.

'Aren't you afraid the excise will take it away from you?'

'Why should they? I'll pay the duty.'

'The problem isn't the duty, my dear. They'll confiscate it. For the general public.'

The woman became alarmed. 'What right do they have to confiscate it? I've worked very hard for it.'

'Don't you know you're only allowed to have as much food as you have coupons? What's in that basket?'

Frightened, the woman owned up: 'Two hams, a small jar of lard, a hundred and twenty eggs. If they try to confiscate it I'll jump out of the train.'

The man in the hunting outfit bent very close to her. 'Listen to me, my dear. I'll try to do something.'

'Are you an official gentleman?'

'No. But the gendarme sleeping over there is my friend. When he wakes up I'll try to have a word with him. For such a beautiful girl . . .'

The manicurist threw all the coquetry she had acquired in both town and country into the scales:

'But how can I thank you for this?'

'Where do you live in Budapest?'

'In Huszár Street. With my mama.'

'Ah, near the Eastern Station. Well, wait a little.'

He plonked himself down again next to the gendarme, who woke up with a start, shook himself and murmured, rubbing his eyes:

'I nodded off. I'm damn sleepy.'

'Sergeant,' the man in the hunting outfit said to him in a low voice. 'Look behind you. Can you see the little woman over there?'

The gendarme turned round. 'Yes. What about her?'

'Dishy, isn't she? A bombed-out girl from Jászberény.'

'She looks like a whore to me. What about her?'

The man in the hunting outfit lost some of his assurance.

'She's got a basket full of food,' he said hesitantly. 'She'd be very grateful if you would help her, too.'

The gendarme lost his temper. 'She can go to hell. I can't get everybody's luggage through the excise. I promised you, but I won't if . . .'

The man in the hunting outfit interrupted him anxiously: 'So, do I tell her it's no good?'

The gendarme turned round again to study the woman more thoroughly. She gave him an encouraging smirk, signalling the promise of gratitude. The gendarme became embarrassed and grinned back gauchely.

'Which is her luggage?' he asked the man in the hunting outfit.

'That wicker basket.'

'I'm not carrying anybody's basket. But tell her to stand next to me at the exit, as if she's with me. I'll do that much, perhaps it'll work. But I'm not going to fetch and carry for everybody.'

The man in the hunting outfit sat down again next to the woman to give her the news.

'What do you think of that woman, brother?' the gendarme asked me, the expert.

It occurred to me that the more people gathered round the gendarme, the easier it would be for us to mingle and be over-looked. Narrowing my eyes, I appraised the woman:

'Not bad. A bit plump for my taste.'

'Not for mine.'

'Go for it, then.'

'I've only got three hours in Budapest.'

'That's enough.'

'I must admit I cheat on my wife sometimes, brother. What gendarme wouldn't if he's dragged away from home all the time? But I'm nervous about these women with red dye in their hair. She could give me some infection.'

'The red hair on its own won't give you an infection,' I said with a coarse laugh.

The gendarme still wouldn't relinquish his main theme. As we were studying the woman, he took the opportunity to praise the charms of his sister-in-law yet again:

'Listen, brother. She's attractive, but she can't hold a candle to my sister-in-law. If you get her into that kitchen . . .'

The compartment door flew open. A strikingly pink-faced young man in lace-up boots, plus-fours and a silk shirt appeared, followed by a vacant-looking, unshaven militiaman with a bayonet, and a creepy civilian with piercing eyes, dressed half like a peasant and half like a bailiff. The young man with the pink face demanded in a ringing, almost cheerful voice:

'Ladies and gentlemen! Identity papers, please.'

As I reached into my inside pocket for Ferenc Pattermann's documents, my glance involuntarily fell on the fake notary. He opened his lids for a moment and then clenched them tightly together, as if he were determined not to let anybody prise them apart. He slept far too knowingly. If I'd been the man with the pink face I would never have believed that he was asleep. My wife also stirred and turned somewhat paler, but her pretence of sleeping looked more plausible. The rest, like me, produced their documents.

By now the passengers in the first compartment at the other end of the carriage had been inspected. There had been nothing wrong. The man with the pink face stepped into the middle of the compartment and said:

'Ladies and gentlemen, as we're running very late and we're also behind with the inspection, I don't want to waste time unnecessarily. So I'll just ask you: are there any Jews or political fugitives among you?'

'Not bloody likely,' somebody said.

'All right, ladies and gentlemen,' the man with the pink face continued. 'No volunteers? Then I'll ask the hopefully Aryan passengers in the compartment whether they have been struck by anything suspicious about anybody?'

He noticed the gendarme.

'Sergeant?'

'Sir,' the gendarme said, standing up.

'How long have you been travelling with these people?'

'All the way from Nagyvárad.'

'Have you seen anything suspicious?'

The gendarme looked up and down the compartment and paused self-importantly. Then he said:

'No, sir. I haven't seen anything.'

The man with the pink face screwed up his eyes, pretending to scrutinise everybody once more.

'Well, then . . . this time I'll dispense with the individual examinations. It's a long train, and we've got a lot to do. But if somebody is caught at the exit at the Eastern Station . . .'

On his way to the door he gave everybody another fleeting

look. As before, he took no notice of me. He seemed satisfied, but when he got to the fake notary with the suspiciously tight lids, he stopped.

'Who's this?' he asked. 'Didn't he wake up?'

'He's a bombed-out notary,' one of the soldiers said. However cruelly he had laughed at the notary earlier, he still felt some gratitude for the juniper brandy of the morning.

'He comes straight from Gyimes,' the other soldier added. 'The Russians are already in there.'

'Well, if they're in they'll be out again,' the man with the pink face said superciliously as if he knew something that we ordinary travellers couldn't dream of. 'All right, done!' And he slammed the door behind him.

The militiaman with the bayonet and the creepy civilian continued to search the passengers' faces as they followed him. Then they too shuffled out and the door slammed once more behind them. The notary and my wife opened their eyes at the same time and closed them again. Mrs Szabó, whose trembling knees had been knocking against mine all the time, relieved her nervous tension by asking the gendarme:

'Tell me, sergeant, what was this man's rank?'

'A court clerk,' he scoffed, even though he had treated him like a superior only a little while before. 'From State Security. Lawyer kids who don't want to go to the front. They do their inspections like kids too. If my company commander heard of a gendarme inspecting a train like he did, the gendarme wouldn't be a gendarme by the evening.'

'That's why the Hungarian gendarmerie is the best in the world,' the man in the hunting outfit remarked.

Now the train was moving at express speed. We stopped at Monor. The all-clear had just been sounded. In the acacia forest of Monor a Hungarian railway unit was camping. The soldiers had washed their underwear in the stream and were spreading it out again on the grass after gathering it up in a hurry because the pants and vests presented a good target to the planes. By now the horses were as scabious here in the hinterland as I had seen them in Russia. The soldiers' faces reflected the same indifference to the fortunes of war as they had when they were out there, too exhausted to care whether they were advancing or retreating. They were sitting on the grass, eating and lost in thought, or lying on their stomachs, asleep. The train started. The man in the hunting outfit was whispering in a huddle with the manicurist from Jászberény. The gendarme went out to the WC. The manicurist stood up, took her basket from the rack and counted out ten eggs for the man in the hunting outfit. It was probably his commission for fixing things so that she would be able to stand behind the gendarme at the Eastern Station when the time came to slip through the chain of excise men. He carefully put the eggs in his suitcase, one by one.

When the gendarme returned, the man in the hunting outfit said to him:

'Why don't you come over here and have some fun, sergeant? There's an empty seat.'

The gendarme seemed a bit embarrassed in front of us. Mrs Szabó tactfully looked out of the window. I encouraged him:

'You go, pal,' I said in a low voice. 'Something might come of it.'

'I don't know,' the gendarme hesitated. Then he growled with a grin: 'Well, let's have a look at this wench.'

He sat down next to the woman and wouldn't leave her for the rest of the journey. Having weathered the inspection, I decided to sleep for half an hour. I woke up at Rákosrendező. The train was at a standstill. There was an air raid. It seemed the British were coming, after all.

Forty-three

Once more there were long rows of burnt-out carriages on the rails, but these must have been hit by the incendiaries somewhere else, because the station and its neighbourhood were unharmed. In stark contrast, on the track next to our train, freshly painted field-grey Tiger tanks and anti-aircraft guns pointed their barrels towards the sky, with juvenile crews swaggering in brand new uniforms as if the war were only just beginning. The scattered industrial zone hadn't suffered much damage, although the ruin of a red factory chimney in the middle of a meadow stuck up as if it had been sawn off at an awkward angle. The whole area was covered by a swirling black cloud interspersed with specks of gold. Grey smoke and a pungent smell of burning oil filtered in through the carriage window. Outside, somebody was explaining that the planes had hit a refinery in the suburb of Ferencváros and were bombing that single target for the third time today. I stared at the city, which looked like the sky in my childhood when I watched an eclipse of the sun through a sooty piece of glass.

Shuffling, creaking and panting, we made a final effort, as we had on the bridge at Szolnok, and set out towards the Eastern Station. We burrowed our way through the oil cloud, which was clinging to the rails and appeared to resist every stumbling lurch of the engine. The stinking mourning band that seemed to hang over the whole world dampened the spirits of all the passengers. Nobody felt like talking or moving. It was only when people saw the distinctive buildings, hoardings and viaducts signalling our approach to the station—just as they used to do in the old days, when we were glad to be nearly home—that they started making the usual preparations for the arrival. They lifted their luggage from the racks silently and anxiously, as if every piece contained something fragile or some forbidden goods or pamphlets. About two hundred metres from the glass roof of the station we stopped again in front of a railway building that looked like a castle keep. I peered through the oily mist, wondering whether any roofs had been blown away by the bombs. But as far as the eye could see they were as undamaged as they had been in Nagyvárad after the bombing that I had watched from the ghetto hospital. There was a lot of smoke, but the spires, the domes, the barracks and the bright red roofs were unscathed. From where the train was standing, I could see the Castle District and within it the Royal Palace with its green dome, rising high above the city. For twenty-six years* every sort of crime, bluster, villainy and incompetence had spread through the country from this palace. Hovering above the oily cloud, the lead cover of the dome glistened provocatively, as if intent on demonstrating that while the unfortunate, mouldering city in the valley might be suffocated by smoke and fear, the Castle District up there was still immune and untouched by the Anglo-Saxons because it housed an admiral,† and the Anglo-Saxons respected a brave sailor. Their bombs only hit the factories and, even more accurately, the proletarian houses in the suburbs and the petty-bourgeois flats on the outskirts of the city . . .

With anger and despondency I gazed at the arrogant Castle District and the dazzling reflection of the sunlight in its hundreds of unbroken windows. Was it conceivable that it would continue to hover over us after the end of the war, because the Anglo-Saxons preferred to see a continental country ruled by an admiral, rather than by the continental people themselves? The train gave a jolt and the Castle District disappeared behind the railway buildings. Until now I had avoided thinking of our own problem, deliberately concentrating on things other than the emotional impact, the technical details and the consequences of our arrival. But now we were here and we had to face the music. The climax

---

* The First World War ended in 1918, twenty-six years before the narrator's return to Budapest. Since the death in 1916 of Franz Joseph, Emperor of Austria and King of Hungary, the Hungarian throne had been vacant, but the residence of the Hungarian head of state remained the Royal Palace.
† Miklós Horthy was an admiral before he became regent of Hungary.

of the drama was imminent. At the station they would examine our papers and that was a scene we would have to play well. It would be no laughing matter. Inexorably, irrevocably, we had arrived in Budapest.

'Well, Róza, you dormouse,' I said to my wife as I lifted her vanity bag from the rack. 'Wake up. We're in Budapest.'

My wife looked up and tried to smile. Her sadness distorted the smile into a lopsided grin, but perhaps that was even better— more convincing, more vulgar, more fitting for a hotel kitchen maid. The gendarme had just come back from the manicurist to look for his box. Seeing my wife awake, he gave her the once-over with the friendly, knowing expression of an accomplice, a man who knew the score:

'You don't half sleep, miss.'

'A person needs a good sleep once in a while,' my wife answered. 'We've been sleeping in the cellar for weeks. And all year . . .'

'Work starts early, does it?'

'It does.'

'Is there a lot?'

'Yes, a lot.'

Even now the gendarme hadn't forgotten the main theme:

'Don't worry, you'll get some help soon. Just keep pestering my mate Ferenc here,' he prodded me with his finger. 'If he gets my sister-in-law into the kitchen, you'll only have half the work.'

'I've told you, pal. I'll get her in,' I assured him. 'And perhaps madam will also speak to the boss,' I turned to Mrs Szabó. 'Madam may carry even more weight with the boss than me.'

'Is he a Hungarian?' the gendarme asked.

'Ethnic Swabian,' I said.

'I'll speak to him, of course,' Mrs Szabó nodded as she was putting on her coat. The train was already under the glass roof.

Everywhere people were running to and fro in bewilderment, as if they had missed a train or been unaccountably delayed. Only the stretcher bearers carrying the wounded brought some order into the desperate chaos. They carried the stretchers in long rows, as the porters once used to carry the luggage before the departure of the great international trains—for instance in August 1939, when they loaded the nine suitcases into the sleeping car in Paris. Shouting to be let through, they carried the wounded in an endless chain, and people stepped out of the way without taking one look at the faces of the men lying on the stretchers.

The train stopped. I took my wife by the arm and planted myself close to the gendarme, who had reluctantly taken the suitcases packed with rabbit and lard from the man in the hunting outfit. Mrs Szabó stood behind us. The man in the hunting outfit and the manicurist from Jászberény positioned themselves on the other side of the gendarme. We stepped down on to the platform. The first person I saw, loitering under a faded pink poster of Viareggio, with the characteristically conspicuous indifference of a secret policeman, was a political detective. This detective knew me personally. In the winter of 1942, when the deputy caretaker had reported me for listening to British and Russian radio, he had even come to my apartment. He had threatened me, but finally submitted a negative report in recognition of a box of Memphis cigarettes. Now he gave me a severe fright in spite of my moustache and waiter's disguise. I hurriedly put my arm through the gendarme's and muttered to him in a fatherly tone, as we walked towards the exit:

'Listen, pal. I'm not trying to put you off that woman, but I don't want you to think that the waiter from Budapest was a bad friend . . .'

'What's wrong?'

'When we were getting out of the compartment just now, I took a closer look at the woman. There are some spots on her neck. They could be just from sweating, but . . .'

At that moment we reached the exit, where a guard took our tickets and a gendarmerie lieutenant with big teeth, gypsy eyes and a mastiff's face scrutinised the passengers one by one, ready to pounce. When the gendarme saw the lieutenant, he pulled his arm free and saluted stiffly. The lieutenant clearly wasn't interested in the gendarme or in the people with him. He saluted back perfunctorily and continued to peer at the stream of passengers following us. A few seconds later we were outside in the concourse: my wife to the left, the gendarme in the middle, the man in the hunting outfit and the manicurist to the right. Then Mrs Szabó joined us. She took my wife by the arm, and I tucked mine again through the gendarme's.

'Perhaps the spots are nothing serious,' I continued solicitously. 'But a man shouldn't take a risk if he doesn't have to.'

The alarmed gendarme had lost his enthusiasm.

'All I need is some disease to take home,' he exclaimed. 'Thank you very much for warning me, brother. Damn it, I almost got off with that woman. And I'll be home with the wife by midnight!'

Having lost his interest in the woman, he once more became the rational, cold peasant, and promptly left her to her fate, together with the man in the hunting outfit, the rabbits and the hams.

'Well, mister,' he said, putting the suitcases of the man in the hunting outfit down on the stone floor of the concourse. 'I'm not lugging your stuff any further.'

The man in the hunting outfit stared at him miserably.

'But sergeant,' he begged. 'The excise. They're standing at the door, and this lady too . . .'

'I'm sorry, I can't wait for you. My train's leaving,' the gendarme said coldly and, taking me by the arm, walked on.

Behind us my wife and Mrs Szabó were chatting calmly, almost cheerfully. My wife seemed to have regained her presence of mind together with her colour.

The excise men were waiting at the exit from the concourse to the square. They saluted the gendarme and asked us casually:

'What's in those suitcases?'

'Slips and knickers,' my wife answered flirtatiously.

The excise men grinned, and the gendarme hooted with laughter at the saucy, quick-witted kitchen maid. It was a quarter to one in the afternoon when we stepped out of the station. The crowded square under the oil cloud seemed to float in the twilight of an autumn dusk. Everybody and everything, even the cars and the horses, seemed to be stumbling about, choking. I reeled as I hadn't done since I had typhus. Not with tiredness, sleeplessness and the suffocating smoke, but with emotion. I was back in Budapest. This was where I had lived for decades, working, loafing, and trespassing against the laws of God, man and nature, and also against women.

Forty-four

I've trespassed against everybody, but most of all, of course, against myself—in addition to the terrible devastations of two wars, I myself have damaged my body, neglected my private life, seen my mother only once or twice a year, and, out of laziness, or in pursuit of some other moral or intellectual passion, applied only a fraction of my abilities to my work as a writer and to the struggle for fame or money. I've trespassed against everybody and everything, except against this city, where anybody who recognised me in my furtive disguise—any good-for-nothing fascist—could club me down like a rabid dog, even though this city is *my* home and was built by *my* urban forebears, whether working- or middle-class, whose urban heroism, regarded by some as wrongdoing, clings to every brick. This city is *my city,* and I still accept the city, warts and all.

But what business was this city of the strangers from the surrounding countryside, who always resented, suspected and hated its rhythm, its outlook, its fashion, its dialect, its press and its literature? To them it meant the West, which they abhorred not so much because of its corruption and frivolity, but rather because they felt that it made demands on their minds, which they might have been able to fulfil but which, in their intellectual indolence, they weren't prepared to take on board. Before the First World War they used to pay short visits around Midsummer Day, countrifying the city, which they despised and envied, and which showed them a falsely boorish face. They vomited into the flower beds in the parks and urinated on the four corners of the Academy of Sciences, before returning to their rural homes, hungover, grumbling and swearing. But then the provinces took up arms to capture the city, stretching that Midsummer Day out into decades. Ever larger legions were let loose and installed not only in the buildings, but also in the city's administration, its spirit, its theatres and its attitudes. Step by step, they took over the city hall, while the taverns and beer halls overcame the cafés, and most of the press also fell into provincial hands. Almost everything now belonged to the provinces, but they hated the city as much as ever, even though it came to resemble them more closely each year. Each year it looked more and more like Cegléd, Kaba or Rimaszombat,* rather than the Athens on the Danube that Csokonai† had dreamt of. And we, the proper denizens of this city, were crushed together more and more and forced to give way to strident types sporting sweaty hats, tooth-brush moustaches and plus-fours, to provincial officers and resolute soldiers' wives. On the promenade in Váci Street, German shepherd dogs strained on their leashes, and dolled-up nursery-school teachers from the country flirted with the village school-masters' sons who were studying at the Ludovika Military Academy. The great concert hall of the Academy of Music was dominated by popular songs, the opera by operettas, and every-body was proud to have destroyed a garden of European culture and to have planted a bit of Hungarian nationalism in its place. What did these people know of our emotional attachment to our bridges, to a new house built on a vacant plot, to an old building with a history and artistic value, or even to our mean petty-bourgeois districts and miserable suburbs, in short, to every-thing in Budapest that we loved, as we loved a woman? Step by step, the strangers from the provinces took all this away from us, without knowing how to treat or how to appreciate it—and now, to make the city look even more like the village, the gendarmes were also here. Yes, the gendarmes had followed them and were now catching us, the locals, one by one—not only the Jews, but anybody who wanted this city to resemble the world's great, beautiful, cultured cities in every way, except where being different was really worth something.

The gendarmes were here—in this square too they were making their rounds with their weapons—but first I had to put

* Typical provincial towns in Hungary.
† Mihály Vitéz Csokonai (1773–1805), one of Hungary's major poets.

my gendarme on the tram to the Southern Station. Up to the very last moment he tried to persuade me to take him to my boss right away, to tie up the job for his sister-in-law. I only managed to talk him out of it by telling him that at lunchtime my boss was always stressed and surly, and if we disturbed him when he was up to his neck in saucepans, it might ruin the whole enterprise. So we embraced each other and said good-bye, having agreed that the gendarme would call in at the Pannonia with his sister-in-law on Sunday afternoon. Then the tram took him away, and we waved after him till he reached the corner.

Now I could set out with Mrs Szabó and my wife to Aggteleki Street, where the Szabós lived. In Rákóczi Road it seemed as if all the natives had vanished—I didn't see a single Budapest face. I stared provocatively at the people coming in the opposite direction, but nobody looked at me. It was a nervous, bad-tempered day, and all the passers-by were in a hurry to join their families in the cellars—not only had the British heavily bombed Ferencváros in the morning and Csepel* as little as a quarter of an hour ago, but the day wasn't over yet, and the night was still to come. At the corner of Berzsenyi Street I saw the first building with a star, where the Jews were being rehoused. A small group was just coming round the corner—an elderly man and a little boy of eight or nine pulling a handcart loaded with suitcases, and a stout middle-aged lady and her daughter, aged about twenty, walking on either side, to prevent the suitcases falling off. As we continued along Rákóczi Road, we met more people with handcarts and suitcases—nine, ninety, nine hundred—stuffed with all kinds of necessary and unnecessary things. Having reached the final stage, they had still packed the suitcases in the optimistic belief that that they might need the necessary things and even some of the things that were not absolutely necessary. My wife, sadly clutching the battered vanity bag, whispered to me:

'You see, even these people are better off than we, at least they can save some of their stuff.'

We turned into Aggteleki Street. When we reached the front

* Two industrial suburbs of Budapest.

door of the second house, Dr B. was just coming out. In the past I had been on friendly terms with this doctor, who was married to a popular comedienne, the niece of a gentle pre-war archbishop. At least once a week we used to meet at the house of my unforgettable friend, the pianist Imre Kéri Szántó, who liked the archbishop's droll niece and put up with her pushy, humourless, insignificant doctor husband for her sake. The company included Béla Reinitz, the composer; Lipót Herman, the painter; Kálmán Csathó, the dramatist; and others. It was a good crowd—a circle of friends who held different views, but who argued good-naturedly and honestly—and we usually had a great chinwag with a lot of witty, malicious gossip about public affairs, high society and the theatre. We had dispersed in the early thirties. The host and Reinitz died, others ended up in Margit Boulevard or in the Ukraine, and some withdrew into themselves, disgusted with public life—but the doctor and the comedienne joined the Arrow Cross party. Of course he immediately recognised me in spite of my moustache and my clothes:

'I'm so glad to see you,' he said. 'I read in one of the papers that you'd been caught. I didn't think you were still alive.'

'I am. But how much longer . . . depends on you, among others,' and I pointed to the Arrow Cross badge on his lapel.

'What do you think I am, an informer? In any case I don't deal with individual cases, particularly if it concerns you . . . I know you're a man of good faith in your own way, just as I am.'

'Then good-bye. You're very kind, but I don't want to hang around in the street too long.'

'You must believe me, I'm sorry for you,' he continued. 'But you must understand what's happening here. You Jews are in the way of a development that has had to happen. Now the strong are pushing the weak out of the way for the sake of that development.'

'That's possible. I'm not going to argue with you, as we used to do at Imre's. But if that is true, then I seem to have double bad luck.'

'Why double?'

'First as a Jew and second as a Hungarian. Don't forget, I'm one of the weak not only as a Jew but also as a Hungarian. The

Hungarians are also supposed to be in the way of that so-called development. You may have heard that the small isolated Hungarian nation is an obstacle to the ultimate development of large homogeneous racial blocks. In fact there are two of those in the neighbourhood, each with at least a hundred million people. If your thesis is correct, each would sooner or later eliminate me as a Hungarian who is obstructing that development. As a Jew I simply get it over with sooner.'

For a moment he was puzzled. Then he retorted:

'That's different. The most we Hungarians will have to forfeit is our linguistic isolation, but we'll be able to save our lives and our masses. What matters is not having a language, but being a uniform race. You Jews forgot how to speak Hebrew, but you still haven't been able to assimilate.'

'Well, yes,' I said. 'If you want to forget how to speak Hungarian, that's of course a different story. Good-bye, pal. Thank you again.'

Feeling that he had gone too far and given too much away, he took his leave with greater warmth:

'I wish you the best of luck. I hope you get out of here safely.'

Yes. It was from the fatherland of this Dr B. that they were trying to deport me in a wagon to Poland and throw me in the fire for being an alien, a non-Hungarian. And it was this Dr B. who now called the tune in my city, while I had to hide, and anybody who recognised me could club me down like a rabid dog without further ado.

The women, who had listened to the conversation petrified, started running towards the Szabós' front door without a word. Inside, my friend István Szabó awaited us. I collapsed in an armchair. For the first time in months I was in a proper home, where the bookshelves really held books and not bedpans, trusses, enemas and greasy paper parcels, and where people slept in beds and on sofas, not on the floor or on chairs pushed together or on window sills. I sat in the armchair for a long time, saying nothing. My wife burst into tears and was made to lie down in the next room.

István Szabó was the first to speak. He asked:

'Aren't you hungry?'

'I think I am.'

He brought in a dish piled with cold meats and another with fruit. I pitched into the food and devoured everything.

'That'll keep me going,' I said. 'Now I'd like to let our friends know I'm here. I'd like to do something.'

I mentioned two names. One was in prison; the other had gone underground without leaving a trace. Szabó tried to reassure me:

'Wait a little. I'll have a look in town in the afternoon. First you'll have a bath and a little sleep. Then we'll talk.'

He turned on the radio to listen to the lunchtime news from Britain. When he noticed that I wasn't interested, he turned it off again. And yet I hadn't heard the radio for four months.

I stood up from the armchair and walked to the balcony window. I looked out into the street through the net curtain. The house opposite had a star. The Jews with the handcarts were just walking in through the gate. On the handcarts were suitcases—nine, ninety suitcases. I stood at the window, drained of hatred but also of compassion for my fellows. I felt nothing. My heart and brain were empty, and my nerves had lost all their tension. I stood there in total apathy. I don't think I would have winced if somebody had driven thorns under my nails.

Some children on their way home from school gathered in front of the Jewish house, forming a semi-circle and sniggering at the Jews. It was only when I caught sight of Dr K., the minuscule high-school teacher with the Henry IV beard and the slight limp, following one of the handcarts, that I bothered to crane my neck a little. Dr K. had been in my year at university and had converted to Christianity while still a student. He was a devout Roman Catholic, who regarded Neo-Catholicism as subversion. He wrote conservative articles on literary history for *Szemle*.[*] He was a friend of Négyessy[†] and a confidant of Count Klebelsberg[‡] and the Bishop of Csanád. At first I had

---

[*] *Budapesti Szemle* (Budapest Review), leading conservative cultural journal from the mid-nineteenth century to the Second World War.

[†] László Négyessy (1872–1963), conservative educationalist and literary scholar.

[‡] Count Kúnó Klebelsberg (1875–1932), conservative politician, 1922–31 Hungarian Minister of Culture.

fiercely argued with him because I thought that he was on the make and a snob. Later, realising that he was sincere in his dreary simple-mindedness, I merely despised him. In spite of his primitive Christomania he married a Jewish woman, after converting her. But he hadn't reckoned with the laws that would one day classify converted Jews as still Jews. Now a man who looked like a worker was pulling his cart from the front, his wife was watching the suitcases from the side, and Dr K. himself was limping behind them with a small leather bag under his arm.

'What do you think he's got in his bag?' Szabó asked.

'Books, I guess.'

When the school children saw the tiny, bearded teacher, who was lame into the bargain, they jeered even louder. Dr K. had always been a timid little man. He overtook the handcart and started running towards the gate. As he fled, leaving his wife behind, his bag opened and its contents poured out into the street. There had indeed been books in the bag. Now they were scattered on the ground, with the wind snatching at the pages. The school children, pushing and shoving, picked them up, opened them and inspected the titles.

At this point the relocation of the Jews seemed to be temporarily halted by the lunch hour. The school children went home. I remained at the window with Szabó, while the table was set behind us for lunch. Returning to an old topic, we were debating which ten books of world literature we would take with us, if we had to spend the rest of our lives on a desert island.

I was talking, when Szabó interrupted me:

'Wait a moment. He's left one book behind. Look! Can you see it? Near the grille in the gutter.'

With my weak eyes I couldn't see it.

'I'll go down and get it,' Szabó said excitedly.

I saw him cross the road, bend down and, in disgust, pick the book out of the muck in the gutter. When he glanced at the title, an expression of scornful and angry surprise appeared on his face. He came running back and almost fell into the room.

'Unbelievable. How corny can things get? This could have been put there by a tasteless director, to make sure that the last moron in the gallery got the message. Such vulgar symbolism! What do you think it is?'

'What?'

He held the wet, dirty book out to me.

'Diabolical,' he said grinning. '*The Imitation of Christ* by Thomas à Kempis.'

'Typical of Dr K. But you're right. What a cheap effect: *The Imitation of Christ* in the gutter.'

Mrs Szabó brought the lunch. My wife had also recovered a little and sat down at the table. While we ate we mulled over what to do. Obviously, having met the Arrow Cross doctor, we couldn't stay with the Szabós very long. After lunch we continued deliberating for hours, but didn't come up with any firm plan. Frankly, I wasn't very interested.

ABOUT THE AUTHOR

Béla Zsolt was born in northern Hungary in 1895. He served in the Austro-Hungarian army during the First World War, until he was gravely injured in 1918. In 1920 he moved to Budapest and, for the next two decades, produced ten novels and four plays, as well as political and literary journalism. In 1945, after the experiences he describes in this book, he returned to Hungary and, in 1947, was elected to Parliament. In 1948, his health failing, he was admitted to a sanatorium in Budapest, where he died in 1949. His wife, Ágnes, committed suicide in 1948 after publishing the diary of her thirteen-year-old daughter, who was killed at Auschwitz.

ABOUT THE TRANSLATOR

Ladislaus Löb was born in Transylvania and grew up in Switzerland, where he worked as a journalist and schoolteacher before moving to Great Britain. He is an emeritus professor of German at the University of Sussex at Brighton and has translated several books from Hungarian and German.